*World Peace and Other*
*4th-Grade Achievements*

# WORLD PEACE

## and Other 4th-Grade Achievements

\*

## John Hunter

*An Eamon Dolan Book*
HOUGHTON MIFFLIN HARCOURT
Boston · New York
2013

For information about permission to reproduce selections from this book,
write to Permissions, Houghton Mifflin Harcourt Publishing Company,
215 Park Avenue South, New York, New York 10003.

www.hmhbooks.com

*Library of Congress Cataloging-in-Publication Data*
Hunter, John, date.
World peace and other 4th-grade achievements / John Hunter.
pages  cm
ISBN 978-0-547-90559-4 (hardback)
1. Peace — Study and teaching — Anecdotes. I. Title.
JZ5534.H87 2013
303.6'9071 — dc23
2012039122

Book design by Melissa Lotfy

Printed in the United States of America
DOC 10 9 8 7 6 5 4 3 2 1

Some quotations in this book first appeared in Chris Farina's extraordinary
documentary *World Peace and Other 4th-Grade Achievements*. Quotations from
Sun Tzu's *The Art of War*, translation by Thomas Huynh, are used with the
gracious permission of Thomas Huynh.

*To my mom and dad, Alma and John Hunter Sr., for their unflagging support, generosity, vision, love, and care; my wise and insightful brother, Malcolm; my wife, Leslie, who is my ocean of calm; my daughter, Madeline, the delight of my heart; our cherished Grandma Catherine; my writing muse, Dorothy Rice; my dear friend through thick and thin, Risa Bernholz; Professors Nathan and Charlotte Scott; and Chris Farina, the visionary who started it all*

609

# Contents

*World Peace and Other*
*4th-Grade Achievements*

# Prologue

# The Power of an Empty Space

To be certain of safety when defending, defend where the enemy cannot attack. Therefore, against those skilled in attack, the enemy does not know where to defend; against those skilled in defense, the enemy does not know where to attack. Subtle! Subtle! They become formless. Mysterious! Mysterious! They become soundless. Therefore, they are the masters of the enemy's fate.

— SUN TZU, *The Art of War*

T HE CLASSROOM IS supposed to be empty. I've been teaching elsewhere in the building, and I've come back to prepare for my next session with my fourth-grade gifted class. The room is so quiet that at first I think it *is* empty.

But no. Three children have made their way into the room, gazing silently at the large Plexiglas structure that represents our planet. It's an imposing, four-level affair—undersea, ground and sea, airspace, and outer space—covered with submarines and ships, soldiers and cities, tanks and oil wells, spy planes and satellites. Every year, my fourth- and fifth-grade classes are divided into four imaginary nations, plus a religious island tribe and a nomadic desert clan. There is a United Nations, a World Bank, two or three arms dealers, and a weather god or goddess, who controls the vagaries of tsunamis and hurricanes, determines the fate of the stock market, and tosses coins to determine the outcomes of battles and coups d'état. The children are provided with national budgets, assets, stores of armaments, and portfolios outlining fifty global crises. Then they are given ten weeks to save the world.

I love every minute of the World Peace Game, even though some of it is harrowing and failure is as much a part of each semester as success. I love watching the endless negotiations, the hurried last-minute deals, the earnest nine- and ten-year-olds plotting their battles and drawing up their treaties. I love listening to my students' discoveries about war and politics and peace. But my favorite moments, always, are the times I enter the room and find two or three children there, not talking or writing or calculating, but simply observing, allowing the silence to unfold. In the midst of this noisy, lively school, full of friends and lessons and activities, they are drawn to this quiet place—the empty space.

David has come back from lunch early, and he's standing on the far side of the room, staring intently at the bottom level of the structure—the transparent undersea layer, where submarines prowl and undersea miners troll for treasure. A small, serious boy with curly brown hair and an occasional crooked smile, David has been involved in several battles lately, and I know he's thinking about his latest victory—and his latest casualties.

The empty space gives David time to ponder, to agonize, to plot his next maneuver. Since no one in real life has yet invented a way to unite the planet in peace, my students have to invent their own unique strategies. There are plenty of rules in the World Peace Game, plenty of protocol and structure. But there is no predetermined solution; this the children must create themselves. And to do that, they need an empty space—the pause in the conversation where they don't yet know what to say; the halt in their creative process where they don't yet know what to do.

I notice Bria, who's crouching on the floor, not far from David. Bria is one of the smartest, most confident kids I've ever taught. I chose her to be prime minister of Linderland because letting her intelligence shine seems to come naturally to her, and I thought she'd inspire some of the more timid girls. A big girl with mahogany skin and a quick laugh, Bria is usually a cheerful, energetic presence in my classroom. But at this moment, her concentration is so deep I don't think she even realizes she's not alone. She's contemplating the ground and sea level of the Game—the Plexiglas layer covered with red and white and yellow and green, one color for each of the Game's four nations, with stretches of clear glass ocean connecting them all. Little plastic figures are carefully arranged across this level, an entire world evoked by toy soldiers and oil tankers and the occasional religious shrine. As one of the Game's four prime ministers, Bria is among the few people allowed to move the soldiers and ships and planes, but she can do so only during the official "declaration" portion of the Game. One by one, the prime ministers announce their actions and move their game pieces, as do the chieftain of the Kajazian tribe and the leader of the tribal Nin. After each declaration, there is an interim period when seeming chaos breaks out and the children engage in intricate negotiations: arms deals, territorial agreements, economic aid packages. It's as close as I can come to re-creating real-life global politics at the fourth- and fifth-grade level.

The World Peace Game plunges my students into complexity —and then gives them the chance to find their own way back to the surface. I support them, of course, with rules and structure and instruction. But I'm also giving them the chance to master this alternate reality by exploring it on their own.

To truly succeed at the Game, my students must engage in all three components of education. First, there is *knowledge*, the realm of precise answers and correct solutions. How do you spell "plethora"? What's eight times nine? These questions have only one right answer, as do more sophisticated questions: What is the United States' position on Taiwan? What are the national incomes of Rwanda, Sweden, Yemen, the United States? These are the knowledge pieces my students need to grasp in order to make the world work properly for them. Although the World Peace Game is played with imaginary countries, navigating it requires a great deal of real-life knowledge: how to calculate a national budget, how to craft a treaty with no loopholes, how to grasp the science behind oil spills and climate change.

But we can't just teach our children what we already know; we must also train them how to discover what is not yet known. So education's second leg is *creativity:* the unexpected insights that come only as we try and fail and try again. These insights emerge from the empty space of possibility, out of which comes Archimedes' *Eureka!* and James Watson's double helix, a sonnet or a sonata, Martin Luther King Jr.'s dream of freedom and Nelson Mandela's vision of justice. The empty space is the birthplace of possibilities that don't yet exist—but might.

And finally, as we try, stumble, fall, and fly, comes the third leg of education: *wisdom,* the deeper, broader understanding that emerges from both our successes and our failures. Sometimes wisdom lies in taking action, rallying others to your point of view, mobilizing your resources for a vigorous effort. But sometimes wisdom lies in simply observing as you allow the possibilities to emerge. For that, too, you need an empty space, and so that is what I try to make for my students.

Kadin is standing just a few feet away from Bria and David, but so deep in thought that he might as well be alone. Wiry and blond, with a sly, delighted smile, Kadin is prime minister of Efstron, the largest, richest nation in the Game, and his precise, thoughtful approach to problem solving has made him one of our most effective leaders. Yet Kadin has a double role—I've chosen him to be the saboteur, tasked with sowing subtle confusion through his conversations and via the mercenary troops he secretly commands. My students start the Game with a whole roster of crises: border skirmishes, fuel shortages, ethnic conflicts, ecological challenges. As if these aren't enough, the saboteur keeps provoking new crises, threatening this fragile planet with never-ending chaos.

Last week Kadin's mercenaries attacked Bria's capital in Linderland. Yesterday they began to occupy an island belonging to David's nation of Paxland. Their mysterious movements have often brought our little planet to the brink of war. I know David is struggling with how to respond to this latest attack, which he has no idea Kadin is behind. In fact, Kadin's and David's countries are allies, and I wonder how David will respond if he finds out that his ally has betrayed him. I watch David now, lifting his gaze from the undersea world to the little battalions of plastic men on the ground level.

Bria's eyes haven't moved from the oil fields in the southern part of her nation. On the other side of the world, Kadin's lips curve into a gleeful smirk as he looks up at the Game's third layer—a clear plastic sky dotted with fluffy cotton clouds that Morgan, our weather goddess, can manipulate with a long metal wand. We have a spinner, too, that she uses to determine fluctuations in the stock market, creating still more crises. Even the saboteur can't control the weather, of course, and Kadin knows that. So what new scheme is he devising? Above the clear sky is outer space, full of black holes and unexplored planets, research and weapons satellites, and asteroid mining. Kadin couldn't possibly be planning an attack from space—could he?

Knowledge, creativity, and wisdom: that's what I try to foster in my students. And then I want to teach them what I believe is the ultimate point of education and everything else, which is simply to express compassion in the world. We can be smart and know how to fix things, and we can be wise and know how not to fall into holes, but what is the point of living if not to express the higher and deeper emotions? Why are we here if not to express compassion—and then to build the structures and relationships that allow the most and the deepest and the wisest compassion to be expressed?

Certainly, there have been moments in history when we have lurched forward toward more compassionate customs, toward social arrangements that are more generous and just than their predecessors. But what no one has done so far is to unite the entire planet in peace. I hope that my students might do that—not just here in my classroom, of course, but someday as adults in the real world. At least I hope that they'll help the world take a few more steps in that direction. How do I educate them for that task, which, unlike the spelling of "plethora" or the solution to eight times nine, has no known shape, no fixed procedure? How do I train them to do something that has never been done—but that must be done?

The best learning tool I can think of is the World Peace Game: training my students in known skills with unknown outcomes. We always begin with an empty space—the possibility, as the Game begins, that anything can happen. Suddenly, the school bell rings, bursting through the silence, and a crowd of children erupts through the door, joking, arguing, jostling, teasing. They run to take their places around the room as I reach for the little silver bell I always use to signal a new Game Day.

"Let today's session of the World Peace Game begin!" I call out. "Ladies and gentlemen, are you ready?"

## What Is the World Peace Game?

I've been teaching the World Peace Game for almost thirty-five years now. The Game began its life as a four-by-five-foot plywood board in an inner-city school in 1978 when I was creating a lesson on Africa. I put all the problems of the world there, and I thought, *Let's have the students solve them.* I didn't want to just lecture or have the kids read books. I wanted them to be immersed so they could experience the feeling of learning through their bodies. I thought, *Well, they like to play games. I'll make something interactive.*

Of course, I didn't use the word "interactive," because we didn't have that term in 1978, but that's what I meant. And so I made the Game, and it has since evolved into a four-by-four-by-four-foot Plexiglas structure that represents the entire planet in four layers: undersea, ground and sea, airspace, and outer space. There are four countries in the Game, each with different commercial and military assets. I choose a prime minister for each nation, plus a chieftain for the Kajazians and a leader for the Nin. Each prime minister puts together a cabinet: secretary of state, minister of defense, and chief financial officer. We also have a World Bank, a United Nations, and two or three arms dealers, as well as a weather god or goddess who controls a random stock market and random weather.

The Game begins when I show the children the Plexiglas model and give them their top-secret dossiers, including a thirteen-page crisis document with fifty interlocking problems. They learn right away that if one thing changes, everything else changes along with it. I throw them into this complex matrix of conflicts and problems, and they trust me because we have a deep, rich relationship. And so they begin to face these crises: ethnic and minority tensions; chemical, nuclear, and oil spills; nuclear proliferation; environmental disasters; water rights disputes; breakaway republics; famine; endangered species; and climate change.

There is also the saboteur, who tries secretly to undermine everything in the Game, even while maintaining an official position as an upstanding leader or citizen. My students know there is a saboteur, a discomfiting piece of knowledge that causes them to suspect one another even as they try to identify the troublemaker. The saboteur's misinformation, ambiguities, and irrelevancies cause everyone to think and question more deeply. The very existence of the saboteur is a reminder that achieving world peace isn't easy, that some people are committed to undermining that possibility.

We usually play for forty-five minutes to an hour at a time, about one day a week, so that the Game extends over eight to ten weeks in the normal school year (or one intense week during a summer session). I've played with high school students, middle-schoolers, and now fourth and fifth graders, in alternating semesters. During summer sessions, I've even had mixed age groups successfully save the world, a nine- or ten-year-old prime minister leading with a seventeen-year-old secretary of state in support. Victory in the Game is defined by meeting two conditions: all of the interlocking crises must be satisfactorily solved, and every country's asset value must have increased beyond its starting point. In almost thirty-five years of playing the Game, students have been remarkably successful in saving the world.

Frequently throughout the Game, we read passages from Sun Tzu's *The Art of War*. Fourth graders use that ancient wisdom to avoid and perhaps even transcend the paths to power and destruction. Even if they decide to follow those paths for a while, they learn, eventually, how to turn away and choose something different. They learn to look beyond shortsighted reactions and impulsive thinking and instead to think in a long-term, more consequential way.

The heart of the Game—the thing that makes it work—is the collective wisdom of the children. I'm just a clarifier, a facilitator. The students run the Game. Once they start playing, I may introduce new crises that they must handle, but I have no say in how they handle them.

That can be a risky proposition for me. More than once, I've watched a child take a path that I could not imagine taking. I've watched her choose what looks to me like a path of war, and my heart breaks because I feel that I've failed to teach her the possibilities for a peaceful resolution. I've watched children behave in ways that I consider selfish, shortsighted, or tyrannical. I've watched them make every mistake you can imagine, and each time I think, *I've failed.*

And then—this happens every single time—I see the collective wisdom of the class take over, and somehow peace is achieved. Perhaps the child who seems to be taking a path of war has a larger intention in mind, a deeper strategic reason for her apparently warlike action. Perhaps the child who behaves like a bully meets his match in a rebel uprising or a series of coups d'état. Perhaps the overwhelming welter of crises—the poverty, oil spills, tribal conflicts, big-power invasions, and insurgencies —resolves itself into a fragile but meaningful peace, a tentative but measurable improvement within even the poorest countries. My students always find a solution, and they always find it together. They find it not because I have devised a correct answer that they might stumble upon or memorize or deduce. They find it because they create the answer together—out of the empty space.

## Learning from the Game

Thanks to the World Peace Game, I've spent most of the past three decades learning to have faith in the collective ability of humankind to solve its problems. For most of that time, my students and I played the Game in relative obscurity. We were known throughout the communities where I taught, primarily in classrooms of gifted fourth- and fifth-graders in Richmond, Virginia; Columbia, Maryland; and Charlottesville, Virginia, in the heart of the Blue Ridge Mountains. But for the most part, we were just another group of ordinary/extraordinary students and their teacher trying to make their way in a complex and contentious world.

Then came the award-winning filmmaker Chris Farina, who discovered the Game when he met me through a mutual friend. Chris spent a year observing in my classroom and then a semester making the one-hour documentary that he called *World Peace and Other 4th-Grade Achievements.* Eventually, the film made its way around the globe to festivals; classrooms; television stations in South Korea, Romania, Hungary, Israel, and other countries throughout the Middle East; and public television stations throughout the United States.

The film also led to my invitation to give a TEDTalk in March 2011. TED is a nonprofit devoted to promoting what it describes as "ideas worth spreading." It began in 1984 as a conference bringing together innovators in technology, entertainment, and design. Since then, it has become an internationally respected organization that sponsors conferences and distributes TEDTalks from those conferences via video. It also offers fellowships and prizes for innovators in various fields. The TEDTalk has become a badge of honor, and the invitation to give a talk kicked off another round of speeches and film showings: at the Aspen Ideas Festival; on the Google campus; and at IDEO, the leading Silicon Valley design firm. I've appeared with the film at the United Nations. My fourth-grade students and I have even spent a day at the Pentagon, discussing world peace with Secretary of Defense Leon Panetta. (You can read about our adventures at the Pentagon in the epilogue.)

Over time, it appeared that my students and I were no longer playing for ourselves alone. We seemed to be playing for an international audience, one that looked to draw inspiration from our miniature but heartfelt quest to achieve world peace. As we attracted more attention, we attracted more questions as well, about what the World Peace Game meant and what lessons could be drawn from it.

I confess, I have spent a lifetime resisting the imperative to summarize or prescribe. I much prefer simply to tell a story, ask a question, create an empty space—and then let my students or my audience draw their own conclusions. But if pressed, I would say that the World Peace Game is the story of individuals confronted by overwhelming and chaotic circumstances. First they must learn to face the reality of the moment. Then they must grasp that moment's deeper implications and interconnections. Finally, they have the chance to organize themselves into a new entity: a collaboration, a collective, a whole that is greater than the sum of its parts. This new collective can devise solutions far beyond the ability of any individual. It has the opportunity to be wiser, more creative, and more farseeing than any one person could ever be. Within this collective, individual members can tap into their deepest strengths, to become their best selves. In a powerful back-and-forth process of mutual transformation—a dialectic, if you will—the group benefits from the contributions of every individual, while the individuals reach their full potential by engaging with the group.

## The Seven Stages of Learning

Forging a powerful, creative group is a process with its own logic and direction. Over the years, I have observed seven distinct stages through which my students pass as they create this new collective entity.

1. *Overload and confusion.* The kids are excited, but they are also engulfed in a sea of information: fifty-plus crises, a plethora of new roles and responsibilities, competing claims, clashing notions of right and wrong. An ancient tribe wants to reclaim its burial ground—which happens to lie within the oil fields on which its host country depends for its economic survival. At the same time, another child playing the role of despot threatens to bully his way into world domination. And meanwhile, yet another country faces famine after a sequence of environmental disasters. At the same time, an escalating nuclear arms race and climate change threaten the entire planet. As the reality of these crises sinks in, along with their interlocking nature

and the seeming impossibility of solving them, my students react as do many adults in the same situation: they are simply overwhelmed and confused.

2. *Failure.* A profound sense of failure usually follows this initial intensity. This is the stage at which my students confront the limits of what they already know and can already do. Individual efforts have fallen flat. Nothing seems to work. Despair sets in. Perhaps my students have not yet grasped the possibilities of the empty space, or perhaps they've become discouraged by their own limitations. Either way, what they're doing has failed, temporarily blinding them to the possible existence of other tactics, other solutions. Often, when we reach this stage, we actively ignore or reject an alternative strategy, just as we may shun those who insist that another way is possible. Yet it is crucial at this stage of failure to ask the following questions: What possibilities have we missed? What lies beyond what we can easily see? How, to use my father's favorite question, are things different than they seem? Although I myself despair at this stage more often than I would like, experience has taught me that failure is often — perhaps always — the gateway to new solutions. Only when the known fails do we have the opportunity to discover the unknown.

3. *Personal understanding.* Out of the depths of failure, individual students may stumble upon new solutions. Forced to go beyond their limits, they create new approaches: a diplomatic treaty, perhaps, with terms that had previously seemed unimaginable. Or maybe they devise unexpected technical solutions to the apparently intractable problems of a depleted aquifer, a blighted crop, a polluted airspace. The decisions of an individual prime minister or even a single country might have an enormous impact on world events, and many of my individual students have much to

be proud of. But given the very nature of the World Peace Game—which is designed to mirror the nature of world politics itself—there is only so much one individual or one country can do. So even with the blossoming of individual effort—and perhaps also individual success—my students also experience a dawning awareness of, again, their individual limits. At that very moment of personal success, they learn that they also must give themselves over to something larger than themselves.

4. *Collaboration.* What happens when individuals become aware of their own limitations? One possible result is that they turn, with ever-growing enthusiasm, to the process of collaboration. At this point, I have observed, my students are ready to experience the awakening power of being greater than themselves. What they cannot do alone, they might well be able to do together. Whether this collaborative effort is directed toward bringing down a tyrant, resolving a military conflict, or combating climate change, students begin to understand that becoming part of a greater process might offer solutions that individuals simply cannot achieve by themselves.

5. *"Click."* At this key point, awareness moves higher or deeper, and suddenly students "get it." They feel the revelation, the sudden wonder, the thunder and lightning of this moment. They see what is possible as they never have before. This is the eureka moment, the abrupt shift from "I have no idea" to "Aha!" In individuals, it comes as an epiphany. In groups, it comes as a shift in energy. This is the moment when the class collectively feels its "groupness," when the collection of individuals *becomes* a group, as palpable a presence in the classroom as any one of us. You can feel that type of click in a church, when the congregation suddenly coalesces around a song or a moment in the sermon; you can feel it at a sports event, when the

spectators unite in wonder or anxiety or desperate hope around a moment in the Game; you can feel it at a rally or demonstration or political event, when a group of strangers becomes one entity, one force, chanting or marching or cheering. *Click!* Now there is not just *I*, but *we*. And now I'm ready—and now we are ready—to move forward to . . .

6. *Flow.* This precious state occurs, sooner or later, in every session of the Game I've played. At some point, the students are simply in the flow, a transcendent time that might last for one minute, or five, or ten, or even for an hour or a day. During that remarkable interval, boundaries seem to dissolve, joy and peace flood the room, and somehow the room (and everyone in it) enters into a uniquely continuous state. Decisions happen sequentially, perhaps, but it feels as though they are happening simultaneously. We become aware of events, but it feels as though our awareness and the events themselves are part of one unbroken whole. We *are*, we *act*, and we *are aware of ourselves acting,* as the activity in the room both speeds up and seems to move into a realm outside of time. In the flow, we continue to experience ourselves both as individuals and as parts of something larger. In this state, there is no longer a distinction between our unique separateness and our boundless unity.

7. *Application of understanding.* Flow, however lovely, is often difficult to sustain. Sooner or later, we are likely to fall back down into time and separateness; sooner or later, things usually go back to normal. Flow is always available to us briefly, perhaps, but few of us can actually live there. What we can do is to take the understanding we've derived from that transcendent state and apply it to the problems—in my students' case, the global crises—that we need to solve. At this point, my students finally un-

derstand that the only way to successfully play the World Peace Game is to play it as a group, to become part of something larger than themselves and decide together how to move forward. Having reached this stage, they are now ready to win the Game.

The stories in this book are mainly my students' stories. But this is also a book about my own journey. Time and again, as I watch my students flounder and despair, I despair along with them. I have often thought, *Okay, well,* this *time they won't get it*—a thought that implies my own failure as a teacher. I have watched my students choose violent responses, or shortsighted ones, or selfish ones, and I have been certain that their limits are a reflection of my own. I have had to accept that I can't control what they do and that, like the adults in the real world, they might fail.

But each time I've given in to my feelings of defeat, I have been mistaken. The selfish student drops his ego-centered approach. The timid student discovers the courage to stand up to her peers in silent, stubborn action. The helpless, confused, or angry student learns to create solutions that take all his fellow players into account and to construct, out of the chaos, a fragile but real peace. And all my students come to understand the power of the empty space—the quiet place where new possibilities can arise and new answers can emerge.

## Entering the Empty Space

> Those skilled in warfare move the enemy, and are not moved by the enemy.
>
> — SUN TZU, *The Art of War*

I first encountered the empty space in my mother's classroom. Alma Hunter was born in Richmond, Virginia, and she taught at a number of schools in the segregated era of the 1940s, 1950s, and 1960s. As it happened, in 1964, just as I was turning nine, she was posted to teach fourth grade in the all-black school near our home. So suddenly, I was in my mother's class.

That was a very quiet year: I didn't make one false step! Unlike the other children, I didn't call our teacher Mrs. Hunter—I didn't know what to call her—so I would sort of sidle up to her desk, hoping that no one would hear me, and whisper, "Mom, may I be excused?"

My mother was a very loving teacher. Her way was very soothing and quiet. Basically—and this correlated with things I learned years later in Buddhist monasteries in China and Japan —my mother approached things in a way that I would now call empty. There was so much space in her approach—she allowed so much to be, so much to happen—that I would often have to come to my own conclusions. I might ask her, "What is the best thing?" And somehow, she would turn me back in on myself. Without exactly replying, "What do *you* think is best?" she would create a space in which I would have to dig deeper and uncover possible answers for myself.

Her habit at first glance appeared counterintuitive. Instead of acting, she chose not to act—to wait, to stop. She might have appeared to be completely inactive, but she was actually quite vibrant. In that quiet pause, awareness could emerge with a sparkling clarity. My mother had no need to direct the action or strive for a particular result, and at such times she freed me from that need as well. She simply allowed reality to emerge, as the two of us silently observed.

I remember often, as a child and a young man, I'd be chattering away, rambling at full speed, and she would just put her hand on my shoulder and call my name. "John. *John!*" she'd say, and then she would stop and wait. It was as if she'd carved out a space of emptiness and stillness amid my chatter and franticness, sometimes with a gesture, sometimes with a word, sometimes simply with a stern tutorial look. It was as if she held a mirror up to me, allowing me to see myself as I was at that moment, allowing me to see as well the possibilities of the moment, so that instead of imposing my own will on the situation, I could choose an action that was right because it fit the time.

My father, too, would simply sit for long periods, letting me talk my way through an idea. "Okay," I'd say finally. "So what do you think?"

He'd never answer right away. He would simply sit, looking at me, mulling it over. I learned not to rush anything but just to wait and see what would happen next. Sometimes he would have something to say—briefly. Then he'd go back into that thoughtful space he had created, still looking at the problem I had brought to him, thinking about it, turning it over in his mind.

As an ambitious young man, I was often too busy or too impatient to appreciate this approach to life. Back then, I wasn't really interested in that quiet place where new ideas whisper or new possibilities emerge. I had been trained by the larger culture to look at the bright lights and to ignore anything that didn't fall within their glare. As a result, it took me decades to understand what both my parents knew, which was that there is plenty of information and depth in the shadows.

Still, I have never forgotten my experience in my mother's fourth-grade classroom. In fact, I think maybe it was one of the biggest influences on my teaching career: spending time within that space, that silence, feeling its discomfort, its fruitfulness, its mystery. In that space, I had to encounter my own questions, the limits of what I knew and what I didn't. I could feel myself unfolding there, tentatively finding my own way or feeling the thrill of a new discovery. My mother didn't hand me—or anyone —the answers. Instead, she created the space for us to be searchers, explorers, pioneers. And so I saw, even as a nine-year-old student, how powerful that space could be. That early experience was reinforced by what I later learned studying Eastern religion and philosophy: that emptiness can be as valuable as the fullness of things.

Imagine a classroom composed only of "fullness." The students within that classroom would be absorbing knowledge every minute. If they weren't doing math problems, they'd be memorizing vocabulary words; if they weren't running laps in the gym, they'd be conducting a well-known science experiment and coming to the correct conclusion about whatever principle was being taught. In such a classroom, not a moment would go by without producing a tangible, predictable result.

The students taught in such a classroom might grow up to be knowledgeable and skilled, but how much training would they have had in coping with problems for which we don't yet have the solutions? How comfortable would they be with their own creativity? How practiced would they be in encountering the unknown?

Of course, a classroom composed only of "emptiness" would not be much better. I would consider it irresponsible to invite children into an empty classroom and simply allow them to sit until they thought of something they wanted to learn. To move forward in education—or in life itself—we need both fullness and emptiness, structure and freedom, knowledge and creativity. The purpose of the empty space is not to remain empty. Rather, its purpose is to make room for something as yet unseen—to allow possibility and potential to be born. That possibility is foreclosed if the space is always full. Children don't have time to think of anything new if every minute of their day is devoted to absorbing knowledge and demonstrating results. Sometimes the best way to solve a difficult problem is to walk away from it for a while and allow it to "solve itself," somewhere in the recesses of your mind or even in a dream. That's what happened when scientist James Watson dreamed of two snakes intertwined during his quest for the structure of DNA. Our culture trains us to go strongly forward until a goal is reached, but sometimes it's more productive simply to *stop*.

When I became a teacher, I turned instinctively to the notion of the empty space, but the lessons I had learned—first from my mother, later from my teachers in the East—were not always so easy to apply. Like any novice in the classroom, I found myself reaching for the things I could count on. Rather than seeking to create an empty space, I filled my students' days with as many activities as time allowed, hoping for results that I could, to some extent, control.

I remember the moment when I was finally able to embrace emptiness. I was still a student teacher at the university, which had me working in a preschool. It was a very lovely environment, with the latest in teaching techniques and generally well-behaved students. But children are children, and like any new teacher, I worried about keeping my kids in line.

The art room in that school contained a closet crammed with items recycled from all sorts of places. There were paper towel tubes, plastic stoppers, glue, tape, glitter, rubber gloves, cardboard this, and plastic that—they called these things "art supplies," but of course they were really just junk, or what we now call "recyclables." Every day, my job was to look into that closet of chaos and somehow create an art project for my students.

At that point, I knew very little about teaching and even less about art. So the idea that I was supposed to look into that closet with no plan, no guide, and no training and somehow find the materials from which my students might make something beautiful—the idea that I had to do this not just one time but day after day after day—well, it was overwhelming. But my advisers told me, "Don't worry, the children will do it. You're just there to help them."

So every day, I would stick my head inside that closet and

pull out an armful of what seemed to me little more than debris and say to my classroom of preschoolers, "We're going to make something magical today." And it worked! Every day, my students and I would emerge from the experience with these astonishing pieces of art, and then the next day, we would do it again. Going into that situation day after day, never having any idea what to do, reinforced those early lessons about the magic of the unknown.

I'm not saying it was easy. Every day, I approached that cavernous, crowded closet with anxiety. I was forced simply to trust that the children, in their collective wisdom, could make something out of nothing. And because I was forced to take this position—because it was the only solution I could see—I eventually became good at it. I learned how to walk into that space of emptiness and magic—not having a map, not having any idea where to go—and not be afraid to say, "Okay, children, here's what we have to work with. What are we going to do with it today?"

I learned to trust that leap into the unknown, to get comfortable with my own discomfort. I never stopped being anxious, just as I feel anxious every time I begin a new session of the World Peace Game and wonder if perhaps this will be the time that a group of students fails to save the world. But I have learned that my anxiety is irrelevant; that if I trust the power of the empty space and the collective wisdom of my class, somehow art will get made or peace will be achieved. Whatever the task at hand, trust and emptiness must be my starting points.

Actually, not knowing the answer can be a genuine advantage for a teacher, because it means that you are not able to impose your own limits on your students. If anxiety and formlessness are one aspect of the empty space, freedom and infinite possibility are the other. There were no restrictions in that art closet: I was allowed to pull anything out of it, and my students were allowed to make anything from it. And so we managed to create something that none of us had ever imagined before. Instead of focusing on success and achievement, I was forced to focus on emptiness and possibility. It was a startling lesson.

That first lesson was soon followed by another. I can still feel the curve of my back as I sat on the bench in that preschool's lunchroom, bent over the long, low table that hardly cleared my knees. The children who surrounded me were, as I thought then, rowdy, noisy, and out of control. They were yelling and shrieking wildly, jostling one another, causing a ruckus—doing all sorts of things we didn't do in that school. As I sat there within the mounting chaos, the only teacher in sight, manifestly failing at my duty of keeping order, I felt my panic rising, because, of course, I had no control over those children. I was sure that any second, the director would walk into that raucous lunchroom and see just how complete and colossal a failure I was.

But just as I was at the peak of my alarm—just as I was ready to yell or scold in a way that I knew would only make everything worse—I felt something inside me shift. I suddenly felt very calm as I thought, *Oh . . . this is okay. This immediate space is small, noisy, and crowded. But all around it is a much bigger space—quiet, spacious, and larger than I can see. And that big space—even though it contains our small one—is full of peace.*

I turned to that little table full of rowdy three- and four-year olds, and I said quietly, "Okay, folks, we're going to settle down now." I know this sounds incredible, but I actually felt a gold light radiating off my face toward them, and it was as if my voice went into this golden ray that settled over the group, and the children all instantly turned and looked at me. Up to that moment, they had been ignoring me so completely, I might as well have been a piece of furniture. But now they gave me their full attention—and they immediately settled down.

That was the day I became a teacher. When I felt that calm come up in me and express itself in that very focused and intense way, I felt as though I had made a direct transmission to my students, a transmission to which they instantly responded.

Somehow I conveyed to them the sense of peace I felt, the sense of openness and emptiness into which I was inviting them to come and join me. They came into that space just as David and Bria and Kadin found their way into my empty classroom years later. We're all hungry for that empty space. We're all looking for a place to just *be*.

From then on, I was able to manage any classroom with just a few words or a gesture. In Japanese zendos and Indian ashrams, I had already learned the practice of mindfulness—the commitment to maximum awareness of myself and my surroundings and the others in my space. Now I understood that mindfulness and profound attention will always invoke an empty space, just as my mother had always done when she put her hand on my shoulder and called my name. At such moments, she seemed to make time stop and to create around me such quiet and attention that I suddenly had the space to just be what I was and observe reality. Now I had discovered how to do the same thing for my students.

That hard-won appreciation for emptiness may be why, when I came to create the World Peace Game, I found myself reaching with deep gratitude for the work of Sun Tzu.

## Lessons from a Master of War

Sun Tzu was the ancient Chinese general who wrote *The Art of War,* a book from which I read to my students at the beginning of every session of the World Peace Game. At first, I admit, reading from a book about war in a peace game doesn't seem to make much sense. What does a man of violence have to teach us about peace?

Yet Sun Tzu's work is not really about how to wage war but rather about how to understand war, as well as the forces of life and death. And in this world, if we are to have peace, war is a thing we must all understand. As a general, Sun Tzu knew that either we must get out of war as quickly as possible, or we must avoid it in the first place. We achieve these noble goals by being infinitely flexible and open, available to switch strategies at a moment's notice—precisely the kind of approach that is fostered within the empty space.

With no ax to grind or agenda to put forward, we are finally free to understand those whom we would consider opponents, truly grasping how they think and what they want. We are free to understand ourselves as well, especially our ego-driven need for dominance, which can poison the prospects for peace. In the world as we know it, war, violence, bitterness, and defeat are givens. But in the empty space, anything is possible, and entering that space, we have the chance to see the opportunity for peace, both with our opponents and within ourselves.

I've tried to build the teachings of Sun Tzu into the World Peace Game, which in many ways is based on his philosophy of sometimes working behind the scenes in a diplomatic, quiet, and gentle way, laboring relentlessly, over time, to achieve one's ends. But I've also seen beautiful moments when a child learns how to wait, nonjudgmentally, to allow a situation to completely unfold while he or she simply *observes*. In those moments, I see that Sun Tzu's teachings are not so far from my mother's. Both of them understood the value of letting things be, of doing nothing —watchfully—until the right action, the *useful* action, emerges.

*The Art of War* has also helped me to realize my own arrogance, to understand the folly of thinking that I can with certainty claim to truly understand anything. I try to share this knowledge with my students as well, to help them find ease with the unavoidable ambiguity of life. As I propel them into the complexities of the Game—the competing claims, the overlapping crises, the contradictory demands—I hope they will see for themselves the value of remaining open to possibility. The teams that suffer most are the ones with preset agendas, fixed personal attitudes, and a lack of thoughtful consideration before reacting. It takes many losses, defeats, and frustrations before they finally begin to discover how harmony might be achieved. The students who move more easily within the Game are the ones who, from the beginning, are more comfortable with ambiguity, flexibility, emptiness. As I observe from the sidelines, I am continually learning from both types of students—seeing how I limit possibilities with my own thinking, seeing ways in which I could create more openness and possibility within myself.

One of my most thoughtful students, a kid named David, found himself in a position where he had to make some very difficult decisions about whether to retaliate for an apparent attack. David's first efforts to combat his enemy were successful —but then he discovered that each victory only set him up for another battle, as the frustrated enemy continued to attack again and again, and as David himself began to feel invincible. (You'll read more about David's story in chapter 4.) As David wrestled with the temptations of victory and the frustrations of defeat, he explained his situation by saying, "Now I'm feeling really weird, because I'm living what Sun Tzu said." I thought David's words pointed the way to the best possible use of Sun Tzu—not as a guide to waging war, but as a way of going deeper into our understanding of it. If we see that we are living what Sun Tzu said—if we see that we are caught up in the web of attack and counterattack, retaliation and revenge—we can allow him to illuminate our situation, and then, perhaps, we can find our own solutions.

When I was growing up, my father used to remind me to look beyond the obvious, beneath the surface, past the easy answers and on into the deeper truths of life. One of his favorite sayings was, "Things aren't always as they seem." I try to share the same lesson with my students. I think Sun Tzu might approve.

## The Collective Wisdom of a Fourth-Grade Class

> The Way is what causes the people to have the same think-
> ing as their superiors; they may be given death, or they may
> be given life, but there is no fear of danger and betrayal.
>
> —SUN TZU, *The Art of War*

Every time we play the Game, it's different. Some sessions are
more about social issues, some more about economic issues, and
some more about warfare. But no matter where a particular session of the Game takes my students, I don't shield them from the
starker realities of being human. I allow them to go to the darker,
more dangerous places and then to learn—albeit in a protected
way—how not to do what they consider to be the wrong thing.
And in this way, they find out what is right, or at least what is
right for them. I hope that they can pick up even a single critical
or creative thinking tool from the Game. If they can, they might
be able to save us all.

Along the way, I've learned so much, right along with them. I
marvel at their last-minute solutions, at their painstaking negotiations, at their willingness to plunge into complexity while remaining flexible and open. But the thing I find most remarkable
is the way, ultimately, they never leave anyone out.

Time and time again, I have seen my students make sure that
everyone is taken care of. Unlike many adults, they don't ask,
"Is someone worthy?" "Is someone slacking?" "Did everyone do
his or her fair share?" They just ask, "Is everyone going to be
all right?" They simply refuse to put anyone completely outside
their concern.

True, for anyone to win the Game, the entire class has to win
it. All conflicts must be settled, and the assets of all four major
countries must have increased. But there are two tribal groups
whose assets could theoretically remain the same, and technically, at that point, the Game would still be won.

That never happens. Even though the students from the major nations don't *have* to make sure that the tribal assets increase, they do—they make sure that the tribal groups and ethnic minorities are not just financially okay but happy with their political, social, and religious arrangements. As the Game nears its end, there is always this spontaneous, informal assessment to find out who in the world is not okay and what everybody has to do about it.

Clearly, I've designed the Game with that hope in mind—with "winning" defined as good conditions for everybody. But it's still up to the students. They still have to decide that everyone is going to win. And they do decide that. I'm in awe every time I see it.

One time, I set up the condition that the Nin had invented a technology that could end global warming but that it was very expensive. For the technology to work, it had to be employed simultaneously by all four nations, and each one needed to purchase a minimum number of factories to manufacture this breakthrough product. Not all of the other nations could afford the technology, and the Nin didn't see a way to lower their prices. It seemed that the economy and the environment were headed for a collision and that the efforts to solve this major world crisis were at an impasse.

Suddenly, one of the students brainstormed a new solution: "Let's plant a trillion trees!" A small group of them went to the weather goddess and asked her if this response would solve the problem. Based on her research on the Internet and her nine-year-old interpretation of what she read, she ruled that they would, in fact, need *ten* trillion trees to even partially restore a healthy climate. The students immediately began to calculate: What would this cost? How would it work? I suggested that they research what the U.S. Forest Service charged for seedlings, so they could see whether this plan was actually feasible for their budgets. The student who came up with this idea lobbied for the rest of the planet to take it up. "If everybody does this, the whole world will be better off—not just us," he explained. The children had learned to think globally and to translate that concept into material reality: international agreements, budgets, environmental planning. But the fundamental collective concern—the wish for everybody to be okay, for nobody to be left out—was there from the beginning.

Although I've observed this as a collective concern, there are usually one or two kids who make it their business to voice this principle for the group. Usually someone takes it upon himself or herself to ask at key points, "Who's not okay?" and to insist that the group take heed.

Outstanding in this regard was Ryan, who played the Game two different times, with two different groups of children—first his regular classmates and then a mixed group of friends and strangers. I could tell that Ryan was special in this way just by being in his presence for a short while. He would get up and say, "Who needs some help?" He'd discern where the weaknesses and trouble spots were, and then he'd bravely negotiate or create a policy to make sure they got some attention. His fellow students saw in him the same quality that I did, and they voted to award him the World Peace Game Peace Prize both times he played the Game.

I also remember Neela, a Tibetan lama's daughter, who was so used to the concepts of collective concern and interdependency. Her way of expressing these ideas was still a fourth grader's, though. One day, she simply leaped up from her secretary of state's chair and lectured the entire World Peace Game team about not having enough compassion. "What about the people who are suffering?" she cried out. "You have to help them have less suffering! You people are just not having enough compassion! You have to have more compassion—everybody does!" Remembering her unique combination of adult wisdom and childlike impatience still makes me chuckle. And there are times, when I hesitate between the upright choice and the convenient choice, when I can still hear her voice lecturing me, too.

And then there was Tessa, who was a spectacular weather goddess. Tessa was a regular Solomon when it came to deciding difficult cases. With no hesitation or self-doubt, she'd come up with the most beautifully balanced decisions. She played the Game more than once, too, and everybody always wanted her to be the weather goddess. Sometimes she'd hand down a hurricane, sometimes a tsunami, sometimes good weather. She was always evenhanded, the way nature would be, with a little bit of something else thrown in. Wisdom maybe. Or mercy.

Her parents came in for a conference once, and I told them how much I appreciated the great role Tessa was playing in our classroom. Her mother was shocked. "At home, she's just terrible!" she told me.

"What do you mean?" I said. "She's beautiful in class."

"Oh, she's always judging her sister, her parents. She's always telling us what's right."

"Well, yes," I agreed, "that's Tessa. But don't you find that she is often correct?"

Her mother grimaced. "Yes, I suppose she *is* right sometimes. But she shouldn't be passing judgment on us! She's only a child."

I'm not saying that I wouldn't have found it difficult, sometimes, to be in the position of Tessa's mother. But as Tessa's teacher, I celebrated her power to make good, true, and helpful judgments, and I was honored to give her the clear, open space in which to make them.

I carry this notion of the empty space into all my teaching, but nowhere does it seem more valuable to me than when I am playing the World Peace Game with my students. Although I've studied the ways of peace—with my parents, in my community, in the East—in the end I don't actually know how to create world peace. And I share my ignorance with my students. I admit the truth to them right up front. I tell them I don't know how to solve the problems I am asking them to solve. I apologize to them as well: "I'm so sorry, boys and girls, but the truth is, we have left this world to you in sad and terrible shape, and we hope you can fix it for us. Maybe the World Peace Game will help you learn how to do that." It's a sincere apology, and they take it very seriously. And because I don't know the answer, they see that if the world is going to be saved, it's up to them to do it. All I can do is arm them with some skills to take up the effort: the practical knowledge embodied in budgets and treaties and the ecology of endangered species; the creative tools of imagination and perseverance and the willingness to fail; and then, finally, the wisdom to be found in the empty space of mindfulness and attentiveness and an openness to the reality of the present moment. As my mother did this for me, I try to do it for them—and the stakes have never been higher.

I find that I keep asking myself who is in charge of my classroom. Who is really in charge? Because over my nearly thirty-five years as a teacher, I've gradually learned to cede control to the students. I don't have to control every conversation and response. My students' collective wisdom is greater than any individual wisdom I might possess, and I admit that to them openly.

Yet my students are wrestling with complex challenges that have no easy solutions. Often they must confront the darker side of their own natures—bullying, deceit, despair, fear. These elements, too, find their place in the empty space.

But here is the wonderful thing: they do save the world, each and every time. In this book, you'll meet Pablo, the quirky, offbeat kid who talked more slowly than anyone I've ever known—until one day, in a flash, the whole world suddenly made sense to him. On that day, he learned what a true leader he might actually become—and he showed me what unlikely forms a visionary leader can take.

You'll meet Amy, too, a quiet girl who was her nation's minister of defense. Against the direct orders of her prime minister, against the wishes of her people, and against everything she had been taught—I thought—Amy sent a tank battalion into a neighboring country's oil fields, keeping that country from accessing its most valuable resource. We all thought she was making war, and I was certain I had failed as a teacher. When we discovered her true motivation, I realized that peacemaking can take some unlikely guises. And we learned that in addition to good and bad, there is sometimes conditional good.

You'll see how, when the Game was almost lost, Brennan found a way to save the world at what was literally the last minute. You'll watch a brave little band of nine-year-olds stage a series of coups d'état trying to defeat a tyrant. You'll see how my students found a way to solve climate change and to balance the religious claims of a native tribe with a superpower's need for oil. You'll watch David wrestle with the price of victory, and you'll see Gary grapple with the lessons of defeat. Seeing how these children encounter seemingly impossible obstacles, struggle to find solutions, and somehow rise to the occasion illuminates our own obstacles on the road to peace and inspires us to imagine new resources for that journey. And seeing how they come into their own as they play reminds us that the future of our world depends on their finding their own wisdom, power, and compassion as they grow, slowly but surely, into the leaders whose decisions might, one day, save us all.

# 1

## John Comes Home

The army achieves victories yet they do not understand
how. Everyone knows the formation by which you achieved
victory, yet no one knows the formations by which you
were able to create victory.

— SUN TZU, *The Art of War*

THE TRUE MEANING OF the World Peace Game came
home to me while I was on a train heading from Shenzhen
to Guangzhou in China in the summer of 1987. For the past fifteen years, I had done everything I could to escape the bounds of
what I saw as my parochial little community of rural black folks
just outside Richmond, Virginia. I had grown a shoulder-length
set of dreadlocks. I had left my churchgoing background to study
Buddhism, Taoism, and the other philosophies of the East. And I
had spent as much time in India and Japan as I could manage. I
fancied myself a true world citizen, one who was equally at home
anywhere on the planet. This was my first trip to China, and I
was savoring the sense of making yet another part of the globe
my own.

In my second-class compartment, sharing some very hard
seats, were two tiny teenage girls who had come from Hong
Kong to visit their grandmother on the mainland. They'd come
into my car because they'd heard that an American was on the
train, and they wanted to practice their English and to learn
about America. In a few years (1997), Britain would cede Hong

Kong to the Chinese, and many Hong Kong residents wanted to get out before it became part of the communist mainland. These girls were determined to leave their childhood home, and their families were trying to arrange marriages for them and have them move to America or somewhere else beyond Chinese control. So they had a lot of questions for me about my native land, and I had quite a few questions for them, too.

The three of us talked for four or five hours, and since this was 1987 and China had just opened its doors, the sight of a foreigner —particularly a black man, and most particularly one with long dreadlocks—was something of an attraction on a train like this. So as we talked, the aisle outside our compartment filled up with people smoking, spitting, eating dinner, and watching our conversation, even though it was taking place in a language none of them could understand.

I was enjoying the discussion, and the audience, until one of the girls asked me a question that stopped me in my tracks: "Sir, where do you belong? Who do you belong to? Who is your group?"

This struck me because I had been in so many different groups since I'd left my home community—so many spiritual and social groups—that I'd begun to feel I had no particular allegiance anywhere, simply because I had come to have allegiance everywhere. After all, I had studied Indian politics and Chinese philosophy and Japanese religion. I had made myself at home (though still a stranger) in a five-hundred-year-old cypress-wood monastery on a bamboo-covered mountainside near the Sea of Japan. I had chanted with monks circumambulating the large reclining Jade Buddha at a temple in Shanghai. I had even swum in the Ganges River in the reddish dawn as saffron-robed monks stooped to dip their hands in their morning ablutions. I would have thought, before that young woman posed her questions, that I had transcended *community* and *nation* as well as *race,* so that I might be equally at home anywhere in the world.

But instead of making me feel elated and free, her questions filled me with a kind of sadness, and all at once I felt homeless. Suddenly, I was overcome with the desire to rejoin my own community of American black people. I wanted to return home. And it was out of this tension I experienced between *community* and *planet,* between loyalty to one's home and citizenship in the world, between belonging somewhere and belonging everywhere, that I finally understood the significance of the World Peace Game.

## Creating the Game

Soon after I returned home, I began teaching in a fourth-grade gifted program. I was given a lot of leeway to create my own curriculum and to do what I liked with my students, and I remembered the "interactive" game about Africa that I had created for my high school social studies class back in 1978. I thought that this kind of game might have some possibilities for my fourth graders as well, but that was as far as it went.

Then one night, I sat bolt upright in bed, seized by a vision of the Game. I had the experience—my own personal eureka moment—of conceiving all the mechanics of the Game in a single instant. It came to me as a diagram, an interconnected matrix of countries aligned in opposition to one another on every possible level—vertically (undersea, ground and sea, airspace, and outer space) and laterally—each country at odds with every other in every possible sphere: economic, military, social, ethnic. I could actually see the multifaceted crises floating there above my bed as I lay awake in the predawn hours.

I immediately reached for a pencil and a scrap of notepaper at my bedside, flipped on the table lamp, and propped myself up on my elbows, scribbling furiously. My vision was like a dream that was fading even as I reached for it, and I was frantic to get it all down before it evaporated completely. I sketched out the diagram I had seen—a kind of flow chart meant to represent an endless stream of crises. Then, in a frenzy of inspiration, I pressed on, trying to list each specific crisis and how it was interwoven with the others. I could feel myself teetering, as though I was balanced precariously on top of a narrow wall, arms perilously extended, desperate to seize my great discovery as it floated skyward out of my reach. I could see the multidimensional matrix of crises, but how could I write it all down? "What if Country A has a nuclear accident with wastes that flow downriver to a common bay shared with Country B, which is heavily dependent on a fishing industry and an agricultural sector situated on the banks of that bay . . . And what if there is combat between a rebel insurgency fighting Country A's farmers on the riverbanks, so that cleanup crews can't get in to stop the flow of waste . . . And suppose that an indigenous tribe has a religious ceremony involving that same river . . . And if Country C's economy depends on selling nuclear materials to Country A . . ." One complication followed another, and I scribbled frantically, my little nub of a pencil flying in the dim light.

But then I thought, *I must allow them some way out. Not an obvious way, not even a specific way, just some other factors that they could use—if they were insightful enough and relationship savvy enough—to pull themselves out of the crisis . . . maybe even to benefit themselves . . . maybe even to benefit others!* Yes, that was important. Maybe there could be a United Nations with funds and some jurisdictional power, perhaps a World Bank whose loans could help bail out a desperate nation . . . Because I realized that I had to overwhelm my students with crises—but not sink them with despair. I had to allow them some way out—but not too easily. I had to make the Game just hard enough—but not too hard. I had to demand the maximum of which they were capable—but not one ounce more.

I wrote until well after the sun came up, feverishly generating scenario after scenario, juxtaposing one disaster with another and "mining" them with trapdoors of good or ill fortune. I began

laying out a grid of two-sentence random cards—both negative and positive—that were to be drawn at each country's turn:
"Tsunami destroys the fishing villages along your coastline; refugees pour into your capital city"; "New invention causes produc-
tivity to rise, and $3 billion is added to your national budget";
"Your stock market takes a sudden downturn, and unemploy-
ment skyrockets." I envisioncd crisis after crisis—the ones they
started with and the ones that emerged as the Game progressed
—as I sought to complicate their every move. I was now walking the fine line between ensuring my students' utter failure by
overloading them with insurmountable crises and driving them
to go deeper and deeper into the risky nuances of problem solving to achieve ultimate success. Victory, I determined, would be
collective, or it would not be at all: "winning" would be defined
as solving every single crisis and substantially raising the asset
value of every single nation.

I began teaching the updated Game the next semester. In
those early days, I used one huge sheet of plywood on the classroom floor; later I started using a Plexiglas tower. From the first,
though, I stocked it with the plastic figures I found at local toy
stores and craft stores, just as I'd done with my two-dimensional
plywood map of Africa all those years before. Since that night,
the crises have multiplied, morphing into cvcr more complex
forms as I seek always to stay one step ahead of my students. I
want them to teeter near the brink of disaster, so that they can
learn to find their way out of danger. After all, this is what wc
adults must do, with our wars and our stock markets and our
climate change. I'd dearly love to see my students succeed where
we have failed, and so while I have the chance, I want to make
their training as rigorous and as useful as possible.

Over the past three decades, my students and I have known
plenty of bleak moments when war is all around us, while famine and all sorts of environmental disasters loom. We have also
known some stunning breakthroughs when the seemingly im-

possible, utterly inconceivable solution presents itself—a startling and sudden moment that I call the click. As we shall see in chapter 6, sometimes this click is an individual epiphany, the discovery of a single player or a couple of players working together. Sometimes it's a group occurrence as every player in the room seems to come simultaneously to a sudden realization of the way out. It's a thrilling thing to watch, and I have learned to anticipate its arrival, usually when things look their bleakest.

Over the years, trying to strike the correct balance between "too hard" and "just hard enough," I have added some crises and taken some away. I have tweaked some crises and allowed others to remain pretty much intact. Whatever else changes, though, I have always held fast to one central principle: all the crises must be connected, so that when one crisis shifts or is solved, as much as possible of every other situation must also change. In the world of the Game, everything must be interrelated . . . because, of course, everything is.

## The Saboteur Is Born

About ten years after we started playing the Game, I realized that some student groups seemed to have no desire for conflict. (Go figure!) They would start the Game with trepidation and almost immediately decide to pull back from all the crises. No matter how many conflicts I presented them with—hostilities between nations, rebel uprisings, disputes over resources—they would simply "declare peace." Countries would immediately lay down their arms, rebels would decide that they had nothing to rebel against, and rival nations would suddenly come to peaceable agreements over natural resources. Students raced to see how quickly they could win the Game by conjuring simple and unopposed fixes for all the problems. When the Game ended— supposedly in victory—everybody felt very smart. Only I knew that they had failed to experience the deep thinking required to work out tough problems—which meant that I, as their teacher, had failed.

So I wondered, *How can I force them into deeper engagement? How can I create an experience that will draw them into greater uncertainty and not allow them to tidy things up so easily?*

The idea of a confusion agent made its way into my mind as suddenly as the initial idea for the Game had. As I conceived it, such an agent would essentially pit the students against themselves. This agent, called the saboteur, would represent the urge toward destruction that lurks within us all. Adding this element to the Game would allow my students to discover that even if they master all the external circumstances, the real problem may lie within—a supposedly upright citizen whom they have accepted as one of their own but whose duty is actually to cause every possible measure of destruction. Students who "cheat" by accommodating one another far too quickly may solve the overt problems, but this covert agent is not so simply conquered.

The saboteur added a new dimension of uncertainty to every strategy a country might devise. Now nobody could take anything at face value. Even a brilliant solution had to be called into question—for perhaps the saboteur had been part of its conception. Even patriotism was suspect, since a cabinet minister's enthusiasm for an idea might in truth be the confusion agent's ploy to push us all over the brink into disaster.

When I first devised the saboteur, I was pretty taken with my own cleverness, thinking that I was somehow free of the internal deceptions wrought by this agent. Later I realized that the saboteur was actually a figure from my own psyche. This trickster harked back to an experience I'd had a decade earlier, sitting on a cushion in that mountainside monastery near the Sea of Japan. As I meditated in that supremely peaceful spot, riven by the lack of peace within, I was forced to see that the greatest enemy to my understanding, my progress, and my hopes for success was my own internal saboteur. My own mind—its predilections, tendencies, habits, and preconceptions—continually undermined my own best efforts. In that cold, drafty zendo, my black robe was no armor against self-delusion; nor could the wafting incense of the meditation hall mask my attachment to my superficial perceptions about who I was, my purpose in life, even my "learned" understandings about the very nature of existence. My greatest obstacle to improving myself was my own concept of myself; the shallow understandings to which I clung so desperately were actually blocking the way to deeper understanding.

Once I was able to see my saboteur, I could work with him, and then, finally, I began to make my way more easily in meditation. In exactly this fashion, the saboteur in the Game often blocks students' easy access to success. A central challenge of the Game is for students either to expose the saboteur and thereby eliminate his power, or, even better, to foil his efforts without ever finding out who he is. In the second case, students play at such a principled and clearheaded level that his efforts to undermine them simply do not land. At that level, there is no need to expose the saboteur, for he has already become irrelevant to the larger play of the Game. Either way, the presence of the saboteur spurs students to greater levels of mastery, which I hope they will take with them into future challenges.

## The Problem of the Nin

Although I never consciously thought of the World Peace Game as mirroring my own experiences under segregation during the late 1950s and early 1960s, I've come to see that the correspondences are there and that it was Sun Tzu who gave me the language to incorporate my early survival techniques into the Game. For example, when I wanted my students to consider the minority ethnic and religious struggles within a larger culture, I created the Nin, a minority within an ecologically minded nation that was neither the richest nor the poorest in the Game but that was deeply committed to peace and human rights.

The Nin, however, were not content to remain within the safe borders of their homeland. They crossed their nation's boundary to stake a claim in a gold-rich mountainous region inside the territory of a much wealthier neighbor. Their boldness was inspired by an independent team of archaeologists, who, in my tricky crisis scenario, announced DNA-confirmed evidence that the skeletal remains discovered in this gold-laden terrain were, in fact, Nin ancestors. The Nin religion requires that ancestral remains are never to be moved or disturbed in any way and that any land where Nin bones rest is to be considered part of the Nin homeland. As a result, in this scenario the Nin believed that they had a religious and cultural duty to occupy their neighbor's land, despite the fact that someone else owned it.

Because the Nin are an imaginary tribe rather than a real-world people, I don't have to worry about my students' preexisting associations. The fantasy thus becomes a kind of empty space allowing for new thoughts and connections. Of course, similar religious and territorial conflicts throughout the world can be read through the lens of the Nin.

This to me has all the elements of a productive crisis and an excellent teaching tool, for there is no obvious right answer. I myself could not solve such a dilemma, so every semester I wait eagerly to see how my students will manage it. One especially intriguing scenario played out like this.

The wealthy invaded nation prepares to oust the Nin, pointing out that the tribal people have no legal right to live inside its borders. For one or two Game Days, there is a tense impasse, with many failed attempts at resolution and no sign of a breakthrough.

Then suddenly, the prime minister of the wealthy neighbor has an idea. What would be the consequences, she inquires, of her converting to the Nin religion and, in effect, becoming a Nin?

As the class ponders this surprising suggestion, the prime minister turns to the United Nations, which has never faced such a proposal before. Discussions begin, approval is given, and a procedure is formulated. And lo and behold, the prime minister's solution of essentially joining the other side immediately eases the tension between the parties, since the Nin now see their former enemy as one of their own. With their new shared loyalties, the two sides are finally able to work out an arrangement.

Of course, my fourth graders' solution seems simplistic by adult standards, and I'm certainly not advocating religious conversion or a leader switching sides as a literal response to the world's problems. What I am advocating is that we divest ourselves of our habit of tightly clinging to a single identity and perceived role. The prime minister's innovative solution enabled her to let go of her role long enough to envision a new identity for herself and a new solution for her people. And that, I believe, constitutes very useful training.

I was struck that this particular solution involved undermining the enemy by essentially "disappearing," as the former enemy became one with her opponent. I think Sun Tzu would have understood and perhaps even approved.

## A Home in the World

All of the diverse influences in my life somehow came together that night I sat bolt upright in bed and created the World Peace Game. I can see now that the Game reflects my own efforts to negotiate those old primal categories: *individual, community, nation, planet.* Inevitably, then, the Game comes with an attractive lure to be nationalistic, tribalistic, and provincial. It forces students to go through the process that we all go through as adults, in which we must examine, as I had done, the local cultures we come from and the world culture we might one day join. The Game makes it clear that, sooner or later, if students remain solely within their own cultures, loyal only to their "own kind," they will put the planet at grave risk. But if they embrace a larger vision, they have the opportunity to heal the planet and create peace. Students learn, in other words, that without a total collaborative effort, no one can succeed.

Of course, it's tempting to hold to an individualistic view and pursue short-term gains. It's certainly possible, over the arc of the Game, to seem to be winning: to increase your territory and your assets; to enter into alliances that benefit you and hurt your adversaries; to expand your military influence; to amass wealth and power at others' expense. But these victories are only apparent. You *seem* to be winning, but you're actually losing. The Game forces you to learn interdependency. If you behave as an island unto yourself, ultimately you will be isolated. And no matter how many resources you might have accrued, the planet as a whole will not achieve the global peace and prosperity that are the Game's definition of victory.

Mindful of the various ways in which even fourth graders already feel some allegiance to various nations and cultures, I decided not to select real countries for the Game but rather to create imaginary ones. I was afraid that with real nations, my students would have enough information to be stuck with the current state of affairs, rather than being a little bit freer to make the world whatever they wanted it to be. Without the baggage of actual countries to start with, maybe they'd be bolder about finding creative solutions. The imaginary world I created for them is yet another version of the empty space—the space of possibility that they themselves must populate, rather than relying on the information and stereotypes, and even the truths, that they already know.

The countries we begin with do have echoes of reality—but only echoes. One nation is extremely poor, with few natural resources and a small population struggling to survive in an arctic terrain. Its budget is a mere $3 billion (or whatever currency we decide to use: euro, yen, pesos, rupees, or yuan). Another is a vast, oil-rich, desert-based land with a large tanker fleet for exporting oil and a considerably larger budget of $789 billion. The wealthiest country—its budget a whopping $989 billion—has an abundance of everything and holds key territories on which many smaller ethnic groups depend. The fourth nation, a middle-income country with a budget of $475 billion, is committed to alternative energy (with some dependence on fossil fuels) and a deep philosophical mandate to protect the earth and life at all costs.

The Kajazians, by the way, don't have any money to start with, although they inhabit an oil-rich territory, while the tribal Nin have $500 million at their disposal. The United Nations has a budget of $3 billion, and it can also charge dues of $10 million per day, which countries can elect to pay or not. The World Bank has a budget of $1.7 trillion, while the arms dealers have $75 million plus a store of valuable armaments. The saboteur's budget is only $20 million—just about enough to buy four intercontinental ballistic missiles (ICBMs) or to support a few thousand mercenary troops—so he has to allocate his resources wisely.

Some students occasionally relate the wealthiest country to the United States or the oil-rich one to a Middle East power. But they name their own countries as the Game begins, which is their inauguration into this alternate reality. They like the freedom to make of each country what they wish, and because the situation changes so quickly and things go so immediately off the rails, they soon stop identifying their imaginary countries with any real ones.

The crises they begin with, however, are real enough. When I introduce the Game to the students, I move around the four-story representation of our globe and call out the problems: tribal, ethnic, and religious minority strife; nuclear proliferation; nuclear waste contamination and nuclear accidents; water rights disputes; desertification caused by overfarming and overgrazing;

breakaway republics and disputes over the sovereign rights of newly independent states; offshore oil spills and cleanup disasters — in combat zones! (I want the crises to be as complex as possible, with multiple obstacles that all interact with one another.) As I move around the game board, pointing to different continents, I continue: revoked and broken treaties; land claims and sovereignty disputes; disagreements over territorial waters and fishing rights; overfishing and ocean destruction; conflict over ethnic homelands and people forced into refugee status. Those are the crises on the ground and sea level.

Then I point to the next level up: problems with planes that strayed into another country's airspace, pollution drifting across the skies, the thinning ozone layer. And then farther up, into outer space: disputes over asteroid mining, countries that develop *Star Wars*–type killer satellites in defiance of international law. And then the undersea level: conflicts over undersea mining, perhaps, and the sunken treasure of ancient civilizations — ships discovered by citizens of one country in international waters or the territorial waters of another country, and the consequent ownership disputes over the spoils.

To link these elements, I have created a chaos formula that generates a series of fifty major and minor crises whose components are based on all the pressing planetary problems that I can think of. The formula ensures that all the problems are interlocking, so that if one element changes, other components change as well. For example, one crisis begins as the following chain: endangered species + oil drilling + eco-protector nation + naval invasion + territorial waters + imminent famine without oil revenue. Translated into English, that crisis becomes, *A microscopic endangered species inhabits a remote island of a poor country that happens to be the location of as-yet-untapped oil fields. The poor country faces an imminent famine without this oil revenue. It wants to sell drilling rights to its rich neighbor, which is eager — perhaps desperate — to find another source of oil. But a third nation, which has a very*

*strong commitment to ecological protection, objects to the destruction of*
*the endangered species and wants to prevent the drilling.*

That's one crisis. There are forty-nine more.

My goal is to create crises in which every party is pitted against every other party in every possible sphere: political, social, economic; airspace, outer space, ground and sea; human, animal, environmental. I'm looking for multiple layers of complexity, problems with no easy answers, crises that require solutions that nobody—not even I—can foresee. As I write these words, it amazes me to think that a group of nine-year-olds has been able to solve these crises—and realistically, with budgets and schedules and very specific trade agreements and debt negotiations and treaties. I love how eager and excited they are to confront these problems, although as soon as the Game begins, the problems take on a reality that is often sobering, even daunting. It's *hard* to save the world.

## Real Crises in Imaginary Countries

A key aspect of the Game is its otherworldliness: real-life crises besetting imaginary nations. This is crucial, because the element of unreality allows me to disturb the conventional leanings and supports that my students have already started to form—a disturbance that I consider part of my mission. I think children's creativity is inhibited when they simply inherit someone else's stale old image that was manufactured in Hollywood or in an advertising agency. Africa, land of the savages and dictators; Middle East sheiks and oil barons; upright American guardians of freedom—these ready-made political categories and stereotypes have already begun to colonize my fourth graders' imaginations, imposing on them the same kinds of limits with which adults struggle. The unreal aspect of the Game preserves the empty space within which my students are free to start over and reimagine politics, economics, and human relations, forging insights that might enable them to view real-world problems with fresh eyes.

Of course, the children are still continually exposed to that mental colonization—the ready-made ideas that curtail what they might imagine or aspire to. When I walk into a classroom, for example, and say, "Today we're focusing on creative writing," my students get all excited and pull out their pencils and paper or their laptops.

Then I'll say, "There's just one thing—today we have some limitations." Well, they kind of like that, because it gives them some direction, but when I announce what the limitations actually are, they're a bit baffled. I say, "Today, no explosions, no death, no injury, no pets, no fuzzy bunnies, no monsters, no aliens."

Once when I did that, one boy, exasperated, said, "So what are we are going to write about?" I thought that was so telling—that the images they usually go for when they start creating come from far outside their own experience. So how do we strip away all that stuff—the burden imposed by 3-D movie animators and cartoonists—and start from zero? What happens when there is no Hollywood or Internet to depend on, no video game scripts to follow, no Harry Potter or car chases or vampires? How do we take away those screens and let them see what is inside themselves? How do we create for them a truly empty space—free of commercial imagery and political preconceptions—within which they might create something genuinely new? After all, our old ways of seeing and understanding and creating political relationships have manifestly failed to bring about world peace. Unleashing the creativity of the next generation may be our only hope—but how do we do it?

One way is simply to overwhelm children with complexity. We often dumb things down for them, making problems and explanations as simple as possible. It's as if we think their minds cannot stand complexity. Well, the World Peace Game is just the opposite. I pack in as many complexities as I possibly can. My students are hit with so much information, so many contradictory needs and demands, and so many competing claims for their attention that they are forced to become critical thinkers. If they are to survive within the welter of those fifty overlapping crises, they have no choice but to discern what is extraneous, what is ambiguous, and what is irrelevant. They must decide for themselves which information is reliable and which isn't—without having to undergo a real-life emergency. I hope that when they do encounter a real-life crisis—whether that crisis is personal or global or maybe some of both—they will think back to some of the lessons they learned while playing the World Peace Game and find themselves equipped with everything they need to move forward.

## The Kajazian Conundrum

One of the knottiest problems in the World Peace Game involves the Kajazians. Like the Nin, the Kajazians are a tribal people, constituted as an ethnic minority within a larger nation. They have their own tribal region in the second-largest country in the Game, and their chieftain is that country's minister of defense.

In one of the inherited crises that are a given for the Game, the Kajazians are living in an area that they want to claim as an independent nation and are petitioning the United Nations for political and economic control over that territory. They point out that they have occupied the region for thousands of years, but it is a region that happens to contain most of the country's oil reserves. They decide to form a breakaway republic and offer to sell the oil they now control to the neighboring country to the north, which is desperately in need of a reliable energy source.

The mother country, of course, is unwilling to recognize Kajazian independence for fear of losing the oil. How are the children supposed to handle that situation?

In one session of the Game, Julianne was the minister of defense of the mother country, and her first solution was to attempt a coup against her nation's prime minister. In the Game, anyone can attempt a coup, which is then settled by a series of odds-weighted coin tosses that favor the leader—who in real life would naturally have more power and resources than the rebels—although the rebels can potentially win the series of tosses. Julianne lost, meaning that the coup failed. As with any failed coup leader, she was condemned to exile. She chose to go into exile in the Kajazian region, which she claimed was actually a separate country, since she, at least, recognized its independence.

Open conflict in the form of a coup had failed, so Julianne found another way. She began soliciting support for her cause from other countries. She became a brilliant diplomat who successfully lobbied every other country and the United Nations to intercede on her behalf with the oil-rich country. Before my eyes, she turned into a super-collaborator.

The students worked out a deal in which Julianne became co–prime minister of the country that was refusing to recognize her people's independence. Instead of forming a breakaway republic, the Kajazians entered into an ingenious form of power sharing, and the contested land was granted to them as a semi-autonomous region. They ended up sharing the oil wealth, too, rather than trying to take it all, and with Julianne operating in her double capacity—tribal chieftain and defense minister of a larger nation—she was able to get her people to lighten up a bit.

## Ingrid and the Ultimate Crisis

One of the most striking examples of tribal versus global came one year when my students had managed to solve all the crises relatively early. World peace and ultimate victory were clearly at hand, and you might think that the children would have been happy. But a small group of them came to me secretly and said,

"Please, Mr. Hunter, could we have some more crises?" Sometimes playing the Game is truly more important than winning —even when world peace is at stake!

I had actually run out of the usual crises, as the kids had already solved all fifty of them. But I still had one up my sleeve; I call it the Ultimate Crisis. It doesn't come up very often, but sometimes there is a need or an opportunity for it, and this was one of those times.

I called the children together and said, "I have been instructed by an unknown third party to move a spaceship down from the sky to land *here*." I placed the spaceship on a deserted island owned by the poorest country, whose prime minister was a thoughtful child named Ingrid. As they all watched, I had some figures step out of the craft, encircling it as if to protect it.

These figures were not soldiers. In fact, they weren't even human. They stood upright, and each one had a little horizontal object pointing outward that could have been a weapon or a gun of some sort, or that could simply have been just a little stick. They stayed there, surrounding their ship, not communicating with anyone. None of the children knew who they were or what the ship was or what was going on.

As it happened, it was Ingrid's country's turn to act. If she and her people hadn't learned anything from the Game, most likely they would go ahead and attack the alien invaders. In fact, I was deliberately tempting them to do something impulsive and dangerous.

Of course, they did have the option to wait. If they waited, they were taking a risk that something bad would happen . . . or something good. Ingrid's people were divided about what to do, and the decision was ultimately hers. She took a long time deliberating, but finally, to my relief, she decided not to attack.

What Ingrid didn't know—but later found out—was that if she had attacked, she would have been attacking her own mother. According to this scenario, the prime minister was actually the child of a human father and an alien mother, who, as commander of the spaceship, had come back to reunite with her long-lost daughter. Had Ingrid attacked, she would have been at war with her own mother.

This was kind of a devious thing for me to do, wasn't it? But I created this crisis because I thought it would provoke a very deep level of thinking among the children—not only among Ingrid and her people, whose decision it was, but among all the students in the Game. They knew that this was the last crisis of the Game and that the wrong move here might undo everything they had spent the past eight weeks working to build. And indeed, it took Ingrid quite a while to decide what to do.

Once she found out who the aliens were, that was almost more challenging. Because now she was being greeted by a long-lost mother who was commanding the spacecraft, someone who was informing her that her father never told her the truth: she was really half alien and half human. How do you deal with being half from one world and half from another?

Having grown up in a segregated black community and then having attended a virtually all-white school, I was certainly familiar with the problem of being half from one world and half from another, which is no doubt why it found its way into the Game. It turned out that Ingrid was familiar with it in real life, too, because her father was British and her mother was Korean. And she brought that experience to bear on her decision whether to attack. For a while, she was torn between the two options. Finally, she told me later, she thought of what her mother would say and what her father would say. She made the connection that just as her parents came from two different cultures and had two different perspectives, her team expressed two different points of view. And just as with her parents, she wasn't free to ignore either of them. She had to take both into account.

"My father would have said *act,* but my mother would have said *wait,*" Ingrid told me afterward. "So I decided to do both

—to wait, but to be ready to act, in case something happened." And it was a good thing she did wait, because the aliens came out and revealed themselves the next time her turn came around.

"My parents come from two different places," Ingrid went on, "so I tried to listen to both of them."

In Ingrid's response, I saw a global future in which each of us experiences diverse influences across the planet at a very personal level. I also thought of a famous Buddhist exercise that asks you to imagine that every person you meet in your life's journey was at some point, in some lifetime, your own mother. In this way, you are asked to cultivate compassion toward everyone —no matter how alien, hostile, or adversarial he or she might seem—because, appearances to the contrary, that person has at some point nurtured you, cared for you, and belonged to you as you belonged to them. What would happen to the planet if everyone understood that every person on earth has at some point given him or her the nourishment and care he or she needed to survive?

## We Are Never Just Ourselves

Stories like Ingrid's remind me that we are never just ourselves. We are always interrelated. We are always continuous, in some sense, with our families, our communities, and our culture. We are always part of our history—the friends and strangers and teachers and enemies who have shaped us. And we are always, whether we realize it or not, part of the larger world, citizens of the planet.

Sometimes I stand at a certain spot in my classroom and look out the window, and it occurs to me that this is something that my mother did decades ago. She stood in a room like mine surrounded by children, and she looked out the window. And I know she paused, just as I do, and allowed herself to just be and to appreciate the experience. At such times, it feels as though there is no separation between us, that she hasn't gone anywhere, that she's right here, and I'm just a continuation of her gesture.

And in a way, I have come home, to teach my daughter in my own classroom just as my mother taught me, to carry on the gestures of my family, my teachers, my community. But I see now that although I belong to this family, this community, I can never belong to them only—I have never belonged to them only. My hunger for experiences that my community could not give me drove me to seek enlightenment in other countries. And my sense of fellowship with people across the planet made it impossible for me to cling to a fixed or rigid identity, even when it might have been more comfortable to do so. I returned home to create the World Peace Game and to play it with children in the communities where I have lived and taught. Now the Game is pushing me to go far afield once more, perhaps to play it with people in Norway and Taiwan, to speak of it to people in Paris and Shanghai and Tel Aviv.

So that may be the answer I keep seeking, the answer I keep hoping my students will someday find. The tensions between individual and community, between community and planet, are continually being created and then dissolving, being re-created and then dissolving once more. I become other people—and yet remain myself. Or I become other people to become myself. As I write these words, I'm not just myself, but many people. I'm here, but I'm not here alone. None of us is.

# 2

# Pablo Sees It All

> Even in the midst of the turbulence of battle, the fighting
> seemingly chaotic, they are not confused. Even in the
> midst of the turmoil of battle, the troops seemingly going
> around in circles, they cannot be defeated. Disorder came
> from order, fear came from courage, weakness came from
> strength.
>
> — SUN TZU, *The Art of War*

THE FIRST FEW DAYS of the World Peace Game are always
an exciting time. Children are studying their dossiers, trying to absorb that they have not one, not two, but *fifty* crises
to solve. They're looking at their national budgets, figuring out
the difference between a minister of defense and a secretary of
state, eyeing their neighbor nations and trying to decide whether
these people are friends or enemies. They are very much conscious of the adult-level responsibilities they have been given,
and even though they understand that this is just a game, to
children—and, in fact, to the adults who have played the World
Peace Game—the experience soon takes on a very intense reality. Although my nine-year-olds understand that their wars and
ecological disasters are purely imaginary, to all of us—myself as
well as them—these crises feel real.

And so we embark on the first stage, *overload and confusion,* of
what is ultimately a seven-stage journey:

1. Overload and confusion
2. Failure
3. Personal understanding
4. Collaboration
5. "Click"
6. Flow
7. Application of understanding

We always begin with overload and confusion as the students are hit with the new environment of the Game and the first welter of overlapping crises. In fact, because I believe that an overload of complexity is precisely what can open the space for creativity and new solutions, I have deliberately designed the Game to begin with a flood of information that makes it impossible for even the brightest, most confident student to feel sure of knowing "the answer."

As the Game begins, the children enter the classroom to find a structure they've never seen before—a four-level Plexiglas tower arrayed with little plastic factories, cities, soldiers, and tanks. On the ground and sea level, they see the trappings of peace and war, leaders and citizens, oceans and deserts, poverty and wealth. The outlined areas on this second level, at just about their knees, reveal four nations: (1) a large, wealthy expanse of green denoting a First-World power rich in resources and enjoying a high standard of living; (2) a sand-colored, wealthy desert country dotted with oil wells, refineries, and tankers; (3) a barren, white icebound country that is sparsely populated and has few resources and not much infrastructure; and (4) a moderate-size, deeper-green country that the children will eventually learn has the mandate of protecting the planet and the people who inhabit it.

The children try to take in the profusion of visual information as their eyes drop to the floor level, beneath the sea, where military submarines prowl, undersea mining takes place, and a sunken civilization, ships, and valuable artifacts lie. Their eyes rise to the air level, supporting dozens of fighter jets, transport planes, and bombers in the designated airspace above each sovereign nation on the level below. On the top level, above the heads of most fourth graders, is the outer space level, with a scattering of stars, a space station, satellites, asteroids and asteroid-mining spaceships, and even a black hole.

These students have heard about the Game—maybe from their older siblings or from friends who played it during summer session—so there's a certain excitement about finally getting the chance to play it themselves. To them, the Game must seem both familiar and strange. On the one hand, those little plastic figures—transport trucks, ships, soldiers, tanks—are like the toys they play with at home or at a neighbor's house. On the other hand, the four-level structure is imposing and mysterious —a code they've not yet cracked. My job is to load them up with even more complexity—enough so that the "overload" breaks through their preset ideas of how decisions are made, work is done, and problems are solved, but not so much that they become incapacitated. A productive confusion, or a useful overload, is my goal, and every year I watch closely to make sure I'm maintaining that delicate balance.

"Welcome to the World Peace Game," I say to them, and slowly they turn their attention away from the structure and toward me. "I'm very, very sorry, but . . . you're going to have to have fun today."

They break into mock groans, and I pretend to apologize. "I know, I know, very difficult to do. Now listen, please, if you would. I'm going to explain the Game. For the next half-hour, you're going to have to absorb a lot."

I walk around the structure as I talk, their eyes darting from it to me and back to it. I explain that there are four nations, and I describe each one. I run through all the different types of crises, watching closely to see if I'm losing anybody. At this point, they're usually still on the "excited" side of feeling overwhelmed, thrilled to think that they'll be entrusted with the opportunity to make these new countries their own. I explain that each Game Day begins with the easternmost country (where the sun rises) making its declarations: the announcement of a treaty, perhaps, or the movement of troops to a new location, or the decision to build a water purification plant—whatever national business its prime minister and cabinet have decided on. I explain that the Game will continue that day until each country has had its chance to declare its actions, with time between the announcements for cabinet members to confer, negotiations to begin, deals to be made, and coalitions to be formed. When each nation has had its say, that Game Day's play is over. It usually takes about eight Game Days spread over eight to ten weeks to solve all the problems of the world.

## Appointing World Leaders

After I explain the ground rules, I announce my appointments for the post of prime minister. Every so often, someone will refuse his or her appointment, but usually the students accept their roles—some shyly bubbling with excitement, others confident and enthused, and still others uncertain but determined. They don't yet know what leadership entails, but watching them step into their greatness, earnest and ready to do their best, is always a moving experience for me.

I choose the prime ministers based on my relationships with them, relying on my intuition as to who might benefit the most from this chance to lead. I am less concerned about the effects these leaders will have on the other students than I am about the learning opportunity for prime ministers themselves. To some extent, this is because of my trust in the random nature of the Game as a learning tool, rather than a results-oriented effort. The goal is not to reach world peace as quickly or as smoothly as possible, but to allow the entire class to wrestle collectively with a group problem. I don't want to put any individual student at risk by asking him or her to step into a leadership role for which he or she is not ready. So I trust my intuition as to which students need the chance to grow into leaders, and I trust the class to cope with whatever situations that produces.

As you'll see in the coming chapters, sometimes my decisions produce bigger challenges than others. In some cases, my selection of a leader has allowed a bully to take power or arrogance to put the world at risk. Ultimately, however, the class as a whole has found ways to overcome the mistakes or shortcomings of any individual leader—which seems like one of the most valuable lessons they could learn.

Then it's time for each prime minister to choose his or her cabinet: typically, a secretary of state, a defense minister, and a chief financial officer, although sometimes the cabinets are larger. These are momentous decisions, and the prime ministers usually treat them as such.

"You can choose your best friends all you want to," I remind them. "However, your best friend may not be good for that job. So choose the person in this room who can do the job for you the best." Sometimes that reminder works; sometimes it doesn't. Children who are already beginning to feel overwhelmed, or perhaps those with a strong sense of loyalty or a love of familiarity, may be more likely to fill their cabinets with close friends. These friends may be the best people for the job, not least because they have already formed a bond of trust with the leader. Still, I'm always impressed by how many of my students cast a wide net and consider their classmates thoughtfully, even the ones with whom they don't seem to have much in common.

After selecting the four prime ministers, or major world leaders, I turn to the Nin, a designated religious and ethnic minority in the environmentally conscious country, and the Kajazians, a tribal minority of the oil-rich nation. The Nin have a religious leader, who also happens to have a cabinet position as secretary of state—second-in-command—of the environmentally conscious nation. The Kajazians have a chieftain, who is also minister of defense of their motherland. Neither of these leaders has a cabinet as such, but they do have some limited political power within their larger governments. The Nin have a budget, although the Kajazians do not. The Nin budget is not as large as even the poorest nation's budget, but it is enough to engage in limited trade or buy arms.

Next I choose a student as president of the World Bank. He or she selects a chief executive officer and a chief financial officer. Together, they review loans for various national and international development projects. One time, the bank made a loan to the poor icebound nation for a special heating system. Another time, it financed a water purification plant that was a joint endeavor of the oil-rich nation and the poor nation. The World Bank routinely audits the "books" of each country's chief financial officer, helping to correct accounting errors and to plan for future financing. Once, the bank's CEO "invented" insurance and sold policies to each country to cover potential losses due to natural disasters. Students who staff the World Bank quickly learn to add, subtract, and make long-term fiscal projections. I can see them now, shuffling through stacks of green bonds and checks, whispering about where interest rates should be set, who has loans outstanding, and how to subtract a billion from a trillion.

I also appoint a secretary-general of the United Nations, who selects his or her deputy secretaries. These august officials might institute their own programs, reprimand nations, or initiate other types of actions. They might also propose treaties, arbitrate disputes between nations, attempt to coordinate relief operations in war zones, collaborate with the World Bank, or even, on occasion, work with the arms dealers. To lead the UN, I want a student who has a deep sense of fairness, is respected by the entire group, and is patiently, even doggedly, devoted to discussion, negotiation, and renegotiation. By the end of the Game, he or she will have learned how to simultaneously manage a wide variety of interconnected crises and prevent looming crises from fully developing.

Next, I choose the arms dealers. Each country comes equipped with a certain amount of armaments, but often, of course, the countries want more. The two ethnic groups—the Nin and the Kajazians—never start the Game with any weapons, but they can choose to purchase or trade for some and often do, especially the fierce Kajazians, who are allotted the role of a breakaway republic petitioning the UN for statehood. The Nin tend to be a peaceful people, but many of the crises are set up to provoke them by creating various real or perceived threats to their homeland, religion, or way of life. They have little in the way of material resources but are long on religious fervor, which influences all their policy decisions.

The arms dealer positions have generally been more popular among the boys. But some girls also seem to enjoy creating their own destinies by both openly and secretly making deals and trades. Whether boys or girls, the arms dealers increase the Game's complexity, expanding the potential for minor conflicts to bloom into full-scale battles or, at the very least, to cause a dramatic increase in military tensions: just one more thing to be concerned about in this fluid matrix of delicate and explosive elements. Although the excitement of being "bad" is inherent in the role, there is also room—and sometimes even incentive—to leverage arms power into something good for the world.

Somewhere along the way, I choose the weather god or goddess, although for some reason, it's usually a goddess. With her long, thin metal wand, she pushes cotton clouds across the sky, pausing to dole out rain or moving on to impose a drought. She is also in charge of the two spinners we use. One is for the Game's random stock market, with options for "skyrocket," "plummet," or "no change." The other is for the weather. The resulting stock market and weather reports immediately affect the fortunes of the nation whose turn it is.

The weather goddess is also called on to make rulings and issue decisions on whether a venture, business, or investment is successful or not. She uses an odds-weighted series of coin tosses to find the outcome of a situation and then relies on her own judgment to decide the magnitude of the effect. A nation cannot appeal any decision handed down by the weather goddess. She is much like nature in that way, seemingly capricious while exhibiting a universal evenhandedness.

On one occasion, an undersea oil gusher, similar to the spring 2010 disaster in the Gulf of Mexico, was spewing oil and fouling the fishing grounds of the poorest nation. The oil leak also endangered a fragile coral reef nearby. Within only two or three Game Days, reef life would become extinct. Financial losses for the nation's fishing industry would be millions of dollars daily until the leak was finally capped. The weather goddess ruled that the ocean currents at first moved the oil closer to the reef, heightening the chances of losing a species while giving a bit of a reprieve to the fishermen of the poor country. The next Game Day, she changed the direction of the currents, now allowing breathing room for the coral reef while threatening the fishing once again. When the students turn to me, as the Game's inventor, with questions about chance, odds, and destiny, I turn to the weather goddess and ask, "What do you think? How will you rule on this issue?" Our best goddesses are intuitively able to handle these complexities with a firm grace and clear wisdom, sometimes calling for a series of coin tosses, sometimes ruling after a period of reflection, and sometimes calling for a recess so they can consult the Internet for information. The students to whom I offer this pivotal role are the type of kids you might expect to see on the U.S. Supreme Court someday: even-tempered, reflective, able to see many perspectives at once and to withhold judgment until the right moment, and ultimately decisive, whether their decisions are popular or not.

Finally, I choose the saboteur. I am more careful about picking the student for this role than for any other, because saboteurs need an unusual set of qualities. On the one hand, they must play a conventional role in the Game—a prime minister, cabinet member, or other type of official—and they must play this role well enough that no one suspects they are not entirely on the up-and-up. On the other hand, they must do everything they can to sabotage the work they are doing "aboveground," sowing the maximum amount of confusion and creating the maximum distress among their fellow citizens and allies. Playing two such contradictory roles requires a very high level of objectivity and insight, and I must weigh carefully whether my candidates for this position have the ability to carry it off.

Usually my top candidate is a high-functioning student (often the class troublemaker) who is able to work for peace collaboratively in public while secretly and subtly trying to bring down the entire World Peace Game. The saboteur's job involves making innuendoes, creating ambiguities, sprinkling irrelevancies in conversation, and generally being misleading in negotiations and even in casual interactions. Not allowed to lie outright, the saboteur plays out his or her public role while simultaneously passing secret instructions on to me. After receiving such a directive, I say, "I have been instructed by an unknown third party . . .," then proceed to the game board to place a battle marker where the saboteur's mercenaries are grouping or remove a shadowy army from its threatening position outside a nation's capital.

When choosing the saboteur, I pull my potential collaborator aside, out of earshot of the other students or while they are noisily involved in other activities, and quickly ask, "Would you be willing to be the saboteur?" Often there is a quick, joyous grin, but sometimes I see a look of consternation or even a definite shake of the head—*No way!* Students have the right to refuse any appointment, so when this happens, I go on to ask someone else. Those who accept are instructed that they may meet with me secretly during the school day or contact me by note or even e-mail or phone.

One of our greatest saboteurs once directed me to launch an ICBM on his own nation's capital in order to distract attention from himself as the possible saboteur. The strategy paid off. "Why would he attack his own country?" another minister asked during the saboteur's trial, but the trial ended, with the accusations being withdrawn, before the truth could be discovered.

The kids all know there's a saboteur in our midst. I tell them so at the very beginning of the Game. A heightened awareness and vigilance charges the atmosphere after this announcement, which has the effect of sharpening the students' discernment and causing them to question every conversation and every action.

As I mentioned earlier, I put the saboteur role in the Game thirteen years ago when I noticed that my strongest teams often unified so quickly and effectively that they made short work of most of the Game's crises. Casting a seed of doubt or a bit of grit into that finely oiled problem-solving machine allows my students to reach new heights of creativity and new levels of rigor and discipline in their problem solving. A side benefit is that the confusion agent's role allows for the participation of a student who seems to have a bit of a contrary nature or a rebellious streak, or one who wants to join the group on his or her own terms and can't seem to get along with others as a result. In general, I don't try to change these students' nature, but rather to play to their underlying strengths in a setting where they can be themselves and still work within the class in a useful way. Playing this role allows such students to exercise their seemingly negative or perverse "talents" as the invisible opponent of, well, everyone —but in a way that makes the Game more challenging and thus helps the entire class.

Initially, students view the saboteur as an obstacle. Later, as the class's excitement about overcoming their massive challenges grows, the saboteur comes to be seen as an integral part of the Game, the net in our tennis match, so to speak. The challenge is what makes the Game fun!

As the role has been developed by some of my greatest players, I've also come to see that in a sense, the saboteur is our best conscience and our sharpest critic. Like a brilliant editor, a good saboteur excels at ferreting out our weak spots and demanding, in effect, that we become stronger, smarter, and more compassionate. The other players can't get away with sloppy thinking, gossip, factionalism, or hasty actions, because all of these provide fertile ground for the saboteur to sow his or her seeds of destruction. If the saboteur lands mercenaries on a nation's borders, for example, the temptation is for that nation to instantly blame a neighboring nation. Or perhaps a frustrated prime minister will attribute the action to a student he or she doesn't like. The saboteur teaches the students to resist such temptations—to make clear, just, and compassionate decisions regardless of any provocation. In this way, the saboteur discovers that he or she can be a positive factor and is ultimately playing for the same goal as everyone else, albeit from a different angle. Accordingly, when the saboteur is finally revealed—usually at the end of the Game in those joyous moments when the winning announcement is made—he or she is always boisterously celebrated and congratulated for a job well done.

Because any student can accuse someone of being the confusion agent, the saboteur is under constant threat of being discovered. An accusation leads to a Game-stopping trial in which evidence for and against the accused is presented by anyone who has something to contribute. A vote is taken after all the evidence is heard, just as in a real-world jury trial. Unlike in real life, though, we ask the accused to publicly reveal whether he or she is the saboteur. If the child is indeed the confusion agent, we award $50 million (or the equivalent in whatever currency we have decided to use in this session of the game) to the accusing nation or party. If the child is not the saboteur, the accuser must pay a $50 million penalty for the false accusation.

The saboteur gets a small budget of $20 million, which isn't much to buy armaments. So to work their mischief, saboteurs mostly have to rely on various types of miscommunication and subterfuge. The intrigue sometimes involves clandestine military action, but the saboteur's strength is less the overt power of overwhelming force and more the subtle workings of deceit. As a result, saboteurs can't just throw their weight around — they really have to think about how to upset the balance of power.

Once all the roles are assigned, I give everyone his or her top-secret dossier, a colored folder stuffed with twenty or thirty pages of vital information. Along with descriptions of the fifty interlocking crises that the students are to resolve, the folder includes detailed instructions on how to play the Game, a thorough explanation of symbols and titles, and a list of all possible cabinet positions. Also included is a legend showing the meaning of every marker on the board, as well as crucial information about it: how much it is worth, what range of movement it has, and the conditions under which it can operate or be moved. There are inventory sheets to allow the chief financial officers to calculate their nations' resources. Likewise, there are expenditure and revenue tables so they can keep track of budgets. There is a form for each country to use to conduct a complete inventory of all its assets. I also include a thorough explanation of combat procedures. The weather goddess has a form to keep track of how many days are left in a particular crisis or how long before a situation returns to normal (since she is often ruling on such matters). There is also a form to keep track of the values of game pieces and/or assets that have changed during the Game. And there are sheets on which students can record their proposed strategy for each day and note their proposed plan of action, as well as their estimation of its possible results and consequences.

I also give students a list of reflection questions, with the idea that they'll answer them after the Game is over. Here are a few examples from that list:

- How did you think of global politics before you played this Game . . . and how do you think of it now?
- Now that you have played the Game, what do you think of possibilities for world peace? How did your attitude change toward your adversaries or enemies during the Game?
- How did your behavior or techniques of diplomacy change during the Game's term, and what caused it to change?
- Describe what you saw in the Game that showed wise problem solving.

I don't define many terms for students. I simply start using words such as "adversary," "insurgency," "protocol," and "emissary" repeatedly in context, and they pick up the vocabulary rapidly.

So closely is the fate of one nation bound to the others that each country is affected by every crisis directly or indirectly. Climate change, endangered species, oil spills, nuclear accidents, natural disasters, rogue satellites, water rights disputes, border disagreements, insurgencies, religious and ethnic tensions, and breakaway republics are some of the complex and interrelated problems they face immediately as we begin play. They quickly begin to study their portfolios and to share them with their cabinets. The crises are designed to pit the four countries and two ethnic groups against one another in every way possible: politically, socially, economically, and militarily. The children have to use their imaginations and thinking skills to solve these problems. They often try to do it without combat, although some kids are more warlike than others. In any case, finding peaceful solutions—or any solutions, really—is meant to be extremely challenging, since the Game starts with situations that teeter on the verge of chaos.

This day of preparation does not include any declarations by the prime ministers. In their initial bewilderment, the students simply try to wrap their minds around the enormous, multifaceted problem-scape and even wonder out loud how they can possibly solve such a load of crises. Heads bent together peering over the details, they shuffle their papers, flipping back and forth, sending pages fluttering around the room. Hands shoot up repeatedly as they seek clarification, latitude in decision making, or escape clauses, anything to help them untangle this Gordian knot of adult problems.

Most urgently, of course, there are the crises to manage.

"You are a brand-new cabinet inheriting a situation that left the world in this state," I explain, as the students watch, open-mouthed. When I was doling out the roles, they were full of energy, dashing across the room to join their new prime minister or huddled in intense conversation with their fellow officers of the World Bank. Perhaps a few budding diplomats have already made forays into neighboring territories, inviting a student from another country to consider a potential treaty or an economic plan. But now, as I reel off the sorry state of the world that they are suddenly responsible for, they grow somber.

"The day you come into office, this is what you face," I continue. "It's not your fault, but there it is. Your predecessors — those who came before you in office — caused all these problems. Now you've got to deal with them."

Around the room, they are watching me, some nodding, some too rapt to nod. My own feelings, as usual, are mixed. On the one hand, I feel I am taking their innocence, word by word. I am transforming them from fourth graders into world-weary statesmen and stateswomen, future adults charged with saving the world, which previous generations — *my* generation — has left in such a sorry state. On the other hand, I am offering them a tremendous opportunity: to become so overwhelmed by the complexity into which I thrust them that they will be forced, or inspired, to discover new depths within themselves—new reserves of creativity, leadership, and integrity that they had not even suspected might be there. The world will take their innocence soon enough; by shining this harsh light on the world, I at least have the chance to show them how powerful, effective, and compassionate they might become.

"Okay," I continue. "We have regular army and mercenary troops from Sandia attacking on this island." I point to the island, a tiny green splotch between Naheen's country and Tony's. "An attack has been launched, and two aircraft squadrons from Sandia are headed for this island, along with ships . . ."

Naheen's mouth tightens. She hasn't been prime minister for more than ten minutes, and already she's facing a military attack. Naheen is one of the most thoughtful students I've ever taught, and I know she has a strong commitment to peace—but I also know that she doesn't like being pushed around. How will she handle this unprovoked attack?

"Napaj wants to start charging a usage fee of ten million dollars per day for the use of this island," I go on. "It wants to pay for a space station project it is building up here." I point to the topmost level of the Game, the dark reaches of outer space. The students' eyes rise and fall, following my hand. Not only am I asking them to think of the entire globe, but I want them to think in layers, too—undersea, ground and sea, airspace, outer space —and to integrate their view of those layers into their vision of the planet as a whole. Gone are the days, if they ever existed, when a nation's leader could think only of the world within his or her borders. Gone are the days when any political entity could simply withdraw into its own culture, its own language, its own economy. At ages nine and ten, these students have already heard their parents talk about high gas prices, dwindling jobs, maybe even foreign wars and rising military expenditures. Today, suddenly, these are *their* problems.

"Why does Napaj want to charge a usage fee for the island?" I continue. "It needs the money! Space programs are exciting, but they are expensive. Even Sandia—the oil-rich nation—doesn't have infinite funds."

The children are listening as hard as they can—not just the ones from the countries involved, but the whole class. This is it: the beginning of deep engagement. This is gratifying, because it means they have already learned the first lesson of the Game: *What affects one of us affects all of us.* Even if they absorb that concept in the most instrumental or functional way—that is, purely as a matter of self-interest, just to keep up with the action —they have begun to think globally. But by definition, thinking globally is overwhelming, especially at first, and it is confusing. In these first hours of the Game, the more you know, the more overwhelmed and confused you become.

"Now, over here"—I point to another piece of land, the yellow-painted desert of the oil-rich nation—"the ethnic Kajazians have taken over a critical oil refinery. They've threatened you, Ms. Casamira, and your cabinet, to destroy the refinery if they are challenged." Ms. Casamira—AKA Madelene—swallows but looks stern. I have enormous faith in her leadership skills, but I'm not sure she does—yet.

"The Kajazian people want to establish a religious homeland for themselves right in this area . . . the area where a lot of your oil reserves are located," I explain. "So you're going to have to work something out with them. Will you find a military solution? A peaceful one? Can you use your economic leverage? Is money something that matters to the Kajazians? Is there something else you can offer them that matters more?"

Madelene nods, taking it all in. Her best friend, Nikki—whom Madelene has made her minister of defense—eagerly leans in and whispers in Madelene's ear. Nikki's passion and fire are a good match for Madelene's slow, steady, careful consideration, and I think this may be one of the times when choosing a close friend is actually a smart political move. As Nikki's whispering grows more intense, Madelene shakes her head, her eyes still on me, as I continue speaking.

"Suddenly, a volcanic eruption occurs — oh, my — right here." I indicate a scrap of white land on the edge of the blue ocean. "Ice-seria has two Game Days to evacuate resources and troops from the southern part of this country, which means from this city down" — I point it out — "or else they'll lose everything *here*."

Ursula, the prime minister of Ice-seria, is already jotting some notes in her spiral binder and pointing them out to Luis, her chief financial officer. Before the Game began, she hadn't had much to do with Luis, so I was struck that she chose him, almost immediately, to be part of her cabinet. Possibly, Luis is someone she has a fourth-grade crush on (at ages nine and ten, the girls are already choosing boys they "like"). Or perhaps she has seen some quality in him that she values. Luis thinks for a moment, gets out a marker, and begins laboriously scrawling a few bright-green notes underneath Ursula's neatly penciled words.

"Endangered species," I go on without missing a beat. "Oh, this is a great one! I love this one! Okay. Oil is just discovered on a remote island, but this same island is the home of a unique microscopic species whose habitat will be destroyed if oil is mined or extracted in any way. Ice-seria desperately needs the oil, but we know the nation of Green is charged with protecting the planet and its creatures. How will world opinion come down, ladies and gentlemen? When values conflict, which shall prevail? When nations don't agree, how do they work it out?"

I want to leave them overwhelmed, confused — but not discouraged; staggering under the weight of these fifty crises — but not disabled; pushed to their very limits — but not beyond. It's a fine line. But as I hear the hum of their discussion and debate rise to fill the room, I feel a familiar relief laced with joy. This time, at least, the confusion seems fruitful. I can't wait to see what my students will make of it.

## Swimming in the Vastness

For most of us, myself included, knowledge and certainty feel far safer than stumbling blindly into the unknown. But to immobilize one's thinking—to select a perspective and to lock oneself into it—is actually very hazardous. There is simply too much of reality that you might miss and, worse, that you might never even realize you are missing. So this idea of being in the unknown, of not knowing exactly what the truth is or even what the facts are, is something I want my students—and myself—to practice every day, until we finally become accustomed to it. Of course, we like to have our set situations that we feel comfortable with; we prefer feeling secure to feeling fear. But life is much bigger than the fixed, secure perspectives that make us comfortable, and so I want my students, without being frightened, to understand the vastness of reality and then to learn how to swim in that vastness—comfortably.

How do I help them get to that point? I try to strip away the conventions. I give them problems for which there are no conventional solutions—certainly none that they have ever worked with, but also none that their parents or grandparents would be familiar with either. I think even the most sheltered student in my classroom understands that previous generations have failed to create world peace. My faith that these students can do it sets the stage for an entirely new reality.

When I've been asked over the years to share the Game with other teachers, by either going to play it with their students or giving them my formula for crises, I've had to warn them that not every group of fourth graders, or even every high school class, is ready to plunge into this challenging game. Here is an excerpt from the e-mail I send to them, identifying the kinds of students who I believe can benefit from playing the World Peace Game.

Students must:
1. possess a certain "intellectual stamina" and be able to wrestle with tough problems that are without quick or easy resolution, over time;
2. be able to interact constructively with others much different from themselves (diversity as much as possible);
3. be able to forestall closure and handle the certain frustrations of endless challenges and conflicts as they collaborate to achieve peace.

In other words, to play the World Peace Game, students must be able to handle the initial stage of overload and confusion. Students who become too anxious, fearful, self-doubting, or frustrated by the enormous amount of complexity within which they are asked to function will have a very difficult time with the Game, just as their adult counterparts might founder when confronted with the complexities of their world. I think that potentially, all of us can learn to tolerate complexity. But by age nine, many children have already been taught that life—or at least school—should be simple, a matter of getting the right answers and passing the right tests. The World Peace Game has enormously high stakes—the survival of the planet itself—and yet within its parameters, there is no such thing as knowing the right answer. It becomes clear to students very soon that even I don't know it. What I do know is that collectively, they can create it: not one single right answer, of course, but a complex, many-layered solution. But the prerequisite for constructing this new solution is tolerating the discomfort of feeling overwhelmed.

Having played the Game for nearly thirty-five years, I am struck by how students' tolerance for that space of *not knowing* has shrunk, decade by decade. In our sped-up world, the gap between problem and solution seems shorter than ever. Where once a student's question required a leisurely, thoughtful trip to the library or at least a careful browse through a reference book, now he or she can push a couple of keys and find the answer on an Internet search engine. Where once students were given diverse tasks and activities, requiring a range of tempos, they are now too often pushed toward the quick, discrete responses appropriate for standardized tests. Where once there seemed to be room to wonder, to speculate, to *not know*, there now seems to be increasing pressure for instant answers, immediate solutions, and narrowly defined results.

As a result, my students are often unused to having much time to think about things. And the typical classroom structure —both then and, too often, now—fosters this sense of "instant answer." The teacher asks a question, and a dozen hands shoot into the air. The teacher calls on the first student whose hand went up, and everybody else understands that their participation is no longer required, and so they may immediately disengage.

These days, the questions are being asked faster than ever because of the focus—even at the elementary school level—on standardized tests. Many teachers' salaries depend on how their students perform that year—bonuses are frequently allocated on that basis—and many more work in schools or districts whose funding is directly or indirectly linked to test scores. So everyone, from the superintendent on down to the first grader, is under enormous pressure to answer quickly, to be certain, to know rather than to wonder, inquire, or sit quietly with a problem and simply let the answer *become*.

Beyond the specific economy of the school system is the culture at large, which increasingly pushes the idea of automaticity: instant, certain responses so that one doesn't lose face or look bad. Both the school culture and the larger culture make students want to answer faster, whether they know the answer or not. There is a huge push to be the one whose hand is up first so that you will be chosen first and most often. Whether my fourth graders are conscious of it or not, many of them have absorbed the message that this is the way to get ahead, and so they place a false premium not just on knowledge, which is problematic enough (since uncertainty is often more fruitful), but on *instant* knowledge. As a result of both school and social cultures, knowledge is increasingly defined as the facts that accord you success on certain test measures, whether those be a standardized school test during childhood or a routinized job performance assessment later on. This is most unfortunate, in my view, because a true and deep knowing is something that I find comes only with time. Time is the empty space that allows knowledge—let alone wisdom—to grow. Knowledge on demand is almost always shallower and less valuable. So I am interested in the knowledge that has time to *become* rather than the givens that are already known.

In contrast to the curriculum that engages only the student who is called upon, the World Peace Game allows me to pose a problem—a whole interlocking network of problems—in which every participant is completely involved in thinking about the entire question. Yes, there are the individual responses—the prime minister who declares an attack, the World Bank officer who refuses a loan, the UN official who issues sanctions. Some of these responses may even be hopeful—a temporary treaty, support for a new green technology, a creative solution to a long-standing hostility or lack of understanding. My students understand, though, that these are all necessarily partial and temporary responses. Whether positive or negative, they all fall short of the ultimate goal of world peace and increased prosperity. Without being told, my students know that they are required to stay involved as fully as they can manage until this ultimate goal is reached. They can't even try to solve a problem quickly: there is simply too much for them to do. And so, because they remain involved for so much longer, their thinking process can grow deeper. Just by virtue of taking more time, they have the opportunity to come up with a more nuanced and reflective answer.

That extra time is another version of the empty space. It's the equivalent of a teacher asking a question and allowing silence to reign in the room for ten seconds, thirty seconds, a minute, before any response is actually called for. That silence gives everybody time to wrestle with the problem, as opposed to coming up with quick responses that can only be based on what we already know. The empty space—the silence—allows time for confusion: it makes room for us to discover what we don't yet know.

As a result, the World Peace Game requires a kind of intellectual stamina that most children are often not given the chance to develop. Building mental muscle, like any other type of muscle, requires time and repetition. The longer students are allowed to wrestle with difficult problems, the more their cognitive and imaginative capacities are able to develop—as long as the referee doesn't step in and prematurely call the match.

I was a wrestler in high school and college, and I was struck, back in the day, by the difference between high school matches, which lasted at most six minutes, and college contests, which ran up to seven minutes. When I moved on to those longer bouts, I understood that the extra time on the mat was what we all needed to develop the art of the master wrestler. We needed more stamina and more finesse to survive those seven-minute matches, and that extra time also allowed each of us to develop his own unique style. That's why you see great wrestlers come into their own only at the college level. And so the first stage of the Game, overload and confusion, is my way of giving my students more time to stay on the mat.

## Rodney Loses Everything

So what kinds of discoveries might my students make when they have the chance to flounder, for a bit, in a state of confusion and overload? One of the first answers that comes to mind is the story of Rodney.

Rodney was a short kid with dark, almost blue-black, hair and pale skin. He was known throughout the school as a sneaky little guy who was always ready to play one child against another. He reminded me of Shakespeare's Iago, if you can imagine that great character at age nine: perpetually anxious about his own social standing, always ready to start a rumor or whisper a well-timed remark in an ally's ear, continually nervous whenever the people he hung out with separately seemed to find common ground and start hanging out together, creating conversations or alliances that Rodney couldn't control.

Anyone would have thought that Rodney would shine in the World Peace Game, because dealmaking and diplomacy came so naturally to him. But as often happens to adults with these propensities, Rodney's power plays began to backfire. He was the chief financial officer of what that group of children had dubbed West Ultra, the richest nation in the world, and he had made a number of deals that involved him buying oil from MechanSand, the oil-rich nation, and selling it to countries without oil supplies of their own. He tried to play a similar role with some anti–climate change technology that had been developed by the Nin; with some raw materials from Lotusland, the poorest country; and with some valuable oceanfront land on the coast of Greenstone, the middle-income nation charged philosophically with protecting the planet.

At first it seemed that Rodney was well on his way to becoming a key power behind the throne, a role that suited him much better, as it happened, than the more overtly powerful position of prime minister. But then, one by one, his deals fell apart. The oil-rich nation cut out the middleman and began dealing directly with its neighbors. The Nin caught on to Rodney's efforts to profit from their technology and decided to offer it at cost to anyone in the world who wanted it. The Greenstonians turned Rodney's potential real estate development into a national wild-life preserve.

By about halfway through the Game, Rodney had lost virtu-ally all of his allies and all of his resources. Disgusted with his apparent lack of honor, his prime minister asked for his resigna-tion. Even the students who had once wanted Rodney to put their deals together were no longer willing to work with him or even, beyond basic politeness, to speak with him. Cast out of his rich and powerful nation, Rodney was forced to take on another role: leader of the Krell, a scattered band of refugees with no resources—without even any territory.

Rodney was floundering in his confusion. He was in a particu-larly tough position because he was now the leader of a small, powerless ethnic group with no resources that was currently under pressure from the larger adversaries that surrounded it. His efforts to manipulate his friends had come to naught. His usual confidence was shaken. Finally, he came to me.

"I've lost everything," Rodney said, trying to keep his voice brave. "I have no assets, no resources, no friends, no allies. I don't have anything. I can't even play the Game."

I looked at Rodney, his large brown eyes blinking in bewilder-ment, and I saw that he had sunk into his own form of confusion, wrestling with questions that he had never had to ask before. Up to this point, he had managed to manipulate each individual transaction separately, but now he was entangled in a plethora of closely knit relationships that had begun to unravel, one by one. Rodney was overwhelmed by the challenge of damage control —what he could say, and to whom, to regain his former power. In a sense, the Game had given him too much material to work with: too many potential intrigues, rumors, plots, and deals; too many machinations; too many opportunities for manipulation. Perhaps a more cynical child could have talked his way out of the bind, or perhaps a more experienced adult could have made all the possibilities work for him. Nine-year-old Rodney, though, was simply overwhelmed.

I was tempted to give him the answer, or at least an answer. I don't like to see a child suffer, and Rodney was clearly suffering. Perhaps it was fortunate for both of us that I honestly didn't know what was right for Rodney to do. I could make a reasoned, detailed critique of where I had seen him go wrong, but I wasn't at all sure that I could tell him how to put things right.

Fortunately, I didn't have to. Instead, I returned to that principle I had learned from my mother, my teachers, and my studies in the East. I gave Rodney the gift of his own confusion and my faith that he could work through it. "Well, Rodney," I asked, "what things are possible now? Is there anything at all that you can do?"

Rodney thought a long while, but the conversation ended in silence.

The next day, I watched as Rodney neared his personal bottom. Now, I felt, was the time for the teacher, the guide, the friend to step in.

In emotional situations like Rodney's, a teacher must be very careful. We know that even the toughest kid can have a delicate heart. There is often no way to know for certain how a given child will respond in a particular situation, so great care is required.

I moved to sit beside Rodney during a moment when the other students were busily planning their next strategy. I made myself smaller by leaning forward in my chair, pulling my shoulders in, and lowering my head. Using my "quiet voice" (a classic teacher technique), I sat with folded hands and leaned down so that we could easily hear each other but our conversation remained private. I did this a few times that day, for just a few moments each time, and each time Rodney opened up, just a little.

The first time I sat beside him, Rodney shared with me his anger at being in what for him was the unusual position of feeling powerless. His regular sly manner and crafty touch weren't getting him anywhere, even with his old friends.

The next time I sat beside him, Rodney spoke of his despair. He saw the excitement, the action, swirling all around him, and yet he couldn't fathom how to be a part of it if his old ways no longer worked.

The third time I sat with him, Rodney had reached a calmer, more grounded place. He truly wanted to play the Game and be a part of our shared experience, and he began looking for someone who might provide him with a way back in.

Rodney looked first to his friends, but none of them were in any kind of strategic position to be useful to him. Then, scanning the room, his eyes lit on Tiffany, the deputy secretary-general of the United Nations. Tiffany was almost Rodney's opposite —effervescent, cheerful, open, and forthright—a natural leader. African American and very proud of it, Tiffany had been taught from an early age to stand up for herself. Not just a fighter for herself, Tiffany automatically stood up for anyone else who she felt was not being given his or her due.

And so she became Rodney's champion—but only because Rodney made a timid yet honest effort to approach her. I don't know if he would have tried his old tricks with someone else or not. But he knew that he was out of his depth with Tiffany, and so he found a way to reach out to her that was new to him.

Tiffany agreed to help Rodney, and a strategic partnership developed. Rodney obtained financial aid from the United Nations in exchange for his promises to, as Tiffany put it, "start being friendlier and stop trying to fool people all the time."

Rodney's more direct and straightforward efforts began to pay off. Other nations began to talk with him. Despite Tiffany's support, most of the students still didn't trust Rodney, and they were careful to make sure that any agreements with him were codified into paper treaties or other binding legal documents from their dossiers.

Gradually, the Krell's position began to improve as Rodney became more of a "player." Because he had found a genuine way to ask for help and had offered to be helpful even with his tribe's limited resources, his honest gestures were well received. Rodney had returned to the world community, where he became a full, participating member despite his tiny nation's limitations. Perhaps for the first time in his life, he began to make friends in a clear and honest way. He still found ways to exercise his genius for dealmaking, but now he did so transparently, in a straightforward and aboveboard fashion, letting all parties know what he was up to and what his motives were. He had a gift for sniffing out potential treaties and alliances, and in his new mode, the deals he helped broker were all mutually beneficial arrangements from which all parties profited. Through these deals, Rodney gradually began to build up his resources, and he became, if not a major power, certainly a major player in the Game.

I would not have predicted that ending to Rodney's story. Out of his overload and confusion, he courageously forged a new version of himself. And that was marvelous to behold.

## Pablo Sees It All

Sometimes the hardest thing for a teacher to do is to keep quiet. I know that my own silence might be just the opportunity my students need to let go of their reliance on me and develop their own resources of creativity and compassion. I am also all too aware that I don't always know the answers that my students seek —when we're playing the World Peace Game, I often don't know them—and so my silence really is called for. So I am highly, almost painfully, aware of the virtues of silence—but it's still often hard to keep quiet.

It's hardest for me to simply allow things to play out in times of confusion and overload, when it seems that my students really might not have at their disposal the resources they need. When they are overwhelmed and confused, they express their feelings about this condition very quickly and openly, and there is no mistaking the atmosphere of frustration, resentment, and self-doubt. As a teacher, how can I look forward to those moments, which I know are painful now but potentially fruitful later? How can I welcome the very confusion and overload that I know, from three decades' worth of experience, will eventually change into the opposite? How can I applaud this uncomfortable state, which I know is going to help my students grow?

The answer is, I can't. As crucial as this stage is for my students' growth and development, I can't look forward to it, welcome it, or applaud it—in fact, sometimes I actively dread it. When an entire class of nine-year-olds is frustrated and fed up, how can I appreciate that moment? It simply doesn't feel good.

I have come to accept that feeling, though. I know that my students are disappointed when they understand that I can't give them a way out, and I would say that's the most difficult thing a teacher has to wrestle with—not knowing the answer when twenty-five or thirty people are waiting for you to break their deadlock and restore them to clarity and certainty. I can't help wanting to make everything right for my students, even as I know that I can't, because I don't really know how.

Over the years, I have taught myself how to simply sit with this discomfort—not to like it or to welcome it, but somehow to let it be. I hang out in my seat at the back of the room, watching my students struggle, watching them suffer, and I try to just observe my desire and do nothing to alleviate my own discomfort. I remind myself that my students and I are practicing this effort together—they for the first time, I for the thousandth—practicing a way to go through the discomfort together so that we can allow something new to emerge. It's hard, I tell myself, because I am traditionally supposed to be the person who *knows*, and I know that I *don't* know, and my students know that, too. I must allow my own unknowing to become apparent, and in doing so, I show my students that they don't have to hide their ignorance either, that they can be in this room as I am, revealed and completely present in our unknowing. Knowing that everyone can see how little I know, how useless I am—allowing that reality to emerge without trying to hide it—is my moment of reckoning, I suppose. Even after all these years, I have to keep reminding myself that the key question to ask is not *How am I going to solve this?* but rather *How can I come through this situation?*

The only reason I am able to approach the situation this way —the only reason it makes sense to do so—is because I am not, in fact, alone. My students are part of the solution, which means that I can afford to let them flounder in their confusion and overload, because they, not I, are the ones charged with winning the Game. Being interdependent with them is what makes these moments of not acting ultimately bearable.

Which brings me to Pablo.

Pablo was a little guy, much shorter than most of the other fifth graders. He was about as wide as he was tall, his hair stuck up, he wore thick glasses, and he talked very, very slowly—in a monotone.

I will confess that it was sometimes difficult for even the most dedicated teacher to wait for Pablo to finish a sentence, let alone a thought, though by the time we started playing the World Peace Game together, most of us were used to his slow, deliberate ways. "Pablo, hurry up," the other kids would tell him. "Just say what you gotta say." No one teased him or was cruel to him. Still, whenever he raised his hand, you could see some other student putting his head down on his desk, rolling his eyes, and muttering, "Oh, great, there he goes again!"

Don't get me wrong. Pablo was bright, maybe even brilliant. It just took a while for his brilliance to come out in verbal expression—sometimes a *long* while. And yet when it came time to choose the prime ministers for the World Peace Game, Pablo was one of the four I chose.

Selecting the four prime ministers is one of the most important decisions I have to make. While every child in the room has
the chance to make a difference, the prime ministers set the tone
for the elaborate negotiations that take up most of the Game.
Each prime minister chooses his or her own cabinet, and unless
someone challenges a prime minister with a successful coup, the
prime ministers largely chart the course of the Game.

As I explained earlier, I don't actually appoint the prime ministers. I offer the position to students, and they have the chance
to accept or decline, although almost always they accept. My
offer is based on my intuition of what is going to be the best
learning experience for them—who needs the chance to grow
into this level of leadership. In this case, something told me that
Pablo deserved the chance to be prime minister.

In this fast-paced, complex game, there was no logical reason
to offer such a great role to Pablo. Perhaps, as a formerly shy,
chubby gradeschooler myself, I remembered repeatedly being
chosen last for schoolyard games and felt some unconscious af-
finity with Pablo. Or maybe I saw something in Pablo that no one
else did. In any case, Pablo had the requisite academic skills, so
there was at least a chance that he would measure up. For good
or ill, I made the decision not to keep him safe, but to challenge
him. But when I announced my offer, I could see several students cringe and put their heads down. I knew they were thinking, *Oh, Mr. Hunter, what are you doing? This is going to be a loooong
game.*

Even Pablo looked a bit stunned. It took him maybe twenty
seconds to stammer, in his typically slow, deliberate way, "Ohh-
hhhh . . . okay . . . I-I-I-I'll be p-p-prime minister."

Initially, it did indeed seem that Pablo was out of his depth.
The Game is played with hundreds of pieces on four different
levels. With the fifty or so crises that the children inherit when
the Game begins, there are literally thousands of possible actions
that a leader might take. After consulting with his or her cabinet,

a prime minister might move troops, offer to make a trade deal, propose diplomatic action, redeploy ships in the country's navy, open negotiations for mineral rights, and so on. The only limits, really, are time, protocol, and imagination.

The declarations announcing these actions are all very formal. A child stands and says, "I am Prime Minister So-and-so, and I speak on behalf of the people of such and such a country, and these are my declarations." The student might say something like, "I'm going to move this ship one thousand kilometers over there, I'm going to offer a peace treaty to this country, and then I'm going to pull these troops back here." The students physically carry out the actions on the board as they speak; indeed, they're forbidden to move pieces at any other time. After each declaration, there's a break for all the other countries to discuss their potential responses, and then play proceeds to the next prime minister.

Players tend to make more moves in the later weeks of the Game, but even in the early stages, they usually make a good five or six moves apiece. But that wasn't Pablo's style. When his first turn to speak came, he ambled through the formal announcement at what felt like one-quarter speed ("I . . . am Pablo . . . prime minister of . . . my country . . ."), . . . and then he very slowly picked up one piece . . . and he very slowly placed it somewhere else . . . Then he stood there doing nothing for a few moments, . . . and then he very slowly sat down.

In his first official action as prime minister, Pablo made just one move. His action was in such sharp contrast to what the other prime ministers had done that I thought maybe the class was kind of embarrassed for him. There was a fidgety silence after he spoke, and again I could almost hear the other children thinking, *Oh, Mr. Hunter, what have you done?*

The World Peace Game normally lasts for about eight weeks, and by Week 5, Pablo still hadn't caught up. The members of his cabinet were impatient with him. The leaders of the other nations felt they had to work around him. Although the students were too kind to say anything, I knew they were worried. The Game requires everyone to work together. If even a single student isn't pulling his or her weight, the process falters. And if a *prime minister* isn't pulling his or her weight . . . let's just say it can get a little nerve-racking.

Then came Week 6. As usual, we had gathered around the four-level Plexiglas structure. I rang the little bell and read a quote from Sun Tzu. The first prime minister stood and made her declarations. The negotiations proceeded. The second prime minister stood and made his declarations. More negotiations. Finally, it was Pablo's turn.

As he stood up, his hands were trembling just a little. His eyes were a little wider and brighter than usual. There was a strange, almost puzzled smile on his face. And I realized that I was witnessing something that I had seen only five or six times in almost thirty-five years of teaching. I was seeing a student who, after weeks of floundering, had finally "gotten it." I was seeing a student who had just witnessed all the widely diverse parts of a complex problem suddenly meld together into a clear and remarkable whole. I was seeing a student who was finally about to come into his own.

But what Pablo did next surprised even me.

"I am Prime Minister Pablo," he announced. (Was he talking just a bit faster than normal, and without his stutter?) "I am Prime Minister Pablo, and these are my declarations." And in the next two minutes, the boy who normally proceeded at a preternaturally slow pace was suddenly moving as swiftly as a Jedi master. His hands seemed to be everywhere at once—undersea, on the ground, in the air, even reaching up into the highest level of outer space. He was moving and he was speaking, announcing troops redeployed and treaties offered and resources unearthed and satellites set in motion. He told the World Bank that he was paying off a debt. He instructed his secretary of state to begin negotiations on a trade deal. He instructed his minister of defense to move submarines, missiles, ground troops, and air force units. In less than two minutes, he must have made fifteen or twenty moves, strategically altering the course of the Game to benefit his country even as he addressed—and in some cases solved—a number of different crises simultaneously.

It was an extraordinary sight. After six weeks of doing almost nothing—six silent, excruciating weeks—Pablo finally saw it all. Between the time he stood up and the time he sat down, he had evolved into a more confident and capable human being than he had been a few minutes before. Somehow the complex vectors and trends and strategies of the Game had all become clear to him: he saw our planet, and he saw it whole. And after weeks of chaos and confusion, Pablo was finally ready to lead his people —his country—his world—to victory.

"Pablo!" I cried, unable to contain myself. "You see! You see!"

"Mr. Hunter," he replied, "I see *everything.*"

"You understand!" I said, watching the calm satisfaction in Pablo's face and the bewildered awe in everybody else's.

"Mr. Hunter," he replied, "I understand *everything.*"

It was such a huge moment of triumph that we all laughed, because we understood, too. Yes. In that one instant, Pablo had seen it all.

## The Value of Confusion

Pablo's moment of triumph is not the typical way learning is observed in a classroom, but it does happen, and maybe more often than we think. Of course, that thunderclap moment of understanding did not really come all of a sudden. The clouds that produced Pablo's lightning flash had been gathering for some weeks, looking dark and hopeless at times, until that brilliant bolt finally shot through the gloom. When Pablo mapped out his thinking at the end of the Game, I saw not a sudden leap, but the steady, incremental development that produced that leap.

As a teacher, I sometimes forget that a perfect solution hardly ever springs fully formed in the first instance of encountering a problem. In such cases, I grow impatient, feeling that students ought to get it after only a few moments' exposure. I frequently have to struggle against my inner push for a quicker resolution and my desire to move on. That is precisely the internal struggle I had with Pablo. I had to allow him his confusion, so that he could attain his insight.

Like most people, I tend to prefer certainty to confusion, and so I must continually remind myself of confusion's value. A child who is allowed a good, long time to try one approach after another—perhaps growing more confused and overwhelmed with each attempt—is not wasting time and does not necessarily need a teacher's help. He may simply, like Pablo, be gathering evidence about the nature of the problem he faces or gaining insight into the problem's inner dynamics. Knowing when to allow that confusion to simply *be,* rather than trying to fix it, is part of the teacher's art.

Later in life, confusion becomes part of the learner's art as well. The scientist wrestling with contradictory evidence or an unsuccessful experiment, the artist struggling with a poem that won't come out right or a melody that doesn't resolve, the political visionary seeking desperately for a way to remake an unjust system or mobilize support for a new alternative—these people are all mired in a long, painful, but ultimately productive confusion. The willingness to bear that discomfort and continue to wrestle with the problem is the gift they give the rest of us—and the reason they achieve so much.

So, I have come to realize, the stage of confusion can have great value. It can give us the time to grow into our full strength and arrive at the deepest, best solution, the one that truly fits the problem at hand. If Pablo had been able to avoid his confusion, he might have given us quicker, sharper answers earlier on —answers that might have been "good enough," but he would not necessarily have achieved the full depth of insight that he ultimately attained. Sometimes confusion is a necessary way to slow things down until we have within us the strength and courage to find the best and truest answer instead of settling for an easier, quicker one along the way.

That afternoon, as I watched Pablo heading off—slowly, as usual—to his homebound bus, I called out to him. "Pablo! You really are a leader, you know that?"

Slowly, Pablo turned back toward me. His face was still, as usual, but he was smiling, very slightly. "Mr. Hunter," he said, "I know."

# 3

# Brennan Saves the World

Those skilled in warfare seek victory through force and do
not require too much from individuals. Therefore, they are
able to select the right men and exploit force.

— SUN TZU, *The Art of War*

USUALLY WE PLAY the World Peace Game during the regular class day. But one year my principal wanted to move
the Game out of the mainstream curriculum, where she felt it occupied too much class time that could otherwise be spent on improving standardized test scores. I believe that the World Peace
Game teaches lessons that can't be measured with multiple-
choice tests or even with essay questions. When students learn to
cope with complexity, respond to crises, and draw on their own
creativity, that seems priceless to me. But those achievements are
essentially unquantifiable, and so they will never find a place on
a standardized test.

In any case, we found our own creative solution by moving the World Peace Game to an afterschool program, during
which we played from 2:30 to 4:00 P.M. once a week for seven
weeks. We didn't have as many hours of game time as we usually do, but the students really put their hearts into it as they
coped with the Game's fifty crises. Week after week, they trooped
into the classroom, pushed their desks up against the wall, and
gathered around the four-level Plexiglas structure to play. As we

approached the Game's final days, the students had solved just about all of the crises and were confident that they could solve the last few within the little time we had left.

But there was one problem that they seemingly could not solve. In addition to resolving the crises, students are also required to raise the asset value of every country. This they had done . . . with one exception. The poorest of the countries, dubbed Snowlandia by its citizens, had suffered one reversal after another. They had begun the Game with few resources, and from that point on, things kept getting worse. The weather goddess—a fair but merciless player, as befit her role—sent a tsunami to destroy much of the country's ocean-based economy. Then pollution from the profitable factories and mining operations of its wealthy neighbors entered its waters, with disastrous consequences for its fishing industry. The country then lost money in a trade deal. The weather goddess's spin of the random weather spinner resulted in a hurricane. A random card, drawn on each country's turn, had one of Snowlandia's nuclear reactors melting down. Poor Snowlandia underwent disaster after disaster, with a corresponding toll on its resources.

It wasn't as though the leaders of Snowlandia hadn't tried. They had put together trade deals that at the last minute fell through. They had appealed to the World Bank for loans that were ultimately denied. They had asked for assistance from the United Nations that the UN couldn't provide. As the Game neared its end, they were becoming desperate, and so were we all. At this point, they couldn't turn to industrialization or internal development, because building factories or exploiting their mineral resources—which were scanty to begin with—would simply take too much time. Essentially, they needed cold hard cash—and quickly.

In theory, we could have extended the playing time, which is something I can do when we are playing during regular class time. But in this case, not only could we not extend our time, but the principal actually wanted to curtail our schedule, because she felt that the students needed to be taking more time after school to do homework. So now we had a hard deadline—a specific hour by which the Game had to end. It seemed impossible that Snowlandia would be able to turn its situation around.

Finally, we reached our last day. The classroom had one of those doors with a half window on top, so we could look out and see parents congregating outside in the hall as they did every time we played, waiting for us to finish. Some of them were chatting with one another, but many of them were leaning on the door and peering through the glass, trying to see what was going on inside.

We often invited parents in to observe our play. But today none of us wanted any guests, because a huge cloud of despair was settling over the room. My students take the Game so personally—they are so essentially involved, especially by the final weeks—that when things go well, they are elated, even ecstatic. But when things go poorly, they are miserable. And today, as we confronted the reality that Snowlandia lacked the asset value to win the Game, we were all struggling with some serious gloom.

We kept looking at the large school clock on the wall, the one with the long, spindly second hand that lurched its way from mark to mark. Ten minutes to go. The negotiations proceeded, but no one could figure out how to make things work, and it was hard for the children to keep coming up with new ideas when they knew that all their efforts might come to nothing very shortly.

Five minutes. The prime minister of Snowlandia appeared unusually calm. He spoke with the officials who came to see him, but he was no longer rushing around the room, trying to make a deal. He seemed to have already given up.

Four minutes . . . three minutes . . . one minute and fifty seconds. I didn't want to say anything, but I felt I had to. After all, it was my classroom, and these children were my responsibility.

They had worked so hard for so long—how could I be the one to confront them with their defeat? But someone had to let them know how little time was left.

"Ladies and gentlemen," I said in a ponderous tone. I didn't want to scare them, but I thought maybe if they knew how serious the situation was, they might somehow pull a last-minute miracle out of the hat—although I had never seen anything significant happen with only a few seconds left.

"Ladies and gentlemen, we have only about a minute and fifty —no, forty-five—seconds left, and it looks like we *may* not be able to win this game." I clung to that "may"; I was still hoping for a miracle.

But what kind of miracle could there be? Snowlandia was so far in the hole, there really wasn't much anyone could do. We had already been through all the possible scenarios. There was no plan that could possibly be executed in the time we had left.

There was a heavy silence for about five seconds, then suddenly, over on my right, Brennan—the prime minister of one of the richer countries—got up and walked quickly to my chair. He grabbed the little silver bell that I ring to signal the convening of the cabinets, and he rushed back to his own chair, frantically ringing the bell.

"Everybody come over here!" he kept yelling. "Come to me, everybody! Come on!"

Well, what else could they do? They went. After all, Brennan had become a respected leader in the Game, and somehow his grabbing and ringing my bell made him seem like even more of an authority figure. Everyone knew that we were down to about a minute and a half, so they rushed across the room as fast as they could. At first Brennan seemed to be talking to them. Then they all started whispering among themselves. I heard one kid yell, and then there was a lot of yelling—arguing, it sounded like— and they were all waving their dossiers around. Now there were only thirty seconds left, but they were still arguing, debating, the volume building with the speed—until outside our door, even the parents were growing alarmed.

I didn't know what they were doing. I'd lost control of my classroom. All I could think was, *Principal walks in right now, I'm out of a job.* And then Brennan leaped up on his chair and rang the bell again, and everybody rushed back to their seats. With ten seconds left on the clock, Brennan cried out, "I am Prime Minister Brennan of Estopia, and these are my declarations. My country and Sandston, Greenlandus, and the United Nations have all pooled our funds together. And we've got six hundred billion dollars. We're going to offer it as a donation to Snowlandia. And if they will accept this donation, it'll raise their asset value, and we can win the Game. So what do you say? *Will you accept it?*"

Everyone turned to look at the poor prime minister of Snowlandia, who still seemed a little dazed. He had been in that huge huddle, too, of course, but I'm not sure how much he understood of this plan until he heard it announced at this moment. He took three seconds to confer with his cabinet—and now there were only two seconds left on the clock—and then he finally called back, "Yes! We *will* accept it!"

And the room exploded. Children were surfing the floor, rolling around on their backs, laughing, kicking their feet in the air, grabbing each other, jumping up and down, cheering at the top of their voices. That room was just a madhouse of glee and exhilaration, because we had done it. We had done the impossible. At the last possible second, we had saved the world.

## Facing Failure

So here is the second stage in the World Peace Game: the dreaded *failure*. To an adult, the solution that my fourth graders devised to overcome that failure might seem obvious, not to mention that this type of "foreign aid" wouldn't really be a long-term solution in the real world. But the benefit of the World Peace Game is not in the real-life applicability of the solutions that students devise. I don't expect nine-year-olds to come up with workable approaches to eliminating poverty or creating peace. What is remarkable is not the answer itself, but the fact that they survived the pain of apparent failure and went on to *find* an answer.

After all, when any of us is facing failure, the pain of the experience is in our absolute certainty that there is no way out. We are sure of that because, after all of our efforts, we still haven't found a way. This is as true at age nine as at age fifty-nine, even if the fifty-nine-year-old can see solutions that elude the nine-year-old. But at any age, failure can be devastating, precisely because it feels so final. The ability to overcome failure—to live through it and move on—is crucial. If we are not willing to face failure —if we don't have the skills to survive it—we have precluded any real creativity or risk. Failure may never become our friend, but if we are to do meaningful work, perhaps failure needs to be our companion.

Failure offers an interesting contrast to the Game's first stage, confusion and overload. Coping with confusion can be difficult, but in the first stage we are still simply observing the complexity. Because there is more going on in the situation than we can handle, we feel overwhelmed—the profusion of information simply overloads our senses. But this can inspire us to determination or even excitement as we seek to master the information or open ourselves up to it.

Failure, by contrast, is what we experience when we have made an effort to sort through the data and it hasn't worked. It's not just an observation ("I feel overloaded"); it's a judgment or a conclusion ("I have failed, and I won't be able to succeed"). Of course, confusion, failure, and all the rest of the phases of learning are not fixed stages—they are more points on a journey that an individual learner or even a class may cycle through many times, even in the course of a single game. But it is useful to identify these stages, because each has its own lessons that can enrich us if we let them.

Failure is a tough stage to talk about, especially in our success-oriented culture, where it is very difficult to develop an appreciation for the lessons of failure. By the same token, it is not easy to give students in our results-oriented classrooms—especially the brightest students—a chance to fail. In this uncertain economy, parents naturally want the best for their children and will do anything to guarantee them success. The specter of not getting into the right college or graduate school, which is supposed to ensure a secure future, looms over even my fourth- and fifth-grade classrooms. The gifted programs in which I teach are under even more pressure to build children's self-esteem, to bolster their self-confidence, and to keep their academic performance at the highest level.

These are worthy goals, and they come from worthy motives. Fortunately or unfortunately, however, failure is an essential part of any great endeavor, and if we can't find a way to allow our children to experience failure—*especially* the best and the brightest—we are doing them an enormous disservice.

What are the lessons of failure?

First, it guards against hubris. For potential diplomats, world leaders, and political activists, this is a crucial lesson indeed. In our culture, we see ourselves as *knowers*. Authority rests on knowledge—in the classroom, in the workplace, in the political sphere. Knowledge comes to seem equivalent to a kind of control, ensuring our ability to get our way: with the economy, with other nations, with nature itself.

But in fact, we actually *don't* know most of everything. Reality is an infinite sea of information, and while we might possess some facts, some skills, some knowledge, it is impossible—as well as stressful and, ultimately, self-defeating—to expect ourselves to know everything about reality, or even to believe that it is something we can fully master. Some part of it will always elude us, revealing to us the limits of our knowledge.

This should not discourage us or even humble us. I don't want my students to withdraw from the challenges of solving climate change, of saving our planet, of creating the peace and prosperity that are our ultimate goals. I want them to throw themselves into the Game—and into their lives—with commitment, enthusiasm, and joy. Paradoxically, though, that openness can exist only among those who are not dominated by the fear of failure, those who are not terrified of being incorrect or incomplete.

So perhaps that's the second lesson of failure: it teaches us that anything can be useful—not good, necessarily, but useful. The most discouraging failures, the most humiliating defeats, the most frustrating dead ends, all have something to teach us. That's not an easy perspective to adopt, but with enough experience and enough confidence, we might be able to see it.

I am not arguing that failure is enjoyable or even that we should necessarily welcome it. I *am* saying that if we are afraid of failure and unwilling to experience it, we truncate our ability to deal with reality, to expand our capacity, to take the risks that our lives—and our world—require of us. In terms of Eastern philosophy, the true master is the person who is evenhanded about failure and success, seeing both as purely temporary conditions that might be useful as sources of pertinent information. Failure might teach us what does and doesn't work, but enlightenment comes from welcoming those lessons while remaining detached from failure (or success) itself. Although few of us are so masterful as to achieve that state of supreme balance, we can come to accept as a natural part of our life experience situations in which we have the opportunity to fail as well as to succeed. We can strive to attain goals that are at least a little bit beyond our current capacity; we can play games whose outcomes are not entirely certain or within our control. We can allow ourselves to know failure—to become accustomed to its contours and tex-tures—and we can become acquainted with ourselves under failure: how we cope, how we react, how we move on.

## Teaching Failure

It's one thing to experience failure ourselves and quite another to let our children experience it. As both a parent and a teacher, I know there are many circumstances in which I would gladly spare both my daughter and my students the pain of failure, even while I realize that I would be doing them a great disservice by doing so. Yet if I shouldn't seek to spare them the pain of fail-ing, neither should I allow them to be in situations where they are virtually guaranteed to fail. I want the World Peace Game, for example, to be winnable—and fortunately, my students have always won it. For that victory to have any meaning, however, failure must at least be an option. And if failure is a possibility, that means it might someday happen. As a teacher, I have to be prepared for this, and so I have to ask myself continually when I am obligated to try to circumvent this possibility and when I am obliged to allow it.

To my mind, this is my most difficult task, as both a teacher and a parent, and I realize that not every teacher wants to work as much "in the dark" as I am committed to doing. After three decades of exploring uncertainty, I have gotten more comfort-able with not knowing than I used to be. But it's still a continual adjustment for me, particularly with regard to letting students assume more and more control over the Game. I truly believe that the more leadership roles they take, the more they learn and grow. But leadership entails greater risk, for me as well as for them. The further they get from "control central," the more will-ing I must be to admit the possibility of failure.

Accordingly, in the e-mail I send to teachers describing the qualities that students must have to benefit from the World Peace Game, I also describe the qualities necessary for teachers:

Teacher/Facilitators who wish to use the game must:
1. know their particular group of students very well, as the game is entirely based upon relationships.
2. must be able to foster (and watch without interfering) and allow opportunities for failure of the students at first, to ultimately achieve success.
3. be able to "not know or understand" just what the students are doing for a time, but have an intuitive understanding of their intent and discern how best to facilitate that.
4. be able to create new parameters/rules/procedures as needed to deepen learning "suddenly."
5. be able to cede control of the classroom direction to the students, while maintaining teacher-student collaboration —to lead without leading.

In short, teachers must possess charisma, compassion, connectivity, creativity, patience, and awareness.

It has taken me almost thirty-five years to develop the skills needed to facilitate the Game, and even now I am quite often in situations where failure is routine, and I am completely in the dark about what to do next. This is normal for me now, but not everyone is interested in adopting the above prerequisites in their teaching or classroom style.

In the e-mail, I go on to explain something about the logistics of teaching and playing the Game. Then I say that the Game is "not a permanent system, but rather a temporary, internalized, flexible, and renewable practice."

This practice requires walking that ever-shifting but all-important line, where I am both allowing my students to experience failure and giving them the opportunity to avoid it. Recently, when I was playing the Game with a group of fifth graders, I had the occasion to intervene with a young man named Dorin, a brilliant but somewhat troubled student who had been adopted a few years earlier from a Romanian orphanage. Dorin had been doing well academically, but I knew he had been having some trouble adjusting socially. He was a very physical kid, very intense—short and sturdy, with an athletic build and curly light-brown hair—and whenever he'd come up to speak with me, he'd put his hand on my arm and hold it there, as if trying physically to hold my attention. Yet if I initiated contact—if I reached out to, say, ruffle his hair or pat him on the head, as I might do with any of my students—he would duck his head and pull back, clearly uncomfortable with the gesture.

I knew Dorin wanted very much to be chosen as one of the Game's prime ministers. He saw himself as a powerful young leader, and I think there's an excellent chance that he'll eventually grow into that role. But at that point, I didn't think he would benefit from the position. In fact, I thought that he would almost certainly fail, very painfully and very publicly. Dorin was still fairly awkward socially, and he would sometimes become very upset at perceived slights from his peers. He would cry if he felt he had been rejected, and then he'd try to recover from the blow by swaggering, bragging, or even pushing his physicality right to the edge of aggressiveness, as though trying to assert his masculinity.

Although some of the students didn't know quite what to make of Dorin, he was respected for his intelligence and his courage, and he ended up getting an appointment as chief financial officer of the richest country, which in this session of the Game was named Awadi. Dorin came to me the day before our first real Game Day—in other words, before the prime ministers had made even a single declaration—and told me that he wanted to stage a coup against his prime minister, Eric.

Coups are an important part of the World Peace Game. If one

or more students object to the leadership of their country and cannot get the prime minister to consider their input, they are free to declare a coup d'état. They then have the opportunity to decide the outcome of the coup by a series of odds-weighted coin tosses in which the prime minister has the advantage but victory for the rebels is still possible.

If the coup succeeds, the prime minister is ousted and has to find another role in the Game. Frequently, ousted prime ministers offer their services to allies, or they may try to work with the World Bank or the United Nations. If the coup fails, the coup leaders have to leave the country, since they obviously can't continue to serve in the cabinet of someone they've just tried to overthrow. They must find some other country or institution willing to take them in, and they might have to endure being left somewhat outside the central business of the Game.

Because the stakes on both sides are so high, a coup is serious business, and students generally understand that they need a serious reason to undertake one. But Dorin was planning to stage a coup before his prime minister had performed even a single action. I knew that the coup would never be allowed by the weather goddess we had at the time, a playful but stern young woman named Rosa, and I thought that Dorin's ability to continue playing the Game would be severely compromised by this effort. If he lost his takeover bid, he would almost certainly have to resign from Eric's cabinet—or perhaps Eric would simply ask him to leave—and who would want to take him in, knowing that he was capable of staging a coup without the slightest provocation?

I knew where this move was coming from, of course. Dorin didn't want to play second fiddle, and he had seized on this opportunity to wrest power away from Eric. I also knew that if I put the matter to Dorin in those terms—if I called him selfish or power hungry—I would be depriving him of the chance to figure out for himself why staging a coup at this time was not a good idea. Likewise, if I pointed out that his effort was doomed to failure—that the coup wouldn't be allowed and that he would forfeit his chance to fully participate—I would be depriving him of the chance to learn a valuable lesson.

So here was a situation in which a student was virtually guaranteed to fail. I was willing to let him fail because I thought he would learn something from it and because the pain of failing would be at least potentially balanced by what he learned. I hadn't been willing to let Dorin fail at being prime minister —that seemed excessive—but I could let him fail in his efforts to stage a coup. If his choices in the Game were to have any meaning, he had to be free to make them.

But then I thought that perhaps there was a way to allow Dorin to learn something else from his situation, which was how to avert failure. Unavoidable failure is one thing, but some failures can be prevented. Could I help Dorin find the means within himself to prevent this one?

"I wonder," I said carefully, "where compassion fits in here."

"What do you mean?" Dorin asked, his dark-brown eyes narrowing with suspicion.

"Dorin, you know you are a great person, and I think you have it in you to someday be a wonderful leader," I said. "But so does Eric. In my opinion, Eric has a big job ahead of him, and he deserves all the support he can get. What do you think about that?"

Dorin shook his head stubbornly. "I want to bring a coup," he repeated. "I don't think Eric should be the prime minister. I don't think he'll do a very good job."

"I understand," I said. "But I'm asking you about compassion. Do you have it in you to show some compassion toward Eric— to give him the chance that you would want to have to try out a challenging and demanding job with the help and support of his cabinet? Whatever you think about him at this moment, do you think he deserves the chance to try? Do you think he deserves your compassion for the difficult position he is in? Would it be a compassionate decision to support Eric in doing the best job possible?"

Again Dorin shook his head. "I don't think he's the best guy for the job," he insisted. "Other people would be better."

"Well, here's what I'm going to ask you to do," I said finally. "You go home tonight and think about compassion. Think about what it means, and why it's important, and who needs it, and why *you* need it. And think about what it means to offer compassion to other people, even people we have criticisms or judgments of. And see—just see—how thinking about compassion might affect your decision."

We left it there that night. Next session, Dorin immediately went to the weather goddess instead of coming to me. I overheard some of the conversation, and the gist of it was that Dorin was still determined to take over his country's leadership. So he quietly asked the weather goddess what his chances of success were in the odds-weighted coin tosses.

Rosa took Dorin to task as only a blunt, honest peer can do. "Dorin, that doesn't make any sense," she said. "You're supposed to be so logical, right? Well, if Eric hasn't done anything yet, there is no reason to stage a coup. So my ruling would be, no coup for you!"

So how do we define failure, and what do we learn from it? In Dorin's case, I would have preferred a better payoff—that the incident would have sparked a startling revelation about himself or provoked him into greater generosity. But those kinds of payoffs are among the first things that a teacher learns to give up, because although they come around occasionally, you certainly can't count on them. Instead, you learn to redefine the time frame within which you define your own failure and success. In the short term, every teacher has to endure a number of disappointments when students don't develop "on schedule." We have to hope that what we give our students survives beyond the time we have them in our class and that both their failures and ours are only temporary.

In Dorin's case, I counted it as a limited success that he had spent time pondering his actions and considering the consequences rather than simply acting impulsively. That seemed like the best step forward that he was capable of at the time. His short-term failure—his inability to stage an unwarranted coup —was a lesson that he had been given, partly by Rosa and partly by me. Whether he chose to learn that lesson immediately, or in a few years, or never was not within my power to determine. Although I felt the pain of my apparent failure to provoke deeper self-reflection in Dorin, I needed to ask myself whether I had truly failed. If I defined "success" as the imposition of my will on people and events, then obviously I had failed. But if I defined "success" as offering my student an opportunity to learn that he could use in his own time, then maybe I had not failed.

Perhaps that is another gift of failure. Failure forces us to move away from results as our primary measure of "success" and toward evaluating ourselves based on process. In a world where none of us can ever truly control our results, that is an extraordinary gift indeed.

## Ezra Falls on His Sword

Yet another gift of failure is the way it drives us to find new resources within ourselves—resources that will stand us in good stead later on even if our immediate circumstances don't allow us to succeed. A few years ago, I was running a summer program in which a sixteen-year-old girl was one of our prime ministers and her twelve-year-old brother, Ezra, was our saboteur. Ezra was a redhead, very feisty and fiery, and he loved being the saboteur more than anyone I've ever seen. He just *loved* being a troublemaker, which of course was why I chose him. He was great at creatively disrupting others' plans and doing it in such a way that they couldn't quite tell how it had happened. I wondered if, as the lively younger brother of a very smart and sometimes bossy older sister, Ezra had had lifelong training for the role.

One day, Ezra called me at home. "Mr. Hunter," he said breathlessly, "something terrible has happened. I think I might have to stop being the saboteur."

"I know how much you love playing that role in the Game," I replied. "What's the problem?"

Ezra explained that as he was leaving our session that day, he overheard someone talking about his or her suspicions that Ezra was the saboteur. He believed that someone was going to accuse him the following day, that he would be put on trial, and that he would very likely be found guilty.

As with coups, there are very strict rules about how to deal with saboteurs. Anyone who thinks he or she knows who the saboteur might be is welcome to come forward with an accusation, which is followed by a large, public trial. All other play stops as the evidence for and against the saboteur is considered. At the end of the trial, the students vote. Then I ask the accused if he or she is guilty. If not, the person who made the accusation is fined $50 million, which comes out of the budget of his or her country or organization. If the saboteur *is* guilty, the Game continues without a saboteur.

The upside to identifying a saboteur is enormous. Everyone benefits from not having to allocate time, resources, and energy to dealing with the saboteur and his destruction. But I don't want to make it too easy to sabotage the saboteur, and I don't want the Game to become only about ferreting him or her out. So there must be a penalty for any false accusation.

The stakes are very high for the saboteur. Exposure can mean the loss of his or her role as saboteur, although the student does continue in his or her original, public position. And indeed, Ezra was devastated at the prospect of losing the role he loved. "I'm so sad," he told me during that phone call. "I love this job. I want to keep on doing it!"

I commiserated with him about what seemed like a highly probable loss — I had heard those rumors, too — and encouraged him to share his feelings with me. Then I said, "Ezra, I know you don't like this situation. What do you think you can do about it?"

There was a long silence on the other end of the phone line. Ezra was thinking so hard, I could just about hear his neurons firing.

Finally, he said, "What if I tell just one person who I am and make him the saboteur if the others catch me? That way, even if I go down, the Game will still have a saboteur. Because, Mr. Hunter, this is a very important job. Somebody needs to do it!"

I was moved that Ezra was thinking less about his own failure — after all, part of the saboteur's job is to avoid getting caught — and more about the needs of the group. The saboteur *is* an important job. It is almost a mythical role — most cultures have at least one troublemaker or trickster in their mythologies, a mischievous figure who tempts, tricks, traps, and otherwise provokes unsuspecting people to think more deeply, to take account of "the dark side," and to understand themselves more fully. Ezra was about to face the loss of this beloved role, but he was thinking not about himself, but about the Game as a whole.

"Well, Ezra," I said, "what you're suggesting is called 'falling on your sword.' Because if you tell anyone — even one person — that you are the saboteur, you are taking a big risk. What if that person turns you in? Once you expose yourself, he can turn around and expose you, and at the trial he can say, truthfully, that you yourself admitted who you were. Are you sure you want to do that?"

I couldn't see Ezra, but I could imagine him nodding, his chin thrust forward defiantly. "Mr. Hunter, I have to try," he said. "They're going to find out about me anyway, I think. At least this way, someone else can be saboteur."

Suddenly his tone changed. "Wait a minute, wait a minute," he whispered into the phone. I could hear shouting in the background. "Nothing!" Ezra shouted back. "Nobody!" Then he whispered into the phone, "I gotta go!" And he hung up.

It turned out that his older sister had overheard him on the phone, and she suspected that he had been talking about the World Peace Game with someone. She was too late to catch him talking to me, but she actually went into the phone's memory to find the number he had called. She couldn't find it, though, because Ezra—ever the saboteur—was one step ahead of her: he had unplugged all the phones in the house so that the history of that call would be lost.

The next day, first thing, Ezra stood up and said, "Can we have an injunction against anyone checking phone records at anybody's house to monitor World Peace Game activities?" The class agreed that would be a good rule, and it was passed. Now his sister, who had been about to share her suspicions, wasn't allowed to use that phone call as evidence against her brother, and Ezra continued as saboteur for a little while longer. When the day came that he was indeed found out (his sister adding to the critical evidence against him), successfully put on trial, and forced to step down, he was able to say, rather theatrically, "I'll have you know that I saw this coming, and I've appointed a sleeper saboteur who will replace me and carry on my work." The other students—even Ezra's sister—were so impressed with his courage and so delighted that they would still have a saboteur with whom they could match wits that they burst into applause. Ezra was one saboteur the other students were happy with!

## August Falls on His Sword

Ezra had chosen to fall on his sword as a way of averting failure. Although he personally failed in his role as saboteur, his self-sacrifice transformed his individual failure into a collective success, as the Game continued, complete with the saboteur it needed.

August fell on his sword in a different way and for different reasons, but ultimately he, too, learned a profound lesson from an impending failure. A short, wiry, and intense man in his early twenties, August had a kind of picturesque cowboy quality that befit the only American in the international group with whom I played the World Peace Game in Bergen, Norway. I had been invited there as part of a European Youth Initiative, which had recruited the group of teenagers and young adults from among the associates of the Bergen International Film Festival planning team. I had met the team the year before when Chris Farina's film about the Game was shown at the festival. In the spirit of excitement about this first-ever playing of the Game outside the United States, an ad hoc group of the planning team's friends from several countries had turned up to join our play: Norwegians, Finns, Bosnians, a Czech, a Brit, and August, the only American.

With his flaring Afro, his neatly trimmed goatee and Fu Manchu mustache, and his unwavering, beady-eyed stare, August bore a striking resemblance to the Latin American revolutionary Che Guevara, a resemblance that he cultivated by wearing a Che-style beret complete with a red star. I thought August's rebellious attitude might serve him well as prime minister of the Game's poorest country, dubbed in this incarnation Subsation. But perhaps I had misjudged how much more quickly tempers could flare and egos could engage when adults played the Game. August's brash, aggressive style soon alienated many of the other players, and at one point he almost came to blows with a fellow player. Although actual violence was averted, August continued to get angry and make belligerent demands. He frequently threatened military action, despite the fact that his country was too poor to afford much in the way of armaments. Yet neither was he able to forge a peace when other military powers threatened to attack him.

As the Game continued, things became very heated, and finally matters seemed to reach a stalemate. Able neither to respond with force nor to craft an acceptable peace, August saw that he had reached the limits of his effectiveness as a leader and was generating an enormous amount of tension in the room. Uncharacteristically, he sought me out for advice.

"All right, John," he began, as if jumping in mid-conversation would ease his frustration and, perhaps, his humiliation. "What do you think I should do?"

I was taken aback, I must admit. August was one of the most strong-minded people I have ever met, and he usually seemed impervious to advice. But I think it had finally dawned on him how deep a hole he'd dug for himself—how many aggressive statements, threats, and demands he had made, to the point where both he and his country would lose face if he took them back.

So we talked for a while. At first August did most of the talking, railing against the other teams, his teammates, and himself. He vented his frustrations, expressed some not-so-oblique criticisms of how I'd handled things thus far, and then went into a long, impassioned recital of his own mistakes. Clearly, August was wrestling with his actions and their consequences in a way that he wasn't at all used to—another gift of failure.

Finally, when he seemed ready to hear from me, I began to speak. I never made any suggestions, only asked questions. August brushed these aside at first, but eventually he began to consider them and then to respond. When I felt that he was truly listening, I asked the question that I thought would be most useful: "How can you move beyond this situation?"

I could see from the way he grimaced that the answer was uppermost in his mind. "The only way things would work now," he said slowly but with force, "was if I wasn't there doing this."

I honestly hadn't expected this answer, but I wanted to give him the chance to play it out. "All right," I said. "What about that?"

"What do you mean?"

"Well, what if you stepped down? Abdicated as prime minister. Let someone else take over. Would that alleviate the tension?"

I wasn't by any means suggesting that August take such a step — I honestly didn't think he would. That hadn't happened in more than three decades of playing the Game. For almost anyone, it would be such a huge blow to the ego, to surrender all your power at one stroke. I didn't think someone who valued power as much as August did would be able to take such an action, even though he was the one who had suggested it. And yet here he was, looking at me under lowered brows, nodding slowly.

"It's very Sun Tzu, isn't it?" he said, half bitterly, half in surprise. "*Not being in the spot where the attack is expected* . . . If I step down, they won't be able to attack me. And some of the ill will, you know, all that bad feeling . . . maybe it'll disappear."

And so, in what I considered an act of enormous courage, August announced his resignation. He was stepping down, he told his fellow players, and he would allow his cabinet to choose his successor. From that point on, he would not be a player in the Game — only a consultant in a lesser role on his team. He hoped very much that the rest of the world could accept this gesture of apology and would not continue to punish his country for what were essentially his own actions.

There were audible gasps as August made this announcement. I could feel the tension dissipating, as if the whole room were sighing with relief.

When I spoke with August about his move some days later, he told me that he had gradually come around to a different view of this action. "At the time, I felt like I was losing," he told me, his mouth still grimacing in discomfort. "But now, I guess I'd have to say I really found a way of, you know, winning. Even though I had to take a pretty roundabout way to do it."

I couldn't agree more. August had taken a moment that might have been construed as a failure and transformed it into an unexpected success. Although there was no way out for him personally, there still remained an action he could take that would enable the rest of us to win. And so, like Ezra, August chose to fall on his sword. His unorthodox strategy changed the entire flavor of the Game. Perhaps it also changed the course of his life, since August had finally chosen to change his own behavior not because he had been forced to, but because he had seen a better way. As it happens, that way was better for others, too. But the important thing was that August saw it as better for himself. I don't know how else he might have learned that lesson, but in this instance failure proved to be his best teacher.

## An Incomplete Perception

When my students play the World Peace Game, they begin, usually, in overload and confusion. And then, often, they move into failure—the sense that the skills and perceptions they can bring to the table will not suffice for them to master the Game. This sense of failure offers them the opportunity for a course correction—the chance to let go of their individual approaches and to think collectively, to see themselves as part of the group. Ezra and August experienced particularly intense versions of this lesson, but to some extent all of my students run up against it.

Once the students make it through this failure stage, they learn another valuable lesson: failure is, to some extent, an illusion. That is, failure is an "incomplete" perception. Failure's gift is to force us toward a more complete perception, a larger vision of what might really be going on. Letting my students experience failure can move them to a more complete perception and a more effective action.

After all, what do we do when we perceive that there is no way out? What actions are left to us when we understand that the obvious, the conventional, the expected, or the habitual actions aren't going to work? In such circumstances, we are forced to take the unexpected, contrarian approach. We may even be forced to simply do nothing. For many Americans, doing nothing is the most difficult choice of all.

One of the things my students learn by making it through the failure stage of the Game is that sometimes they must simply observe, wait patiently, and allow events to develop. Since the actions they expected to work have not actually worked, they realize that some other type of action might be in order. And when they don't yet know what that other type of action might be, they must stop, do nothing, and wait for a way to open or reveal itself.

This, again, is a version of the empty space. In that newly opened place of inaction, there is room, perhaps, for something new and bigger to grow—something we had not previously been able to imagine. If my students can have this experience of failure with the World Peace Game—if they can see failure as an incomplete perception, a call to a course correction, and an opportunity for something new to appear—then perhaps they can carry that experience with them into the rest of their lives. In that sense, the failure stage of the World Peace Game serves as a kind of vaccination. In real life, when the fate of every living creature on the planet may be at risk, the stakes might seem unbearably high. "Inoculating" my students with a protected version of that experience might enable them to develop a relationship with failure that will serve them well when they encounter the real thing.

## Spontaneous Compassion

Significantly, the solution to failure—the one found by August, Ezra, and Brennan and his classmates—is often a form of compassion. As I watch my students struggle with the forms that failure can take, I am struck by how often spontaneous compassion emerges in situations where you would least expect it. Over many generations of students, I have seen amazing inventiveness and innovation—creative thinking and problem solving that I could not have begun to imagine myself. They continually exhibit the will to do good and a commitment to the tireless work of negotiating and renegotiating until everyone wins. I am sometimes moved to tears by their deep, spontaneous compassion and their creative thinking to "make it so."

I love seeing how compassion arises among my students. It reminds me, always, of how much our ideas of success and failure are self-created. As I see it, these are arbitrary states that have been culturally agreed on. Once we understand that, we see that they can be changed. The key is to realize that "success" and "failure" aren't absolutes; they are simply labels we have collectively decided to affix to certain circumstances. Once we understand the fluid and flexible nature of things, this cultural agreement can be called into question, as can our entire sense of reality, and of right and wrong.

So perhaps this is the final gift of failure: sometimes, when it seems that there is no way out, failure forces us to make a new way. It may not be the solution we're expecting. It may not be a conventional solution. But it spontaneously resolves the situation—or takes it to another level.

What I loved about watching Brennan and his classmates save the world was realizing that before they acted, there was no solution. A solution had to be created, spontaneously, at the last possible moment. It might be easy for us as adults to see their solution as a simple and obvious one, but those nine-year-olds were unaware of the possibility until it suddenly appeared in their minds, in their hearts. The lesson we can learn is to ask ourselves what seemingly obvious solutions to our dilemmas we might be missing. What possibilities in our own situations exist that will seem embarrassingly plain to us once we have discovered them, but seem impossibly obscure to us now?

I was also struck by the depth of compassion my students showed as they looked for a way to win the Game. Significantly, nobody asked, "Are the people of Snowlandia worthy? Are there any slackers there? Do they perhaps not deserve our help?" They didn't ask, "Should we or should we not help them?" They didn't say, "Those people did not work hard enough, and we did." They simply did what they thought was right and necessary, and they did it quickly and spontaneously. And in that huge gesture of spontaneous compassion, out of emptiness, out of nothing . . . appeared a way.

That way came from a profound understanding that often emerges in failure's wake: *I am not the center of the story, but only a very small part of the whole. And yet, when I apply my effort to the collective action, so much change is possible.*

This understanding is not a matter of faith. I don't have much to do with faith, because I've found that faith and belief are very unstable and useful only up to a point. In my experience, knowledge trumps faith; and beyond knowledge is wisdom; and beyond wisdom is compassion—just flat-out compassion. In the end, that is what we really have to count on. If failure can teach us that, it is a stage well worth passing through.

# 4

# David Learns the Dangers of Victory

He looks upon his troops as children, and they will advance to the deepest valleys. He looks upon his troops as his own children, and they will die with him.

— SUN TZU, *The Art of War*

ANY GREAT GAME begins as the World Peace Game does: with empty space, a lot of complexity, and an overwhelming amount of information. A great game is designed to counter the overriding effects of our own personal "operating systems," which are typically so large and so practiced and so firmly established that they automatically supersede whatever reality presents to us, shaping our view of the world in relentlessly familiar terms. Most of us never even realize how limited our outlook has become and how many new possibilities we unknowingly filter out, seeing only what we are used to and believing that's all there is.

But if we flood ourselves with so much reality that our operating system is overloaded, we are forced to see beyond our ordinary view of the world. We might even realize the limits of that view, seeing how shortsighted or partial our habitual vision has become.

This, to my mind, is the value of games, or at least it's the value of complex games: they expand our perception of reality, forcing us to broaden and deepen our vision in order to achieve what the game demands of us. Some games teach us patience, requiring us to stretch out our rhythms, waiting and trusting in what might emerge. Other games teach us strategy, the ability to think two, three, four, five moves ahead. Still other games teach us teamwork—giving us the ability to cooperate with others or perhaps even the capacity to become so deeply integrated into a group that we and our teammates begin to think, feel, and respond as a single entity. At their best, games demand more of us than we knew we had, forcing us to expand our sense of our own potential and requiring us to let go of self-imposed limits.

At its best, the World Peace Game makes those sorts of demands as well, beginning with the challenges of confusion and overload, followed closely by those of failure and despair. Then a new phase of the Game begins to emerge: *personal understanding*. In this stage, an individual begins to develop new ideas about how to respond to a complex situation. He or she begins to glimpse new solutions: a new global approach, perhaps, or at least new suggestions for how to proceed.

Our individualistic culture places a great deal of emphasis on this stage, and so do the teachers in many classrooms, where children are expected to learn by themselves and are inevitably rewarded—via grades and other honors—by themselves as well. Likewise, the biographies of great achievers in business, science, and the arts often focus on the exemplary striver whose victory follows a painful defeat. We often view spiritual journeys in the same way, emphasizing the individual's emergence as stronger, wiser, and more powerful after an apparent failure. Generally, we are taught to think of victory and defeat in individual terms and to focus on the personal understanding that might come from them.

That approach is valuable, and individuals certainly have an important role to play in the World Peace Game. That's why I consider so carefully who should be offered the role of prime minister, since these four children's leadership can have such a crucial effect on the Game as a whole. The children who accept these positions invariably evince a keen sense of responsibility for their nations. Most of them understand from the beginning that each one of their decisions—as well as each failure to act —will affect not just themselves, not even just their cabinets, but hundreds of thousands of unseen others.

And yet, as in real-world issues of peace and war, there is ultimately only so much that one individual can do. In the World Peace Game as in life, one is tempted to rise to the occasion as an individual, to single-handedly craft the treaties or trade agreements or military strategies or alliances that will unilaterally solve the nation's problems. Each individual nation—whether rich or poor—is also tempted to solve the planet's problems on its own, so that an individual prime minister or even a cabinet might believe for a time that his or her own superior wisdom, insight, or good intentions are enough to save the world.

This wish isn't entirely wrong-headed. We have to try, as individuals, to understand a situation and to craft the response to that situation that seems wisest and best at the time.

And then, still as individuals, we have to come to terms with the limits of our own response. We have to accept that any action we take might promote an equal and opposite reaction that we do not want. We have to realize that even the most noble actions or most obviously correct course can have its dark side that we cannot control or reason our way out of. The fighter of the "just war" must understand that her actions will result in the deaths of other humans, many of whom may be innocent. The pacifist who refuses all war must realize that his inaction might likewise result in the deaths of the innocent. There are no actions without contradiction—and yet we must act, for *not* to act is also a contradictory action with both positive and negative effects.

And so, as individuals still, we have to discern the lessons in any outcome, no matter how seemingly straightforward. There is a kind of collective wisdom that we can move toward, and that is the topic of the next chapter. But in this chapter, I'd like to stay with the lessons we learn as individuals and to consider in particular the lessons learned by my student David, as he struggled with the power and excitement of being the prime minister of Paxland.

As you recall, there are four nations in the World Peace Game: a wealthy country (called Efstron by David's classmates), a poor country (in this session of the Game, Iceania), an oil-rich country (called Linderland here), and a country philosophically mandated to preserve the planet, which David and his cabinet dubbed Paxland, "land of peace." As prime minister, David wanted to create peace single-handedly, drawing on his own strength and skill. What he actually did—well, let's not tell the end of the story before the beginning. To fully grasp what David learned, let's begin where I began in the prologue—with David, the individual.

## The Prime Minister of Paxland

As we saw in the prologue, David was a small, serious boy with dark curly hair and a crooked smile. One of his parents was a New Yorker, and even though he had spent all of his life in Virginia, I always thought of David as a New Yorker born and bred: he was savvy, quick, intelligent, and very well-read, with, as it happened, a thing for maps. Perhaps that was why he had such a strong grasp of the World Peace Game geography and such a good feel for the economic and political ramifications of the shoreline's shape or the mountains' challenges.

David was very outspoken and politically oriented, and he loved above all a good discussion—maybe even a good argument. He was adept verbally and intellectually, and he was quite skilled, even at age nine, at negotiating the careening curves and turns that come with philosophical debate. David demanded a lot of himself and others. He was also very generous and good-hearted—a kind of noble being, in my opinion. I selected him to be prime minister because I wanted to test that nobility against the realpolitik that even my fourth graders struggle with in the course of the Game. I was curious how his sense of generosity would hold up against the challenges of creating peace in a frequently hostile world. And I was eager to see how his strong, almost harsh, sense of right and wrong would survive the inevitable compromises that are called for even on our pretend planet.

David's moderately wealthy country, Paxland, bordered Amelia's impoverished nation of Iceania. Amelia was a rangy, physically dynamic kid, tall and skinny with a carefree smile and short dark hair. She had an intense, analytical, probing intellect and was gifted with a strong sense of fairness. Early in the Game, Amelia had responded generously to the Nin, the religious group that occupied a small island in the sea that separated Iceania and Paxland. Technically, the island belonged to Paxland, but the Nin were now seeking their own homeland, and Amelia agreed to let them have an island within Iceania's borders. This didn't hold any particular advantage for Amelia or her nation, but she saw no harm in making an alliance with the Nin, and she was willing to do them this favor.

Under the terms of their treaty, the Nin assumed dual citizenship—in their new independent homeland within Iceania's borders and in their native Paxland. David was clever enough to see in this arrangement the chance to make some mischief and to poke Amelia just a bit by catching her in a fine-print oversight and then exploiting her mistake. With a slight, unconscious smile, he argued that since the Nin were technically citizens of his country, their land was his land. In ceding territory to the Nin, Amelia had, in effect, ceded it to David.

Amelia was first puzzled and then extremely frustrated. David was technically correct, but both he and Amelia knew that he was violating the spirit of the agreement. Amelia had intended to give the homeless tribe some land; she hadn't planned on ceding a portion of her territory to another country. The two of them, along with the students representing the UN, went out into the hallway, where they had a big argument. At the end of the day, the UN was forced to rule in David's favor. Whatever Amelia had intended, the agreement was worded as David said, and so he won out.

Because he was technically correct, David was able to square his "land grab" with his own sense of justice. But I was struck at how his maneuver showed the extent to which he was still thinking of the Game in individual terms. He wasn't yet thinking about how to create peace on the planet, but only about how to win the greatest advantage for his own nation. Nor had he worked cooperatively with his own cabinet, at least one of whom might have disagreed with his questionable action. The prime minister of Paxland was very much acting on his own to shore up his country's fortunes, and I wondered, as I watched Amelia flop into her seat with a fourth grader's disgruntled sigh, what lesson David was ultimately going to learn from taking this individual-istic approach.

I didn't have long to wait. The mercenaries—directed by Kadin, our wily saboteur—began attacking the Nin within Ame-lia's borders. As a result of David's legal maneuver, however, the little island that had once belonged to Amelia now belonged to David, and so the mercenaries' next attack was on him.

## Saboteurs and Subterfuge

"I have been instructed by an unknown third party . . ."

That is how I always begin my explanation of the saboteur's action. Since the saboteur can't act openly, the student charged with this role has to find some private way to instruct me how to deploy the mercenaries and weaponry at his or her disposal, usually by finding me alone in the classroom or arranging to meet me sometime during the day, but occasionally by calling or e-mailing me at home. Then, at the beginning of the next Game Day, I announce the action and carry out the saboteur's directive myself.

A hush always falls upon the class while I am describing these third-party instructions, and the students watch me intently, half-fascinated, half-unsettled. They know that the saboteur's explicit purpose is to disrupt the Game, so they generally suspect that this "unknown third party" is the saboteur and that the influence is malign. But there is always the possibility that one of the legitimate parties is simply acting secretly. Or perhaps there is some other element of the Game that I have not yet disclosed — another source of my mysterious instructions. This is the power of the saboteur: his or her very existence sows the seeds of doubt and discomfort, creating the idea that no one can ever be wholly sure of anything.

In this session of the Game, the saboteur was Kadin, who in his public role was prime minister of Efstron, the planet's richest country, and, as it happened, a close ally of David. Just as David was taking advantage of Amelia's treaty with the Nin to annex her island, Kadin was launching a series of relentless attacks on Amelia's nation. These attacks had created confusion for Amelia and for everyone else in the Game as well.

To the saboteur's delight, Amelia was growing increasingly paranoid. Why was she being attacked? She couldn't understand it. Hers was the poorest nation in the Game — what resources could she have that someone else would want? Hers was the weakest nation as well — what actions could she be taking that someone else would want to stop? The less able she was to understand the saboteur's attacks, the more disturbing she found them. Being attacked for an obvious reason is upsetting. Being attacked for no apparent reason is infuriating. As a result, Amelia now suspected everybody of being behind these maneuvers, even though she couldn't figure out what the hidden agenda was.

All the other players were equally baffled—and equally demoralized by their inability to understand. Since there was no apparent reason for the attacks, everyone was driven into a fury of confusion and frustration as they tried to figure the situation out. Either the hidden motive was so subtle and nuanced that it involved a prize of vast importance, or it was so irrational and meaningless that it was simple misdirection. Not knowing which was driving everybody crazy.

Nor did Amelia know how to respond to the attacks. Should she put her defenses around the saboteur's target and wait to see what the saboteur would do when he or she could not get through? Or was that playing right into the saboteur's hands and distracting her from defending another, more important asset? Should she focus on a military defense? Or should she spend her time and energy trying to figure out who the saboteur was, knowing that unmasking this villain would end the sabotage?

In fact, some of the students had begun to suspect that Kadin was the saboteur, so he had more reason than ever to misdirect attention while continuing to sow maximum confusion. By attacking Amelia, he had performed the role of the saboteur to perfection, causing the other players to look in all the wrong places for answers, keeping everyone thinking on the superficial level of isolated actions instead of trying to go deeper to see the patterns and connections. Amelia and her classmates should have been asking, How might this be an example of how the saboteur divides and conquers? or How might this be a way that the saboteur confuses and misdirects us? Instead, Kadin had succeeded in getting them to ask far less useful questions: Why Amelia? What does she have that someone else wants? What action is she taking that someone else wants her to stop? Whom has she offended? What could someone get out of targeting the poorest country in the Game? Of course, these questions were meaningless. The saboteur's target was not Amelia per se, but rather the entire class's peace of mind.

As it happened, Kadin would eventually go on to attack his own country. By that time, some of the students were getting even closer to accusing him, so his attack on himself threw them off the scent completely. Although the saboteur is given only a tiny budget, Prime Minister Kadin had access to the entire treasury of Efstron. He had so much money, he could keep on attacking all day. And no one would ever suspect him of attacking his own country! It was a supreme instance of misdirection.

But that would be several Game Days later. First, Kadin had another trick up his sleeve. Just after David got the United Nations to cede him Amelia's island—the island she had given as a homeland for the Nin—Kadin secretly sent his troops to attack that very island.

This was a brilliant move on Kadin's part. First, no one would suspect him of being the saboteur, because in his official role, he was David's ally. Second, because of the recent conflict between David and Amelia, the obvious conclusion would be that Amelia was somehow controlling these mercenaries and trying to get back at David. So David might well suspect either that Amelia was the saboteur or that she had somehow managed to stage this attack.

At the same time, Amelia was likely to take this attack personally. Although the island was technically no longer hers, it had just been hers, and she still had an emotional attachment to it —it was still color-coded as her land, and it was also within her borders and within striking distance of her nation's capital. So Amelia was affected by the mercenaries' attack at least as much as David was. She stormed over to David and shouted, "Did you put those mercenaries on *my* island?"

David caught the implication—that despite the UN ruling, Amelia still considered the contested territory to be *her* island.

"*Noooo*," he said, stretching out the word with indignation of his own. "*I didn't.* I would *never* do something like that, and you know it!"

As the two prime ministers stared at each other, I wondered what David was thinking. I know what I was thinking! Here he had just made an enemy of Amelia by taking the land she had meant for the Nin, and now, suddenly, he and she were in the same boat, facing the same mysterious adversary. First she had been the saboteur's target, and now he was. But if David hadn't found a way to make Amelia's land his, he might never have been the saboteur's target at all.

Did David regret his earlier land grab? I don't know that he did. To my mind, David was more of a pragmatist, who took things one step at a time, than a moralist or master strategist, who looked continually at the big picture. Yesterday it had been practical to take Amelia's land; today that might seem impractical, because he now needed her help against this new enemy. I wondered whether this lesson might teach David foresight, if not a greater sense of justice, but that is the type of question I'm always asking myself about my students, and there are rarely any immediate answers.

"Remember what Sun Tzu has told you," I commented after I announced the saboteur's move. "You do not have to fight to win every battle. Are you smart enough to know what to do? You are, but you can also ignore your own knowledge if you want to."

David, however, was more than ready to battle the mercenaries. Even as he had been conducting his own routine state business, he had been growing increasingly frustrated with these nameless troops, who had been doing damage here, there, and everywhere. He was not happy that none of the other prime ministers had taken on this problem, and even before his own territory had been attacked, he had been gearing up to propose some kind of retaliation or defense. "Nobody's doing anything about this, but we're going to do something!" he vowed. That had been a harder position to take when David wasn't involved directly. But now he was.

## Living What Sun Tzu Said

As it happens, just after I announced the decision of the "unknown third party" to stage an attack on David, the next turn belonged to Linderland, the oil-rich desert country, and the one after that to Efstron. And then Game Day was over. That was on a Tuesday, and we wouldn't be playing again until Thursday. So David and Amelia had an entire day to think about what to do next. Neither one of them was happy about the situation, but Amelia was inclined to wait and see what happened, while David was itching to take action.

Sure enough, when David's turn came on Thursday, he announced that he would be sending his country's troops to retaliate against the mercenaries. He wanted to use blunt force to unequivocally settle the situation—to make sure this threat to his nation and to world peace in general was squashed.

"We're sort of upset that these other countries who've been attacked by these mercenaries have not done anything about them," David said. "But *we* are going to do something. We're going to attack!"

I always let it be the children's decision whether to attack, but I had to at least ask, "Is that the best way to deal with it, sir?"

David nodded vigorously, his determination growing. "Right now, we're sick of attacks."

"All right, sir," I said. "Airstrikes or infantry?"

David thought a moment. "Infantry," he said decisively.

"This is a thousand troops you're risking," I pointed out. "If your troops lose, of course, you will have to write a letter to their parents." I have all the students write letters to the parents of any of their troops lost in battle. They can engage in war if they choose to, but I want them to understand at least some of the consequences.

As David announced his decision to attack, I could see the little girl behind him, David's chief financial officer, in agony over her prime minister's declaration. Her face was contorted, and she pounded her fist hard against her knee. Startled by the slight sound, David turned around and looked at her. I watched him take in her anguished expression. I knew he had consulted his cabinet, but clearly his chief financial officer had opposed him or had at least counseled very strongly against this action. I wondered what impact her response would have on him as the situation continued to play out. David had been making the kind of individualistic decisions that are so much a part of the American tradition, and he had been making them boldly, even fearlessly, with great certainty about their rightness. I wasn't sure whether I wanted those decisions to succeed or fail.

Luckily, it wasn't up to me. In the World Peace Game, all battles are decided by the weather goddess, who tosses a series of coins to come up with a random answer. The coins are weighted in favor of the bigger nation, which has, as in real life, the greater chance to win. The ultimate outcome is random, however, and either side might emerge victorious. In this case, the winner was David.

"All right," I announced. "The mercenary attack is over. Paxland's troops have done the job!" There were cheers and claps from the other students, who were relieved to be done, as they thought, with the mercenary attacks. With his characteristic slight smile, David took the "enemy troop" pieces off the board.

"David risked war to gain peace," I pointed out. "Now before the prime minister continues, think about whether his actions were right or wrong. Was that a good thing or not? Lives were lost —they weren't his people, but lives were lost."

I couldn't tell whether that message got through to David or anyone else. So far, for David, going it alone was proving to be a success.

But the battle that day was not the end of the cycle. The next Game Day, I was again announcing, "I have been instructed by an unknown third party . . ." At the saboteur's instruction, I sent yet more mercenaries into battle, and despite the anguished face of his chief financial officer, David sent yet more troops to engage them. The weather goddess tossed her coins of fate once more, and once more, David's troops emerged victorious. The next Game Day, the saboteur attacked a third time, and yet a third time David fought back and emerged victorious.

And all this time, my heart was breaking. I could not help asking myself if there was not some peaceful solution, some permanent way out of the cycle of violence. Each time David engaged in battle, I knew that there were going to be more flames, more explosions, more deaths. Perhaps war is inevitable, even justified, in some circumstances, but when I see someone choose it repeatedly, it gives me great pause. As a teacher, I hope that I've given my students a path to avoid this cycle and not get stuck in this quagmire as armies sometimes do. But when I see a student like David choose war again and again and again, I wonder whether I've given them all that I might have.

At this point, I viewed David as stuck in a cycle of endless war—a cycle that he had no idea how to escape. The enemy attacked, and he retaliated. Then the enemy retaliated, and he was forced to attack. I wanted him to find a better way, but he didn't seem to even be looking for one.

Finally, David began to change his leadership style. He began to rely more on his cabinet and his allies, to look more to the big picture of international alliances and planetary goals. He had to listen to his cabinet, to view things in global terms, to consider outcomes he hadn't expected, and to be open to points of view he didn't share. He had to enlarge his sense of himself, perhaps, so that his individualism became, in a way, larger. And he had, sometimes, to open himself up to the wisdom of the group rather than trying to change the world single-handedly.

Still, it wasn't until I watched the film made of that particular game that I realized how much David had learned from this experience—and how much farther his vision had extended beyond mine. When the filmmaker asked David about all the battles he had been winning, David just shook his head and said, "We've really had enough of people attacking. I mean, we've been lucky. But now I'm feeling really weird. Because I'm living what Sun Tzu said. He said those who go into battle and win will want to go back. And those who lose in battle will want to go back and win. And I've been winning battles, so I'm sort of going into battles. More battles. And I think it's sort of weird to be *living* what Sun Tzu said."

When I first viewed that part of the film, I silently cheered for David's ability to imbibe Sun Tzu's wisdom. I was glad the great Chinese general had taught him such an important lesson about war and peace: that the victor is as much a prisoner of the cycle of violence as the loser, and so each will be drawn back into battle again and again—the loser because losing is so painful, the victor because winning is so sweet. I liked to imagine that the next time David was faced with an important decision, he might rely less on his individual ability to attain victory and more on his awareness of the effect on the group as a whole.

Someone asked me to identify the exact passage from Sun Tzu that David was quoting, and I discovered that I could not find it. Although David thought of himself as "living what Sun Tzu said," the insights he articulated were his own hard-won wisdom, culled from his own struggles—with Amelia, with the mercenaries, and with himself.

I was struck again by the importance of this phase of individual discovery. Yes, I wanted David to move to what I thought of as a more advanced phase—understanding his place within a larger whole. But I would not short-circuit, even in my own thinking, the need for that earlier phase, where each of us is thrown back on our own resources, our own personal experience, our own moral compass, trying to make sense out of the specific events that have occurred.

I was struck, too, by how my own need for right and wrong answers had clouded my ability to view David's journey objectively. In my mind, peace was "right" and war was "wrong," and so I yearned for David to choose peaceful responses, even when he was being attacked. But maybe David had achieved a wider vision than I had. He was seeing beyond right and wrong to perceive the entire cycle of violence. When he told the filmmaker that he was now "living what Sun Tzu said," he wasn't making a judgment. He was simply observing that he was *in* that cycle.

What I ultimately wish for my students — and for myself — is precisely that type of observation without judgment: to be able to hold different perspectives simultaneously — to view a situation from all angles — and then to decide, without judgment, what is called for. After all, David's victories put an end to the mercenaries' attacks. I wish there had been another way, but that is the perspective you can take only from the sidelines, where you have the luxury of wishing for a supposedly perfect response. As the individual charged with taking action *in* the situation, David had to go beyond good and bad, seeing only necessary action and its consequences. I was pleading silently with David, saying, "Oh, no, war is bad; please don't fight." But David was going through a cycle of violence, seeing for himself how victory leads to resentment and retaliation, how one victorious battle often requires another, and then another, and then yet another.

As a result, I believe, David found a genuinely admirable way to deal with the specific demands of his situation (and perhaps made it clear to me, once again, why I am happier as a teacher than as the leader of a nation). Taking all the risks into account, he finally concluded that attacking the mercenaries was the only choice, and so he did it, without regret, without too much enthusiasm, but with the firmest of convictions. David did what he saw as his duty—and then, later, he could acknowledge that his duty had put him into a cycle of violence that he still did not know how to master.

These are the contradictions that all of us must face when engaged in questions of war and peace. Should we use violence to prevent greater violence? Is even justified violence too dangerous to consider, because it will lead to even greater harm? Suppose it is correct to take a violent action. What are the consequences that will arise afterward, and how can we best deal with them? How do we keep even a "just war" from poisoning our chances of ever finding peace?

A couple of years ago, after one of the parents in our program, a university professor, observed the Game, she took me severely to task. "This is all wrong," she said. "You should not be teaching them to use war or even letting them use war—don't even go there in the first place! Peace is the right way for the world, and you should be teaching your students that and that alone."

But I believed then, and I believe even more strongly now, that if I put my bias onto the Game—my preference for peaceful rather than warlike solutions—it lowers the chances that my students will learn for themselves. Certainly, if I restrict their actions in that way, they have no chance of learning anything that goes beyond my own position—as David was able to do. After all, my opinion is only one of many. And if my students rely on it to the exclusion of their own individual visions, I will have done them a great disservice. I will have deprived them of the opportunity to face the reality of our warlike world: the unintended consequences, the uncontrollable results, the collateral damage that may or may not be avoidable.

Imagine the following scenarios. An oppressed people is battling an oppressive regime. Is it more compassionate to send them arms and material support or to leave them to fight their own battles, knowing that our intervention may cause greater problems than it solves? A tyrannical nation faces economic sanctions. Do we support the sanctions to bring down the tyrant or decide that, in the end, the sanctions will hurt innocent citizens more than the tyrant? These are not easy questions, and there are rarely any a priori correct answers. Our principles can help us find a solution, perhaps, but they cannot predict what it should be. For that reason, I believe, nobody can tell my students how to shape their own individual visions—not even Sun Tzu, whose wisdom about war and peace fell short of David's own insight in the particular situation he faced. That is why David had to come up with his own response and his own analysis, even if he chose to believe that he was only "living what Sun Tzu said." David went into the World Peace Game with an open mind—with an empty space—and he managed to achieve one of the greatest goals of my teaching, which was to withhold his judgment while holding multiple perspectives, at least for a time. I salute him, and I am grateful to him. I hope we can all go on, as he did, to find our own ways of "living what Sun Tzu said."

## *"We Regret to Inform You . . ."*

One of David's duties as commander in chief was to write condolence letters to the parents of the troops killed in battle. I think this is an important part of developing self-awareness: that in positions of leadership, you have to take responsibility for your actions, particularly when they turn out—as they so often do —to have larger consequences than you expected. Having my students write condolence letters to parents is like holding a mirror up to them, so that they can examine their own thinking and intentions. Victory is often its own justification, enabling us to avoid looking closely at what we did or why we did it. Why should we reflect when it all turned out so well? But losing a battle provokes a moment of reckoning that can often lead to a productive internal dialogue.

The condolence letter is a relatively recent addition to the World Peace Game. It was inspired by a meeting I had a few years ago with someone who had been a soldier for many years. This man told me something about how families are affected by their loved ones being in the military: the worry when they are abroad; the relief when they are home; the grief when they are lost. I came to realize that a soldier is never a singular entity—he or she is never just an individual. Every soldier is part of the military—unit, company, battalion, army—and also part of a family—spouse, children, parents, siblings, cousins, aunts, uncles, grandparents. The family is almost as involved in the military as the soldier is.

The soldiers who fight World Peace Game battles are hardly likely to inspire those thoughts in my students. They are tiny molded-plastic figures, dyed green or brown, holding indistinguishable weapons in fixed poses. If you prick them, they do not bleed; if you wound them, they do not cry out; if you annihilate them, they do not die. How, then, could I bring that broader perspective to my students—how could I get them to see these little plastic figures as part of a larger web of relationships—without inappropriately overwhelming them with worry and grief?

Of course, these days, even fourth graders might have participated in video game killings and other types of electronic warfare. Even nine-year-olds have seen countless men, women, and children die in the movies and on TV. Many of them have read books—including fantasy and science fiction novels—about combat and warfare on every scale imaginable, from the personal to the intergalactic. I wouldn't say that my students are used to warfare and human suffering, but they certainly have had a lengthy exposure to it, far more than I had at their age.

Still, I thought, most of their exposure is to the dramatic side of war—armies clashing, heroes prevailing. I wanted them to have a more complete picture of war's consequences and some real feeling for what those might be. My challenge was to bring some of that broader awareness to the situation without damaging them. I thought a letter might do the trick.

So I began to tell my students that anyone responsible for sending troops into battle had to write a letter to the parents of those who died, and I have continued that tradition. The students are required to write just one form letter to all the parents, but I tell them to really put their hearts into it. They usually find somewhere quiet to work on it, or sometimes they take it home and share it with their own parents. I tell them, "You can keep it short, and you can keep it simple. Just express the feelings you would have if you were in command of these troops. Imagine what the parents of those troops might be feeling. And speak from your heart to them."

This is a new task for most of my students. The ones who have relatives in the military can already imagine the situation, of course, because they are living it. But the ones who don't are being asked to imagine something they have never seen in pop culture or the media. Without any models, they have to invent their own solutions.

In most cases, students keep these letters childlike and simple. "I'm sorry!" they write. "Sorry that your sons and your daughters were killed." I'm struck that they don't say, as an adult might, "We were defeated" or "A lot of lives were lost." They just say, "Your child was killed—and I'm sorry."

I instruct them to tell the parents what happened, why it happened, and how they feel about it. They don't usually know the word "condolence," but they understand that this is an apology, and they almost always begin with the words "I'm sorry" or "We're sorry." Some of them add, "Your sons and daughters were heroes." Some say, "They died trying to protect our nation." They never say, "They died attacking someone" or "We were trying to get a military advantage." Instead, they say that the deaths were necessary to protect the rest of us.

The mood when a condolence letter is read aloud to the entire group is always very quiet and subdued. I wouldn't call it sad, exactly, just very subdued. It's almost as though there is more space in the room, as though the letter itself creates more space. I see a seriousness come over the students' faces, and sometimes I see the dawning of a new understanding: *This, too, is what war means.*

One summer, when it was time to read one of these letters, a student said, "Mr. Hunter, there's a parent over there"—someone who happened to be visiting that day. "Let's ask that mom to read the letter. It'll be more real."

So we asked her, and she gamely picked up the letter and began, "Dear Parents: We regret to inform you . . ."

She read one sentence. She read two sentences. By the third sentence, she was in tears. I was in tears. Everybody understood that when even one person is killed—even a single, precious individual—the winners cannot gloat. At those moments, we all lose.

## The Benefits of Defeat

David had to learn about the dangers of victory. But I hope that my students also learn about the benefits of defeat.

This is not just wordplay. I want my students to understand that appearances are illusory—that we almost never know, at the moment we make a decision, what the ultimate consequences of that decision will be. As individuals, our perspectives are limited. We do our best, but we can't really know what we have done or what it means. Unless we are very, very lucky, we may never know.

Sometimes, though, life gives us a chance to see the results of our actions—to understand more, eventually, than the individual can ever understand at the time. Several years ago, life afforded me such an opportunity.

I was a new teacher at a middle school in Maryland. I'd been teaching there for about a year, and it was already clear to me that the principal had, well, some problems, shall we say. In fact, the word on the street was that she was crazy! She did make some odd decisions, I thought, in a kind of draconian fashion, but for most of that year, she and I got along fine.

For that whole year, my homeroom class had been working on a literary magazine. Now it was April, and we were nearing the end of the term. They had worked really hard, and in my opinion they had done a great job, including a great range of materials that showed a lot of dedication and commitment. Of course, they were their usual snarky, funny middle-school selves, but I thought the magazine benefited from that. Not surprisingly, the magazine was full of innuendo and slang, and it included some putdowns of the administration.

As with anything to be published by students at that school, the principal had to review the magazine, and she simply decided that it was not a proper publication for her establishment. She didn't suggest any editing or any kind of limited changes—the whole thing was just going into the trash, and that was that.

We got this news late in the afternoon, and although we were all fairly disappointed, we just went home. But the next morning when I was opening up my classroom, I heard a roar out in the hallway. I looked outside to find a mob of students, banging their lockers, slamming their notebooks on the floor, and heading for the principal's office. I realized that these were my students— my homeroom kids—and I understood, with concern, what they were doing. As I stepped out into the hall, wondering what to do, I saw their leader, Chad.

"Hey, Chad!" I called out. "Where are you guys going? What's going on?"

Of course, I knew exactly what was happening, but I was looking for a way to slow them down.

"We're going to the office!" Chad said. "That principal is wrong about our magazine, and we are going to tell her exactly what she needs to do!"

Their protest would lead to suspensions and expulsions, no question about it. I had to figure out some way to prevent them from doing that kind of damage to themselves. So I said, "Okay, but before you go, just step in here a minute and show me what exactly in the magazine she objects to."

I knew that this made no sense, but for some reason the students bought it, and Chad led the group into my classroom. As soon as they were all safely inside, I locked the door behind them and said, "Now we are just going to talk about this. We are going to take as much time as we need to figure this out."

Well, it was a madhouse in there. It was hard to calm the students down, let alone figure out what to do about it. But we kept at it for about an hour, and finally we hammered out a solution. The students worked with me to write a letter to the principal, explaining their reasons for disagreeing with her decision, offering a solution, and asking her to approve their solution. They also offered to meet with her face-to-face to discuss the problem.

The hour the students spent in my classroom meant that the entire school schedule was totally derailed. All of us—them and me both—were in deep trouble. Some of them got detentions simply for being late to class, and all of them got punished in some way. When it was my turn to be called into the office, the principal suggested that she was going to terminate my contract.

"You were talking about my decision," she told me. "But that's *my* decision to make. Not yours."

That was my worst day ever as a teacher. I was thoroughly disheartened, and I seriously thought that if I wasn't fired, I should consider leaving the profession.

I didn't quit teaching, although I did leave that particular school. For many reasons, my family moved that summer from Maryland to Virginia, and I began teaching at Venable Elementary School in Charlottesville, where I remained for many happy years.

I had been there for about a decade when out of the blue, I got a phone call from the University of Maryland. I didn't know anybody there, I hadn't gone to school there, I had no connection with the place whatsoever. When they told me they were giving me some kind of award, I actually thought it was some kind of scam.

They explained that I'd been nominated for this award by one of my former students who was now at the university, and that there was going to be a ceremony and a luncheon. Would I like to come? They would even send a car for me. The free lunch sounded pretty good, but I politely declined the car.

When the day of the ceremony arrived, I got into my Volkswagen Beetle and drove to Maryland. When I got to the university, the parking lot was crowded, and there were limousines everywhere. It turned out that I was one of twenty-five people nominated by students as a teacher who had had a profound influence on their lives. The university had spared no expense in making sure all of us would attend. One teacher had been flown in from Germany, another from Indonesia. I was stunned. I had no idea this was such a big deal.

I came to find out that it was Chad, the ringleader of that rebellious group at my old school in Maryland, who had nominated me. We had a lavish lunch, sponsored by the Philip J. Merrill Foundation, and each of us received the Master Teacher Mentor Award. All of the students sat with their teachers in this giant hall at tables covered with white linen, and all of the officials made speeches. The thing that really floored me was when someone announced that the award included a partial college scholarship to be given to some worthy student in my name.

Now this scholarship was going to some high school student I didn't even know. It suddenly occurred to me that someone I had never met was going to get a shot at going to college simply because I had had the worst day of my teaching career.

I don't want to take a simplistic view here. I would never say that there's good in everything. I can think of plenty of events in life — on both the personal and the global level — that can't be broken down in terms of good versus bad, positive versus negative. I don't look at things that way.

But I will say that there's always a *deeper* view than what seems obvious, that we can never stop with, "Well, he fired a missile at me, so I'm going to have to fire one back at him." That can never be the end of the story. We have to know that even when things seem really, really bad, there's something deeper in the situation that we can use. Because there it was: Ten years earlier, I had undertaken some risk and danger, experienced some misery and depression. Yet the action I took with my students, an action that seemed so useless at the time, turned out to have a greater effect than I ever could have imagined.

Perhaps it's that way with many — or even most — of our actions. As individuals, we just have to do the best we can, but we almost never know the power of what we do. What if every action we take is that important? What if every single one has meaning?

More important, I saw that the roots of my actions connect me more powerfully than I had ever suspected to a larger whole of which I am a part. Chad, that troublemaking kid I had taught ten years before, was not out of my life — he was part of it. And some other student whom I had never even met, the one who was getting the scholarship, he was part of it, too.

I learned then that if I see myself only in terms of myself, I am always going to be wrong. To fully understand who I am and what I am capable of, I need always to see myself in terms of a community, even a community I have never met, like the one that organized the scholarship; perhaps even the community of the planet as a whole, which I am affecting and affected by in ways that I am both aware of and cannot even imagine.

David was forced to learn a similar lesson, as he took what he thought were individual actions as a leader—his legal battles with Amelia and his military battles with the mercenaries—and then had to confront the fact that those actions did not begin and end with him, which meant that his identity didn't either. David's identity—my identity—everyone's identity—might *feel* like an individual matter, and certainly there is a level on which we have to take individual responsibility for the choices we make and the consequences we set in motion. But on another level, that individual responsibility has meaning only in terms of the communities of which we are a part. Just as on one level, we can speak of individual body parts—a foot, an arm, an eye—on another level these individual parts only acquire their true meaning and ultimate identity as members of a living human body.

This dialectic between the personal and the communal seems to me a profound truth about the nature of the human species. The individual expresses herself through language, but she learns that language from the people who raise her. The individual expresses himself through writing a book, teaching a class, building a business, or discovering a cure for cancer, but to bring these actions to fruition, he needs tools, students, workers, and a preexisting body of knowledge from which he can learn and to which he can add. Even the individual mystic, who believes she speaks directly to God, needs a religious tradition to shape the images and language through which she understands her experience, through which she and the people around her distinguish a divinely inspired experience from a demonic possession or a schizophrenic break. Our most intimate, personal examples of self-expression can flourish only in a human context. Children raised by wolves are not spontaneous artists or natural toolmakers; without a human community from which to learn, they are barely able to walk upright.

The stage of personal understanding brings us inevitably to the Game's fourth stage, *collaboration*. Once we truly understand ourselves, we have very little choice but to work with others. Or perhaps it's more accurate to say that once we truly understand ourselves, we have very little choice but to understand that, despite our illusions of autonomy or self-sufficiency, we have been working with others all along.

# 5

# Standing Up To the Tyrant

In ancient times, those skilled in warfare make themselves invincible and then wait for the enemy to become vulnerable. Being invincible depends on oneself, but the enemy becoming vulnerable depends on himself.

—SUN TZU, *The Art of War*

I'M GOING TO FIX IT. I'm going to make everything come out right!"

That was my student Micah, or maybe it was Channey, or maybe it was Russell, or maybe it was Beverly. Over the years, I've seen many students who enter the World Peace Game with a kind of sanguine self-confidence that borders on arrogance, and I never know whether to applaud their goodhearted intentions or dread their inevitable disappointment when their wish to solve all the world's problems by themselves runs up against the reality that this simply cannot be done. Like our planet itself, the Game just isn't built that way. Peace is not a puzzle waiting for the right genius to discover the solution, nor is it a complex mechanism waiting for the right engineer to figure out how it works. Peace is a delicate ecosystem that requires a kind of organic harmony among all its many participants: from the richest nation to the poorest tribe, from the nomadic Kajazians to the deeply religious Nin, from the World Bank to the weather goddess, from the United Nations to the arms dealers.

As we saw in the last chapter and shall see even more clearly in this one, individuals can make an enormous difference. An individual leader—and in the Game, all the children are potential leaders—can come up with a brilliant idea that saves the world, as Brennan did; or he can fall on his sword for the good of the group, as August and Ezra did; or he can learn to compromise while still holding firm, as David did. These individual actions—and the individual talents of the students involved—have had an enormous influence on the course of human events, both inside my classroom and outside it, in real life. But the key lesson that must be learned for the Game to be won is that the individual is able to contribute most effectively through collaboration. Without the ability to work with a group, an individual reaches a certain natural limit of what he or she can accomplish.

I believe this principle of collaboration—and the notion that it allows the full flowering of individual talent—applies to virtually all aspects of human endeavor. A scientist emerges from a community of scientists: the process of dialogue and peer review is what pushes an individual genius to new heights while also advancing the field. Even the most isolated artist creates in response to work that has come before, in dialogue with some imagined audience, in conversation with some form of community: that is how the work grows, educating and reshaping the artist even while influencing and inspiring the world. An athlete benefits from years of accumulated knowledge about how to train, reach peak performance, and preserve and extend his or her individual ability. Those years of knowledge represent the embodied wisdom of the community, to which the record-breaking athlete contributes by revealing to the community that humans can accomplish even more than was previously understood. Even a mystic, shaman, or monk operates within the community that created and maintains the spiritual tradition and that produces the food, clothing, and shelter that sustains material life. I celebrate the flourishing of any individual talent, inside or outside my classroom, but I want my students to learn that they will flourish most fully in dialogue and collaboration.

So when a cocky or earnest or excited student tells me that he or she knows what to do to win the Game, I just smile. "I've never yet seen anybody win the Game by themselves," I say as lightly as I can. "So let's see what happens. Maybe you'll be the first!"

Yes, it is a warning. But it is also an invitation. Perhaps that quixotic effort, which I know is doomed, is precisely the lesson that the student needs to discover his or her own personal dialectic with the group—his or her own process of mutual interaction whereby student and group change each other, a back-and-forth process that leaves both sides transformed. Perhaps the other students need their own opportunity to watch and learn from the folly of trying to do individually what only a group can do. And perhaps I, their teacher, need to remember the limits of my own foresight, my own predictive powers, since in the end I know as little as any of them about how any particular session of the World Peace Game will unfold.

When I think back through my years of playing the Game with hundreds—perhaps thousands—of students, one incident emerges to exemplify what I see as the ultimate instance of how individuals transform themselves by collaborating in community.

## The Birth of a Tyrant

Jared was a bully. He was my student about ten years ago, before the problem of bullying got the kind of attention it gets now. Bullying is part of the national consciousness these days, and many teachers are trained in how to deal with it. But that wasn't the case back then. So I was more or less on my own in figuring out what strategies might help Jared get past the impulse to bully.

Now, when I call Jared a bully, I don't mean to imply that this was all he was. He was in many ways a likable character—powerful, charismatic, and handsome—all the girls considered him "really cute"—with sparkling blue eyes; thick, wavy, dark hair; and a devilish grin. At first glance, you might even think of him as a natural leader, and I suppose bullies do sometimes tend to be leaders. But Jared turned his leadership in a direction that wasn't helpful to our school. He could be very sophisticated and very sneaky about how he did things, very clever at somehow setting things up so that he always got his way. Somehow every group that Jared was a part of ended up doing exactly what Jared wanted, and any dissenters found themselves silenced. Perhaps it was through social pressure—Jared would give the dissenter a stern look or a mocking glance, or he would make some kind of joke that would turn the other kids against the unfortunate boy or girl who had tried to make an alternative suggestion. Or perhaps it was through veiled threats. Jared was taller than most of the other kids, and he had a kind of natural grace that many of my fourth graders were somewhat intimidated by. At that age, many children haven't yet grown into their bodies, and they may carry themselves shyly or awkwardly. But Jared had a powerful physical presence even at nine years old, and if he seemed to be annoyed with you or ready to take action against you, it could be somewhat frightening if you were smaller and less confident. I don't know that Jared ever actually threatened anyone or caused actual physical harm, but the force of his presence was such that he didn't really need to. He had enough physical and mental power that he could carry on his bullying any way he chose, and although he was occasionally caught and punished, it was very hard to pin down exactly what he had done wrong if you weren't on the scene at the very moment it happened.

Today we talk about bullies who threaten and mock and organize children into "gangs" to harass other children, and even that is hard to identify and respond to. Jared's methods were far more subtle, which made his bullying almost impossible to prevent. What was most troubling about him was the gleeful look that passed over his face every time another child suffered, whether it was someone who missed an answer in class or someone who lost a verbal sparring match with him. Clearly, for Jared, the world was divided into winners and losers, and every time another child lost, Jared felt a little bit more like a winner.

What is maybe harder to understand than Jared's tendency to bully is my decision to offer him the post of prime minister. That is not what you would normally do with a child who has that kind of difficulty, and I'm not quite sure what was in my mind when I proposed it to him. Did I hope that giving him formal power would counteract his bullying tendencies, maybe ease his need to be on top? Did I imagine that he would learn, through his new position, a kind of responsibility that he had not exercised among his peers? Did I think, in some devious way, that the students who succumbed to his bullying in the classroom or on the playground would stand up to him in the context of the Game?

All I can say is that I saw something in Jared that was greater than his current behavior, but of course you could say that about any human being. Still, it appeared to me that Jared could change — in fact, it appeared to me that he could change *now.*

In my defense, these kinds of seemingly magical transformations do frequently occur. Assuming a prime minister's responsibility seems to entail a kind of awesome power to a fourth-grade student, and I have seen many children rise to the occasion with surprising speed. I have seen timid girls step into a natural authority that surprised them and everyone around them. I have seen boisterous boys access a calm and almost delicate style of negotiation and alliance building. Recently, one boy in my class who previously talked about nuclear war and weaponry with a kind of rising glee did an abrupt one-eighty after becoming prime minister of the nation dedicated to preserving the planet. One of his best friends, whom he had chosen as minister of defense, began their first cabinet meeting by saying exuberantly, "Dude! Let's nuke somebody!"

To my surprise, the new prime minister—who was studying a thirteen-page dossier of world crises—looked troubled. "Let's try a peaceful way first," he said slowly.

"No!" said his friend. "Peaceful is boring!"

I could see that the minister of defense had not yet made the transition from boy playing with toy soldiers to responsible leader of a crisis-ridden nation—and maybe some adults have some trouble making that transition as well. But the prime minister's face remained thoughtful, almost pained. I could see that the citizens of his new country were becoming real to him, as were the ecology of the planet and the notion that his actions had weight and meaning, and the power to harm or help at a level that he wasn't used to thinking about. Just assuming the leadership that I had offered him had given that boy the chance to step into a hitherto unknown capability, with all the distress and concern and uncertainty that overwhelms real-life leaders in those positions. So it *is* possible for children to change. Children given the opportunity to transcend themselves often seize that opportunity and, as if by the miracle of time-lapse photography, grow more rapidly than we could ever imagine.

However, sometimes they don't. Jared didn't. Or at least for the first few weeks of the Game, it didn't look as though he was going to.

I began to question my decision from the moment I made it. I could see that Jared's classmates were shocked when I offered him the post of prime minister of the richest, most powerful country on earth (which Jared and his cabinet eventually called Golden Land). More significantly, I could see that Jared himself was surprised. Although he had somehow found his way into this summer program where children played the World Peace Game every day for one intense week, he made no secret of his love of war—or at least, given that he was only nine, his love of the *idea* of war. But lots of boys that age, and even some girls, think that war, weapons, and fighting are cool, and the Game is designed to

make room for those feelings. Although I have named this venture the World Peace Game, I include armaments and arms dealers as an integral part of the Game. Jared's nation had a nuclear
arsenal, and his closest rival, the oil-rich nation, had a program
for developing nuclear weapons. The other two countries were
free to buy nuclear warheads, or any other kind of conventional
weapons, their budgets would allow. There is no reason for anyone to believe that his or her excitement about fighting will dis-
qualify him or her from a leadership position.

Maybe Jared was shocked by my offer because his bullying
tendencies had already come to his other teachers' attention and
he was used to being steered away from power, not toward it.
That was perhaps why I wanted to give him this opportunity. Yes,
it was a surreal kind of logic, but I thought there was something
in him that could be brought out by the experience — something
that could be good for him and maybe good for us.

Maybe. But when Jared leaped at my offer and then immediately started talking about going to war and blowing things
up, my familiar internal debate began yet again. Had I done the
right thing? *Was* Jared the right guy for the job? Did he need this
chance to grow, or had I been misled by my own idealism, my
own hope, my own willingness to see another side to a situation?
Was my choice going to create new possibilities, new openings
for growth, or was it only going to cause more suffering in the
Game?

I am forced to learn, over and over again, that I can't ever
think of the Game in terms of results. If I take an action hoping
for a particular outcome, I am doomed to second-guess myself
forever, because I can never guarantee the outcome. I have to
learn — apparently each time I play the Game — that my actions
must make sense to me on their own merits and not in terms of
the results. I have to be able to live with my actions however they
come out, since there is no way, really, to know their ultimate

impact. I can never be satisfied with any action unless, by coincidence, it happens to match my intention.

As far as what my specific intentions were with Jared, I honestly can't say. I make these appointments based on a combination of reason and intuition, which means that sometimes I can explain myself and sometimes I can't. Whatever my motives, whatever my hopes, the fact is that I offered Jared the post of prime minister, and he took it. And then the bullying began.

## A Fourth-Grade Quest for World Domination

Jared had a real gift for maximizing his power, and so he began to pursue his quest for world domination. He quickly made deceptive alliances with other nations that allowed him to effectively take over their governance, and as his power expanded, so did his cabinet. Although most prime ministers are content with a secretary of state, a defense minister, and a chief financial officer, they are allowed to expand their governments as needed. Jared quickly staffed his with the defeated leaders of the countries he had conquered, creating a ten-person cabinet that he ruled with an iron fist.

Every time Jared was victorious in battle or negotiations, he burst into an exaggerated celebration. The Game moves pretty quickly once it's under way, and there's never time for much of anything except clear, focused play. But Jared managed—while he conquered here and annexed there—to cheer and self-congratulate and do a little victory dance every time he racked up another win. He didn't cast any negative remarks toward any of the other players—I didn't allow that, and Jared wasn't interested in testing me—but he did puff up his chest, strut about, and celebrate every accomplishment as publicly as possible. Although battles in the World Peace Game are settled by a series of odds-weighted coin tosses, meaning that Jared couldn't justifiably take credit for any victory, he had uncanny luck in winning battles and forcing other countries to accept defeat, and he *did* take credit for those victories, exaggerating his prowess and his ability to win.

Jared had one close friend, kind of a sidekick, a short fellow named Connor. Connor had a sly manner—he reminded me of the stereotypical used-car salesman—and he dressed like a little businessman, with his button-down polo shirts and upscale slacks. He also had a chip on his shoulder—it wasn't a big chip, but it was a chip nonetheless—and like his powerful friend, he seemed to take delight in other people's suffering. He genuinely seemed to enjoy having power over other people and making them pay the price for being weaker than he was. He savored the moments when he could get others to pay homage to the military victories that were, in his mind, clear evidence of his own superior ability, simply because he was associated with Jared. Like Jared, Connor liked to puff up his chest and strut after a victory. He enjoyed his powerful friend's status, and, to my mind, he also egged Jared on.

Jared and Connor were much too sophisticated to break any rules or even to engage in what you would call actual bullying. Watching them day in and day out, I was hard-pressed to find reason to criticize them, let alone censure them or impose any type of punishment for their behavior.

Yet in a sense, these two boys seemed bent on destroying the Game. Certainly, they were destroying the pleasure the other children took in playing the Game, which seemed to have shifted from a complex planetary network of diplomatic and military encounters into the fearsome progression of a steamroller making its inexorable way across the planet. Except for the help of Connor, who was completely under his thumb, Jared was playing the Game more by himself than any child I had ever seen. He didn't need other people to do what he was doing, and he looked to be well on his way to dominating the world and winning the Game all by himself. I had always believed that couldn't be done—but maybe, in this case, it could. And if Jared won, the Game would be completely lost. Yet nothing he did was, strictly speaking, outside the Game's parameters, and I felt completely helpless to stop him.

To some extent, of course, the Game is designed to allow that kind of thing to happen. I want to give my students a chance to make the worst mistakes that world leaders actually make, because I have a secret faith in their collective wisdom and compassion. I believe that if given the chance to collaborate and create solutions, they are not going to do the worst things that people can do. But it seemed, in this case, the worst *was* going to happen.

Then one day, the smallest girl in Jared's cabinet, a shy, almost speechless child named Lily, announced a coup d'état.

## The Coup d'État Collective

Students in the World Peace Game can engage in a wide variety of conflicts. They can mount rebellions, announce breakaway republics, and even seek outside assistance for their revolutionary activities. Jared, however, was such a feared figure in this classroom that no student had dared to organize a resistance movement. Only Lily, it seemed, could stand up to her ruler, and so she announced her coup.

In the Game, all play stops until a coup has been resolved, which occurs through a series of odds-weighted coin tosses. The odds favor the ruler, as they do in real life, but it is certainly possible for a coup to succeed. If it does, the deposed leader has to go into exile. He or she must find another nation willing to offer asylum and risks being condemned to relative inactivity and isolation from the ongoing business of world affairs. Deposed leaders often have the chance to reinvent themselves in a less powerful role, in which they are watched intensely until they prove themselves to be trustworthy. But there is definitely a cost.

If the coup fails, however, it's the unsuccessful rebel who has to go into exile. In practical terms, he or she is likewise doomed to irrelevancy—or at least to reinvention—in the continuing play of the Game.

So Lily's coup was, I thought, an act of great courage. First, she was risking her opportunity to remain relevant in the Game. I have often wondered about the political rebels and freedom fighters who have chosen throughout history to go into exile, as well as the draft resisters who left the United States during my own era. I've pondered their decision to give up the familiarity and comfort of home, the nearness of family, and the certainty of knowing how things are done—even little things, such as paying a bill or finding an apartment or enrolling your children in school. I have imagined what it would be like to give up the opportunity to function in my own language, to abandon the professional or business credentials I have accrued, and to let go of my possessions, status, and citizenship and embark on a new life in a country that may not make me feel welcome and that certainly won't regard me as a fellow citizen, a person who belongs. I have thought about all the sources of nourishment that going into exile might sap—indeed, it was the sense that I had become less a world citizen than a man permanently in exile that finally drew me back home to my own family and community and native ground.

And so when I saw Lily standing up—Lily, the shiest, quietest little girl in my class—I marveled that she was willing to risk such an exile, even in the attenuated, temporary terms of the Game. I knew that if she lost the coup, she would have only one country to flee to—the others having effectively been annexed by Jared—and she would then face the prospect of being conquered by Jared a second time.

In real-life terms, of course, Lily risked nothing. She would still go home that night to her family; she would still remain among familiar people and possessions. But in the imaginative life of the Game, she was risking everything, and I saw, as I watched her pale, narrow face, how frightening she found this whole experience.

Above and beyond the imaginative exile, of course, was the real-life challenge of standing up to Jared. I saw her watching him as the coins were tossed. I saw her almost trembling with fear at the retaliation that he might exact. Would he rally the other students against her? Would her friends in his cabinet view her as a traitor? Would her girlfriends, who maybe still thought Jared was cool or cute, ostracize her to curry favor with him?

There was no doubt that Jared was displeased. He stood, chin lifted, barely deigning to cast his eyes on the weather goddess as she began the toss. Jared had won every coin toss up to now —every battle, every dispute—and I could see that he fully expected to win this one. But like any tyrant, Jared had come to think of himself as not only invincible but also unassailable. Even the idea that someone could challenge his rule disturbed his fantasy of himself as all-powerful and, perhaps, universally loved. I could see him glancing quickly at Connor, worried, maybe, about losing face with his underling, worried that if Connor knew that it was at least theoretically possible to challenge Jared, Connor himself might not remain as admiring or loyal.

And then the coins were tossed . . . and Lily lost. We all watched as she quietly gathered her dossier, her backpack, and her little sweater, preparing to leave Jared's country and find another home. She would have to get permission from Claudia, the prime minister of the last remaining independent country, to settle there, and I could see by Lily's tentative steps away from her chair that she hadn't yet made this arrangement.

But before she could get very far, Marisol stood up. She, too, was in Jared's cabinet, and she was almost as small and as shy as Lily. Her voice trembling, she said, "I am Deputy Minister Marisol Guajardo of the Golden Land, and I would like to declare a coup against Prime Minister Jared Forrest."

Was she simply copying Lily? Marisol had never struck me as a copycat, but then I'd never had two coup attempts one right after the other before. I looked at Marisol standing there, hugging herself, her eyes downcast, and I could not figure out what she was doing.

Unsettled before, Jared now looked positively disconcerted. For one student to rebel against him was bad enough—but two? Again he glanced at Connor, who would not meet his gaze. I wondered whether Connor was indeed deciding that his idol had feet of clay, simply because it now seemed possible to attack him.

Yet if it was possible to attack, it was not yet possible to win. Marisol, too, lost her coup, and she followed Lily around the circle of chairs to Claudia's country. The prime minister, a tall, sturdy girl, quietly granted the girls asylum.

A heavy gloom was settling over the room. Watching Jared rise to power had been bad enough. Watching him defeat two attempted coups made us feel, as perhaps happens in real life, that the tyrant was indeed invincible. Yes, you could attack him, but you could never win.

Then Olivia stood up. Normally cheerful and mischievous, with bright-blond hair and red pixie glasses, Olivia had grown increasingly somber with each passing day of the Game. I had wondered how she was reacting to Jared's growing power—she had been his original chief financial officer—and now I saw that she, too, was ready to lay her political career on the line as she stood ready for the coin toss. Was she simply copying the other two girls? Or was there some other type of strategy going on?

"I am Chief Financial Officer Olivia Strachan from the Golden Land, and I declare a coup against my prime minister, Jared Forrest."

Lily and Marisol watched intently from their side of the room as the fate of Olivia's coup was decided, and I couldn't help wondering just how lucky Jared could be. He had won every battle he had entered, and now he had triumphed against two coups. Was he going to be able to prevail against a third?

He was. But instead of bringing him relief, success seemed to make him even angrier. Gone was the puffed-out chest, the self-satisfied strut, the Cheshire cat smile that had followed every other conquest. Now Jared seemed positively injured, as if he was thinking, *How dare you challenge me? Don't you know who's the big dog around here?* He looked around the room with a put-upon air, and most of the other children looked away. Connor, for his part, had sunk into his seat and twisted around until his back was facing Jared. He looked as though he wanted to slip away from the room entirely.

I was about to declare that Game Day over when Tyler got to his feet. He had been the first player to be added to Jared's swollen cabinet. The minister of defense of his former, defeated country, he had been brought in as deputy minister of defense to assist Connor. Tyler was a small, skinny kid, wiry and alert, but he was quiet and hadn't said much when Jared had brought him on board. Now he stood up and said in his oddly deep voice, "My name is Tyler Johnson, deputy minister of defense of the Golden Land, and I declare a coup against Prime Minister Jared Forrest."

Jared snorted in disgust, but Tyler only stared at the coins. They were thrown, he lost, and he began to cross the room toward where Lily, Marisol, and Olivia were standing.

"I am Deputy Chief Financial Officer Mina Fiske, and I declare a coup against Prime Minister Jared Forrest." Mina had plump red braids and freckles. She was usually giggling at something or other, but she was deadly serious now.

We all stared at the weather goddess as she brought out the coins once again. Jared had survived four coups. Was it possible he could withstand five?

He couldn't. When the weather goddess announced the outcome in a flat, neutral voice, nobody cheered, nobody shouted, nobody even smiled. Everyone simply looked at Jared, who looked shocked, shaken, and close to tears.

"You must leave the Golden Land," the weather goddess intoned, with all the solemnity of a fourth grader. "Prime Minister Jared Forrest, you have been deposed."

## Coming to Terms with Tyranny

I don't know quite when I realized, watching the incredible series of coups, that the entire action had been planned right down to who would stand up when. I don't know how the children in Jared's cabinet came up with the idea, or where they found the privacy to organize it, or how they decided which child would take the risk in which order. I don't even know how many more volunteers they had waiting in the wings, in case Jared's luck held and he survived a few more coup attempts. What I do know is that the series of coups was one of the most remarkable examples of collaboration I had ever seen in my classroom, and I am still in awe every time I think of it.

Clearly, the rebels were not interested in power for themselves. None of the students who stood up to Jared had ever shown much interest in becoming prime minister; none had insisted on getting their way in group discussions. I believe they were motivated, rather, by a very deep-seated feeling that what Jared was doing was not fair, it was not right, and it was not just.

Jared, for his part, was floored. A look of bewilderment came over his face as he was finally forced to step down, and I could see how shocked he was that so many children had wanted him out of power, how confused he was by their passionate efforts to depose him. I don't know which surprised him more: that they had found the power to defeat him, or that they had wanted so badly to have him gone. He knew, as we all did, that the price of a failed coup was exile, so at least five children had been willing to pay an enormous price to get rid of him. He had to be wondering about the effects his bullying had had on the others. He had to be discovering that even a bully can run into a power greater than his own.

Or maybe not. Maybe he blamed what had happened to him on bad luck. Maybe he assumed the other kids were mean-spirited, petty, or simply envious. Maybe he was already plotting his revenge, if not on these children, then on some others, who might not be as successful in their organizing efforts.

Connor was even more shocked than Jared. I think it never occurred to him that anyone could be more powerful than Jared, and certainly not any fourth grader he had encountered in my classroom. The idea that these small, weak, insignificant children had banded together to defeat his leader, I believe, was a totally new idea for him.

The thing about bullies—whether top dog, like Jared, or sidekick, like Connor—is that they are always sure of exactly what they can get away with. Neither Jared nor Connor had broken any rules, challenged my authority, or done anything else to draw down punishments or restrictions they couldn't handle: they knew their limits. And then came that series of coups, which took away their limits and turned the whole world upside down. They felt the weight of the collective rebellion, but they didn't know how to defend against it or what to do about it. The action was all the more difficult to deal with because clearly, no one was angry at either boy personally—they were simply carrying out a duty. So the smaller intentions of Jared and Connor were ultimately subsumed in the larger wave of an intention that was carrying them in a different direction, to the place of unknowing.

In a sense, although only Jared had gone into exile, both boys had lost their usual social identities. Accordingly, they responded first with denial, then with anger and frustration, and finally with a kind of acceptance. What else could they do? Now they were the ones who had to leave their homeland; there was simply nothing else left to them. Stripped of their weapons and tools by the nonviolent but persistent efforts of those around them, they were vulnerable and bare—and for a bully to be vulnerable in front of others is the ultimate transformation.

Jared had only one place left to seek asylum, and it was in the last independent country on the planet—a country that everyone knew he had been planning to attack. In complete humility, he had to ask for acceptance into the country and then hope that Claudia, the country's prime minister, would have mercy on him, despite his previous threats. I wondered what would happen if Claudia said no—I had no plan for such a contingency and would have had to invent one—but luckily for all of us, the prime minister said yes.

The moment when Jared was received, despite all that he had done, was, for me, magic. My students showed that two wrongs do not make a right, and so Jared was taken in. And to continue the irony, he was put in the position of having to work for peace —though no longer in the leadership role he had so enjoyed. With no social avenue for him to bully the other players, he had to "go along to get along" and to find a way to work with those whom he had formerly bullied. It was a humbling process, but I was impressed that none of the children seemed to rub it in. They simply let Jared become part of the process in this new capacity.

With the cessation of hostilities, a peace treaty was immediately established between Jared's old country, now governed by Mina, and Jared's new country. The most touching thing was that Mina asked Jared to be the one to sign the treaty. Jared was never reprimanded—nor was Connor—but he was shown the error of his ways by this extreme gesture he now had to make.

Since this was an afterschool program in another state where I had been brought in as a guest teacher, I couldn't follow up on what Jared might have ultimately learned. But I do know that the rest of us had learned a powerful lesson. The "coup collective" discovered that they had within themselves the courage to take a stand and make a difference. They had learned that what they couldn't even dream of doing as individuals, they could undertake as a community. I like to think that all of the children who stood up to Jared that day were transformed by the experience —that they had seen that what the community could empower them to do would carry them well beyond their individual limits. They had moved, decisively I thought, from the phase of individual action into the phase of collaboration. It seemed to be a powerful shift.

I learned something, too. I learned that if I am frightened into forgetting the wisdom of peace, I will always be wrong. Sooner or later, the tyrant will be deposed, the cruel warrior will be defeated, the unjust leader will be overthrown. Many individuals may have to suffer—perhaps they will even have to die—before justice is done. But the collective wisdom of the group will ultimately create a kind of counterforce that will not rest until the right action is taken—and succeeds. Even fourth graders can see that.

## Forging a Community

Sometimes a peace-loving collaboration forms on a much smaller and more spontaneous scale. I remember in one session of the Game, Prime Minister Brian gave an order to fire on the plane of a neighboring country that had come too close to his border, which Brian thought might thwart his own plans for a surprise attack. Tall and thin, with a head a little too large for his body, Brian was a geeky kid—very intellectual, very suave and polished, but a bit awkward at times, and a little off-center socially. When he told Eamon, his minister of defense, to fire on the plane, we had to throw the coins to see whether the plane was hit.

It was. Now it was up to Rachel, our weather goddess, to determine where the plane came down—in the ocean, where minimal damage would be done, or on land, where the crash might kill more people and destroy vital factories and government buildings.

Rachel was firm but tenderhearted. She was a large, imposing presence, ready to stand up for herself or for anybody else who needed it. She was usually brimming with cheer and good humor, but the thought of the damage the plane might cause made her unusually somber.

"The plane falls in the ocean," she announced sternly. "That is my ruling!" The other students breathed a sigh of relief, and the Game was about to proceed.

But Brian was not yet done.

"We've got to continue the attack!" he said. It was almost as if, having begun an aggressive action, he couldn't imagine changing course. "We have to shoot down more planes! We have to finish what we started."

Eamon was all for it. He had been one of the loudest voices urging Brian to mount the attack, and now he was more than ready to keep it going. But suddenly, spontaneously, a group of students—from Brian's country as well as from other nations and the UN—began to argue with Brian.

"You were lucky this time," Emily said. "But, Brian, you came *so close* to having that plane crash into your own country. Is that what you want? I don't think so!"

"Dude!" said Mason. "Think about it. Quit while you're ahead."

"You can at least *try* negotiating first," Loren pointed out. "If you shoot down any more of their planes, it's gonna start a whole *war*, man. It's gonna cost a fortune, and lots more people will get killed."

I looked at the three children who had gathered with Rachel around Brian. It was almost as if they were trying to create a defensive tag team, eager to prevent any more bloodshed.

"Think about the people in the ocean, all drowning," Emily said quietly. "Maybe you had to shoot *them* down. But you've made your point."

"It's kind of a waste of resources," Loren added.

"Yeah, think of how much it's going to cost if the plane crashes into our own territory and kills a bunch of people and smashes up our factories," Mason continued.

"And then you'll lose people *and* money," Emily said.

"Plus you might start a *war*," Loren repeated. "A whole war, Brian. I don't think that will be good for our country. I think that will be a disaster!"

Their arguments continued, weaving a net of words around Brian but also, I thought, giving him time and space to calm down, to rethink, to change course. Finally, Brian nodded and stepped back. He agreed to a meeting with the prime minister of the country whose plane he'd shot down, with the goal of crafting a treaty to stop the flyovers. War, at least until the next Game Day, had been averted.

Rachel, Emily, Mason, and Loren seemed to breathe a collective sigh of relief, stepping away from their cluster around Brian to become individuals once more. I shared their relief, but I was haunted, too, by a memory I couldn't quite access.

Then I realized what it was: I was torn between sorrow and wonder. I was remembering the Air Florida crash into a bridge over the Potomac River back in 1982. All of us living in Maryland and Virginia had heard about this crash for days, because although the crash itself was a massive tragedy, leaving only a few survivors, it had sparked the formation of an extraordinary spontaneous heroic community—disparate strangers in many locations—who had somehow organized themselves into a single collaborative rescue unit. The incident stuck in my mind as a shining example of what human beings can do in impossible situations.

The crash occurred on a freezing January day after struggling with a failed takeoff from Washington National Airport. There was no tenderhearted weather goddess to control the fate of *that* plane, which crashed into the Fourteenth Street Bridge and Interstate 395, crushing seven occupied vehicles and then plunging into the Potomac River.

Most of the passengers, flight attendants, and motorists on the bridge were killed. But because of a remarkable, spontaneous, collaborative response, a few were saved. Out of the chaos, individuals with little or no experience in coping with emergency situations suddenly found themselves members of a rescue team operating under seemingly hopeless conditions.

For example, flight attendant Kelly Duncan clung to the tail section of the broken airliner in the midst of the icy Potomac. She somehow managed to inflate what was later found to be the only remaining flotation device and passed it to one of the most severely injured passengers. Meanwhile, passenger Joe Stiley tried to swim a fellow passenger to shore.

Duncan and Stiley might be seen as two exceptional individuals who simply rose to the occasion. But the rescue community kept growing larger. Roger Olian, a sheet metal foreman at a local hospital, was making his way across the bridge when the plane struck. Hearing that there was an aircraft in the water, he actually jumped into the ice-choked river, trying to reach any survivors. At the same time, three military staffers from the nearby Pentagon ran to the water's edge to try to help, despite the two-foot-high snowdrifts and freezing temperatures.

Olian was able to get only a few yards into the river, and when he came back onshore, ice was sticking to his body. The men onshore asked him not to try again, but he insisted. Yet another individual joined the group, grabbing some rope and battery cables to make a lifeline for Olian so that he could make another foray into the water. This time, he went a bit farther, but soon the men were pulling him back. Someone else had joined the effort by this time, backing his jeep toward the river so that the team could put Olian inside to warm up.

By this point, a crowd began gathering on the riverbank. The survivors screamed for help, and the crowd shouted back, telling the drowning passengers not to give up hope.

Eventually, a second Park Police helicopter arrived with a rescue crew, who tried to airlift survivors to shore. The crew collaborated with another recently arrived group of fire and rescue personnel, and all of them worked with the Pentagon staffers and civilians, who helped pull the survivors from the shore up to waiting ambulances. As one of the helicopters returned to the river, passenger Arland Williams caught the lifeline—but instead of saving himself, he passed it over to flight attendant Kelly Duncan. The helicopter made another trip out over the wreckage and dropped two lifelines. Williams caught one of them and again passed it on, to injured passenger Joe Stiley, who in turn grabbed passenger Priscilla Tirado. Another passenger, Patricia Felch, took the second line. When Tirado and Felch fell back into the water before they reached the shore, another bystander, Congressional Budget Office assistant Lenny Skutnik, stripped off his coat and boots and dove in to try to help them. Meanwhile, paramedic Gene Windsor dropped from the helicopter into the water, also trying to rescue one of the fallen passengers.

At the end of the day, only four passengers and one flight attendant survived. But even they would have been lost without the extraordinary spontaneous collaboration of the random group of strangers who somehow created a complex system of on-the-spot problem solving. Within that collaboration, ordinary people became heroes, creating makeshift tools and improvising solutions.

In such situations, decisions are made very quickly, and ideas are implemented almost as soon as they are formed. And yet somehow it is a team, a collective, that acts, not simply disparate individuals. "I'll dive in the water—you pull me back"; "I'll throw the lifeline—you grab another passenger." In these urgent conditions, where there is no chance to plan and no time for do-overs, failure is at least as likely as success. But in the press of events, the participants seemingly give no thought to either. They think only of the collective demand that is upon them, the collective drive that must be fulfilled in order to survive the situation.

When the push is for survival, a group may evolve rapidly—but what is striking to me about the Air Florida disaster is that the group continued to evolve. From a single flight attendant passing a flotation device to an injured passenger, the rescue team expanded to include dozens of separate individuals, each collaborating at a progressively higher level. In such cases, we seem to be able to watch both individual and communal potential expand right before our eyes.

Just as the rescuers lost most of the people they tried to save, the little band of students rebelling against Jared lost the first several coups they attempted. As the battle against the tyrant went on, the conditions of the struggle demanded that more and more people become willing to sacrifice—to voluntarily remove themselves from play at the very climax of the Game. How many people are willing to sacrifice for the greater good, and how much are they willing to give up? When times are tough, we think we know the answers to those questions, and pessimism sets in. And then the rescue effort develops or the rebellion begins, and you realize that there is no predicting what human beings are capable of, particularly when they form communities that extend the abilities of every individual who participates. With that type of collaboration, there is no telling what individuals can accomplish as they rise to extraordinary heights of courage, compassion, and power.

# 6

# The Arms Dealers Choose
# Right over Might

The intelligent general contemplates both the advantages
and disadvantages. Contemplating the advantages, he
fulfills his calculations; contemplating the disadvantages,
he removes his difficulties.

— SUN TZU, *The Art of War*

LADIES AND GENTLEMEN, let the World Peace Game session begin! There will probably begin to be some changes
or adjustments in the Game, so be prepared for things to shift
radically today. We know we don't hold on to things, because
things do change, so change is the name of the Game! Be ready
to roll with everything that happens today. Are you ready?
Really? Good luck!"

That's me beginning another day of the World Peace Game,
reminding the students that everything shifts and changes, in
the Game as in life itself. And indeed, there are many different
types of changes that we experience in playing the Game, individually and collectively. There are slow, gradual changes that
seem to occur almost imperceptibly, such as when a group of
strangers meets to play the Game (say, in my summer acad-
emy), and for a few days we all still feel like strangers — and then
one day, everyone realizes that we all know one another's names.

There are the laborious changes that we work hard for—trying to solve a crisis or craft a treaty or start a new industry to raise our country's gross national product—where we measure every day's progress toward our ultimate goal, and then finally we're there. There are the confusing changes, when we feel that we used to understand how to play the Game, but suddenly everything is going backward, and we know less than we did before.

All of these changes have something to teach us, and I want my students to be ready for each of them. But the most thrilling type of change in the World Peace Game—the one I look for every time a new session of the Game begins, the one I count on and am grateful for—is the one I call the *click*—the click that precedes the *flow*.

The click is the moment when we get it, when everything seems to just snap into focus. Sometimes the click takes the form of an individual epiphany: a single student or a couple of students suddenly see themselves, the Game, or the world in a new way. Sometimes—as happened with Pablo in chapter 2— this epiphany puts the individual into the extraordinary blend of joy and peace that psychologist Mihaly Csikszentmihalyi has dubbed "flow": an almost timeless state of creativity in which thought and action seem to meld into one and the individual experiences oneness both with the activity he or she is doing and with life itself.

Sometimes, though, the click is a group transformation: the moment when the class truly begins to act as a unit, as a single entity with a purpose and personality that all of its members have internalized. A group click also can generate flow: the process by which the whole suddenly becomes greater than the sum of its parts. In this case, not just one student but the whole class transforms.

And that's when the World Peace Game really takes off.

## Eurekas and Ahas

The defining characteristic of a click is that it divides our experience into two eras: *before* and *after*. There are many different flavors in which this division might come. It might pertain to problem solving: Before the click, there is no answer—indeed, it seems as though an answer is incapable of being found. After the click, the answer is right there in front of us, and it seems so obvious, we can't believe we never thought of it before. For example, when Brennan saved the world in chapter 3, that was a problem-solving click. Before Brennan came up with his literally last-minute idea, the problem of how to win that semester of the World Peace Game seemed completely insoluble. Suddenly —*click!* Brennan had a new idea, and now the answer seemed obvious.

Or a click might pertain to worldview: Before the click, the world looks one way. After the click, it looks another way. I think my students experienced a click of this sort when they saw Jared defeated in the series of coups d'état in chapter 5. Certainly, there was a click of that sort for Jared, the bully, and for his sidekick, Connor. For as long as they could remember, they had lived in a world where their power was unshakable and Jared was unbeatable. Then suddenly—*click!* A handful of frightened children toppled the tyrant, and the world appeared to be a very different place.

A click might also pertain to identity: Before the click, we experience ourselves one way. After the click, we see ourselves quite differently. Pablo exemplifies that type of click. For most of his life, he might have seen himself as slow, isolated, and ineffective. Then suddenly—*click!* He was a powerful leader who saw and understood everything.

What all clicks have in common is that they are sudden and transformative, and as they are occurring, they feel total. At the moment you feel the click, nothing else matters. The transformation is overwhelming and all-absorbing. It's a quantum leap that catapults you to a different state, a change so profound, you almost can't remember what you thought or saw or felt before.

The moment when a baby takes her first steps has the quality I'm talking about. Of course, from an adult's perspective, the baby's first steps aren't sudden at all, because you've had weeks to observe her slow progression. First she stands holding on to your hands; then she stands clinging to a solid object but dependent on no other human being; and finally she takes a few tentative steps—before, inevitably, falling down! But even though you, the adult, perceive an incremental development, you can see by the startled, delighted look on the baby's face that she experiences her click as abrupt and total. Before the click, she could only crawl. After the click, she can walk! She's a different person, and if you catch that look of wonder on her face, you can see that she somehow grasps the totality of the change.

Riding a bike works the same way. There is that moment when you get it, when you have the power to make the bike carry you without falling over. *Click!* You are different, the world is different, everything is different, to the point where you can barely remember what it was like just a few minutes before, when you couldn't keep your balance and didn't know how to ride.

Sometimes a click involves an intellectual or emotional discovery—that wonderful feeling of *Now I get it!* Learning to read works that way. You don't know how—and then suddenly, looking at the page, you're not seeing letters, you're reading words. Falling in love works that way, too. "*Now* I see what everyone's been talking about," the teenager or young adult might say. "So *this* is what they meant."

Researchers tell us that what I am calling the click has two essential features. First there is the impasse, the sense that we have hit a problem that we cannot solve or a situation that we cannot master. Brennan, the coup d'état collective, and Pablo all had their moments of impasse, when it seemed they had gone as far as they could go.

And then there is the breakthrough, the eureka moment, the revelation that arrives with an overwhelming sense of certainty —leading Archimedes, for example, to jump out of his bath and run stark naked to the king's palace, famously shouting, "*Eureka!*" (I have found it!). Brennan, the rebels, and Pablo all had that experience, too.

Scientists have found that these eureka moments seem to happen in a region of the brain known as the anterior superior temporal gyrus (aSTG), a small fold on the right side of the brain located just above the ear. Apparently, this part of the brain does not engage when people solve problems through analysis and logic, but it is extremely active when people have their aha moments.

I think it's significant that the aSTG is on the right side of the brain, the hemisphere that is associated with meditative and religious states of oneness. I would suggest that part of a click is suddenly feeling, if only for a moment, what Buddhists call satori: the experience of being one with everything. The writer who finds just the right words in a moment of ecstatic insight feels at one with language, as though the words are coming through her. The jazz musician who enters into that zone of inspiration feels as though the music is washing through him, as though his hands and mouth and body are so at one with the music that the music is playing *him*. The scientist who solves a difficult problem sees the entire solution in a flash, as though she has always known it, as though it was an actual part of her brain, and at that ecstatic moment of revelation, she feels at one with the universe, which seems to be sharing its secrets.

Pablo, I believe, was suddenly at one with the Game, which was why he was able to see everything at once and to make the moves that expressed that oneness. One of the characteristics of that "*Now* I get it!" moment is that you feel everything coming together, everything swimming into focus at once.

Brennan experienced that oneness when the answer for how to win the Game suddenly dawned on him. I believe that at the moment of his epiphany, he felt that he saw everything and understood it all. That's what gave him the power to seize my bell and call all the other students to him, inspiring them with the idea that he had just discovered.

The coup d'état collective must have had that shock of oneness at their moment of victory, when they suddenly saw a startling truth that changed their understanding of both the world and themselves. Perhaps at that moment, they felt at one with the world.

When I observe the click, it is always a startling moment: an individual student, often bewildered and confused for some time, suddenly grasps enough of the entire equation of the Game to feel a change within his or her mind, or even within his or her heart—a true "change of heart." The awakening is so sudden and sometimes so wrenching that I often see the dramatic alteration manifest itself physically.

The child's eyes grow wide as her head snaps away from the problem she has been considering on the game board, her mouth open in astonishment. Suddenly, she *sees*, and even I can see the click. Sometimes she rises up out of her chair almost as if she were pushed up by some kind of surge or explosion. Sometimes she breaks out in raucous laughter for no apparent reason. Her arm almost always immediately shoots up, waving to be called on. If she's granted a turn to speak, she jumps up out of her seat, and her words tumble out in a rush.

The excitement is palpable. We all know that something momentous is happening, and we can all feel the force field rippling out from this powerful, sudden storm. For the next moment or so, the child enters the joyous flow state, and I sit in awe as she literally dances in the exposition of her enlightenment.

Sometimes, like Brennan, a student who has had such an experience can bring the rest of us with him. Sometimes, like the jazz musician who is clearly transported before an uncomprehending audience, the click remains a private event. Either way, the student feels, at least for a few moments, at one with himself, the Game, and, perhaps, the entire world.

## *The Arms Dealers' Epiphany*

One of the most powerful clicks I've ever seen occurred with Michael and Jamal, who in a recent session of the Game became arms dealers. Michael was a wide-eyed boy with blond bangs so long and thick you never saw his forehead — his characteristic "helmet" hairstyle. He was spontaneous, impulsive, and unorthodox in his movements. I never expected him to do the same thing that everybody else was doing. He was a fairly quiet child, but he was always moving, and he definitely marched — or dashed or skipped or strutted or sashayed — to the beat of his own drummer.

Jamal was also very active. In fact, we saw Jamal's mother a lot, because Jamal was always involved in some kind of mischief: somehow things just *happened* around Jamal. He was always into something, instigating some exploration or creating some new game, or just doing something physical, and sometimes that got him into hot water. But there was no malice in Jamal, and everybody seemed to recognize that. He had a kind of wide-open expression, and, in fact, his mouth was often literally open in a state of wonder. He wore large, round glasses that he was always taking off and losing. He was a little larger than most of the other children, slightly chubby, and he always wore short pants, even in winter (though granted, winter in Charlottesville is usually not very cold). He loved to grab the armaments out of the box and play with them—rearranging them by color, and then by size, and then by type, and finally by some other system known only to himself. When I picture him, that's how I see him, his hands always busy with those game pieces.

I chose Michael to be our arms dealer because he seemed to have kind of a restless spirit that made him hard to fit into any one country or group. I considered Michael very talented, but I thought his talents lay far outside the box. He was one of the most inventive, creative children I have ever taught, and I thought he would make the most of the arms dealer role. In a way, this can be kind of a limited role, since the arms dealer's only function is to sell weapons. But Michael was just the sort of child not to be limited by that one-note role, and so I asked him if he would like to have the job. He eagerly accepted and promptly declared himself president of Acme Arms Dealers, a company name he came up with himself. Then he chose his best friend, Jamal, to be his chief executive officer.

From the beginning, both of them were thrilled to have charge of the Game's weapons, as many little boys might be. I handed them the small cardboard shoebox crammed with the plastic armaments that were not already distributed on the game board, and they immediately began to root around in the box, sorting and counting and inventorying the fighter planes and submarines and missiles that were not yet assigned to the four nations, the Nin, or the Kajazians. They got to keep the little plastic figures on their desks, ready to sell to anyone who wanted to purchase them.

At first this seemed like an exciting job, since the boys assumed that all the players were going to want weapons. But in this particular session of the Game, for some reason nobody was buying. The wealthier nations seemed to have enough weapons stockpiled, and the poor country didn't have enough money.

Michael and Jamal were fairly enterprising young men, and

so they devised all kinds of discounts and advertising schemes. They had a two-for-one sale on ICBMs—buy one and get one free—and made all sorts of posters and signs advertising their wares. It was really quite impressive. But they didn't get any buyers.

So then Michael said, "I know what we'll do. Only one country in the Game has nuclear weapons. We're going to offer nuclear weapons–grade material. We'll figure out a cost, and we'll start selling a whole weapons program to the other countries so they can catch up."

This idea had actually begun when the minister of defense of the oil-rich nation, a girl named Cynthia, had approached the arms dealers secretly. I was made privy to the conversation, but none of the other children were supposed to know. Cynthia's clandestine visit had been ordered by her prime minister, Nia, who had realized that despite its enormous oil reserves, her country was at somewhat of a disadvantage relative to the richest country in the Game. After all, the richest country had nuclear weapons, and her own country did not. So these secret efforts to procure nuclear weapons began, causing Michael to ask, "Mr. Hunter, can me and Jamal sell dirty bombs?"

That was one of those moments when the responsible adult in me wanted to yell, "Of *course* you can't sell dirty bombs. Don't you think we have enough trouble and misery in this world already? Your job is to make peace, not to equip nations with a new level of destructive weaponry!"

But the teacher in me had already created and assigned the role of arms dealer, and I knew that role was there for a reason. If the children were going to truly explore issues of war and peace, they had to have the chance to try out—at least in theory —everything that adults do to make war, so that they could see for themselves what the consequences of war might be as well as why war is so hard to avoid. So when Michael asked me if he and Jamal could sell dirty bombs, I said cheerfully, "Sure, if you can afford it and think it's a good idea, and if you know what the consequences are and you're prepared to deal with them."

There weren't actually any nuclear weapons in the box of plastic armaments I had given them. So the two boys went to check with the weather goddess about what it would take for them to put part of their budget into creating some of these weapons and whether she thought it was allowable under the rules of the Game. The weather goddess said, "Yes, you can make these weapons, but it will cost you a lot of money to create enough inventory." Then she told them how much she thought it would cost.

Michael and Jamal were very excited about this new business that had seemingly fallen into their laps, and when Cynthia came back to see if they would be willing to sell her nuclear weapons, they were prepared to respond with a resounding *yes!* The sale was just about to go through when Michael suddenly said, "Wait! Uh . . . But, but, but . . ."

I remember him sputtering like that, three *buts,* even though no one had said anything for him to contradict. You could practically see the light bulb flickering over his head, struggling to light up. He wrestled with his own thoughts for a few moments, and then he said, "If you use these dirty bombs, and you destroy most of a country, then that country will come and buy some more nuclear weapons from us, right? And then they will destroy most of *your* country. And then everybody else—I mean, all the other countries—they'll all want to do the same thing. Right? And then if that goes on, we're gonna lose most of our customers!"

He turned to Jamal and said, "I don't think we should sell dirty bombs."

Jamal was still busy with all the little plastic weapons, sorting the submarines from the tanks from the jets. He had been listening, his mouth half-open, but he hadn't quite followed Michael's train of thought.

"Why not?" Jamal said. "Why *shouldn't* we sell dirty bombs?

Mr. Hunter said we could. The weather goddess said we could. So why can't we?"

Michael was still struggling with the weight of his discovery. He took a deep breath and repeated, "They're going to blow everybody up, and then we're not gonna have any customers."

Jamal paused with the weapons in his hands. "So you think we shouldn't sell dirty bombs?"

"No, we shouldn't!" Michael said, shaking his head as if to get these new thoughts out of it. "Because if we do, there's gonna be nobody left to buy any more weapons from us! These dirty bombs are gonna put us right out of business!"

This wasn't exactly the first time an arms manufacturer has had such thoughts. Alfred Nobel, the inventor of dynamite, was so horrified by the uses to which his invention had been put that he established the Nobel Peace Prize. Still, as I witnessed this conversation, I had to laugh. There was something about Michael's logic — if everyone gets blown up, "we're not gonna have any customers!" — that seemed to say it all: nuclear war doesn't benefit even the arms dealers, it seems.

What happened after that, however, caught me by surprise. Horrified by their vision of a world with no customers, Michael and Jamal became the first arms dealers in the history of humanity to vehemently oppose nuclear weapons. They had no problem with war per se — they would have been delighted to do a brisk business in conventional weaponry had they found any takers. But they wanted battles with survivors, not mutually assured destruction. And because they weren't doing enough business in tanks and guns and fighter planes — a problem no arms dealer in the history of the modern world has ever had, as far as I know — they began to diversify.

Although economic experts before them had already explored the notion of investing in multiple sectors so that they are protected against a downturn or crisis in any one industry, Michael and Jamal were actually figuring this out for themselves. Michael, with his wonderful talent for thinking outside the box, started the ball rolling.

"Hey, Jamal," he said soon after they had decided not to sell dirty bombs. "Let's buy some farmland!"

"Okay," Jamal said cheerfully. "But where are we going to put our farms?"

Michael thought for a moment. "We could rent them or buy them from poor people," he said. "Because they need money. So they'll make a deal with us."

The two arms dealers went to the poorest country on the planet—the icebound country with few natural resources, called Snowlandia in this session of the Game, and they offered to invest in that nation's agriculture. They worked out a deal in which Snowlandia sold them some of its farmland, and they invested their capital in developing the farms and then returned a percentage of their profits to Snowlandia.

Now the boys were dealing in both arms and farms. But for some reason, weapon sales remained slow. I don't know why that was happening in this particular game, because often the arms dealers do a brisk business from the first day of the Game right up until the end, but that wasn't happening this time. So Michael and Jamal had to keep looking for other ways to invest their time, money, and energy.

The next idea was Jamal's. He suggested that they continue to work with the poor nation, which couldn't afford to buy much oil, and invest in a wind farm. The deal was struck. The boys were making money, and Snowlandia's economy took another turn for the better, since they were no longer spending as much precious currency on oil.

Next the boys started a solar panel factory in the oil-rich desert nation, so that this country could sell solar panels to the countries that couldn't afford to buy oil. As they invested in alternative energy sources, they fought hard to decommission nuclear power plants (for fear that the plants would be the targets of terrorist attacks) and to limit the use of nuclear weapons (because of the danger to their customers). From being strictly arms dealers, Michael and Jamal went on to found their own thriving energy company, which had customers all over our world. Their personal click had led to a transformation of the entire landscape of the Game. And as they created new possibilities for themselves, they helped shift the dynamic for the entire class—economically, environmentally, and politically. As they saw things differently, they helped the rest of us see things differently, too.

## Moving into the Flow

Michael had experienced an individual click, which he shared with Jamal. But sometimes there is a group click, a moment when, simultaneously, the entire class seems to "get it." Like the individual click, this group click is a movement toward oneness, but even more dramatically so—a oneness among the group that becomes almost physically palpable.

This group click is often evidenced by an abrupt stoppage of . . . *everything.* There is a kind of suspension as the room freezes, with everyone seemingly in a state of shock. That moment seems to last forever, but only a few seconds pass. I can feel it and see it, and so can everyone else. This is the moment when everyone gets the full equation of the Game all at once. The whole room shifts from dullness, low-grade despair, and hopelessness into an eerie quiet that holds us all in place.

Then, like a glacier calving, an almost audible *click!* sounds, and the entire room explodes. Everyone suddenly comes alive —moving into high gear, seeing everything, understanding everything, seeming to apprehend all the solutions and resolutions we have been searching for. There they are, bright and shining and almost literally visible.

Suddenly, all the children are moving as one. They are all on their feet, or talking loudly, frantically all at once. Dossiers are being waved about, documents spilling out like a blizzard, as the room seems to blur with their hyper-celebratory motion. They race back and forth to rushed conferences. They know what to do, and they move to do it, *now!*

At this point, the click has led us into a whole other state: the oneness that Mihaly Csikszentmihalyi describes as "flow" in his remarkable book by this title. In the flow, the children are no longer playing against one another, team against team, as the original constellation of crises had tricked and trapped them into doing. Now everyone is playing as one—playing against the Game itself.

In the flow, everyone speaks faster and louder. They finish one another's thoughts and happily shout, "I *know!*" even before the other child has a chance to finish his or her sentence. Then they both giggle. It's a marvelous, miraculous experience. Instead of a roomful of soloists, we have suddenly become an orchestra, all flowing together in symphonic unity.

When I finally call them to order, ringing and ringing that little bell until they finally dash reluctantly to their seats, they are still bubbling with joy, still tingling from the flow. The entire cabinet of whichever team is ready to take its turn all bolt up and dash toward the game board. Sometimes they all speak at once, the noise augmented by a cacophony of shouts—against all the rules of order, yes, but the rules have been cast aside at this juncture. Together, they ultimately make sense and make themselves heard in relating the obvious array of solutions. The Game is handily won.

Sometimes, however, I am amused to see them holding back on sharing one last solution—obvious to all—just to keep from finishing the Game. They smile knowingly and announce that there are other crises they need to solve. Or a leader will suddenly declare that he or she wants to initiate an attack—unprovoked—on an ally. Why? What are my students doing? They are toying with me! They clearly recognize that they have mastered the World Peace Game. Reluctant to let go of that feeling of supreme ease and skill, they simply want to prolong the Game, to make up new crises just for fun, just for the pleasure of solving them.

## *Savoring the Flow*

The remarkable thing about the flow is how frequently it grows out of despair. The players in the World Peace Game often stumble dispiritedly through a landscape of intertwining difficulties, stubborn adversaries, and mutating crises, becoming progressively more certain that they will be unable to solve the problems that they face. Then there is the click of great clarity, in which they are somehow able to grasp not only the entirety of their dilemma *and* a way out but also their connectedness to one another. *Click!* There's a sudden spike in energy, focus, and awareness. But there is also the opening to joy . . . and the beginning of *flow*.

Coming into the flow during the World Peace Game might look something like this. Jacki, prime minister of the richest and most powerful country, suddenly announces a troop withdrawal from two fronts against two different countries, even as her chief financial officer offers $50 million to help a refugee population return to its homeland, all for no apparent reason. A stunned hush falls over the room. The tensions engendered by Jacki's military adventures have been building for several Game Days, and her abrupt withdrawal is unexpected to the point of being counterintuitive.

After a moment, Ben, the fiery minister of defense for the oil-rich nation, glances wide-eyed at Rosalind, the UN secretary-general. The cabinet members of the Game's other countries begin to look at one another as well, quickly, almost covertly. Even the arms dealers sense a change in the air.

Gradually, the room begins to move, to come alive, slowly at first, then accelerating in speed and intensity. Laid-back young-sters who were simply taking it all in suddenly snap upright in their chairs, fully alert. I see what I can only describe as a jewel-like shimmering of movement as other students, whipping side to side in their seats, plunge into intense whispered conversa-tions. The energy is rising, swelling, until I call the group back to attend the next set of declarations.

But Jacki's declaration was the click they had been waiting for, albeit without realizing it. Now they know that they are somehow set free into this new state of oneness, where suddenly, instead of playing against one another, they are all playing against the Game. When I raise the little silver bell and ring in the next nego-tiation period, there is a mad, careening rush, as all the students jump up from their seats and dash into the now apparent flow.

Up until now, the Game has been slow, calculated, even plod-ding, full of blind-alley turns and hit-or-miss unskillful actions. But now, suddenly, everything is smooth and spontaneous. The students are diving in without a plan and yet with supreme as-surance, understanding full well the entire equation of the Game and needing only to execute the fully fledged plans that seem to be in everyone's mind simultaneously. There is no procedural protocol now, no ordered steps to the ultimate solution. Instead, the solution seems to have appeared all at once, and everyone seems to grasp it. There is an urgency, a dynamic tension, that renders time irrelevant. Instead of structuring the action, rules and protocol have become the children's playthings. They sud-denly *see*, as Pablo did, and they are moving like some kind of martial arts masters, in their confident, flowing moves on the game board.

The tide of energy surges around me at waist level as I stand observing the room. No child is disengaged, not one is distracted or distracting. They are all at full power: thinking, expressing, and doing simultaneously. I feel their thrill at finding themselves in the flow. In his book *Flow*, Csikszentmihalyi speaks of the effortless flow of psychic energy, in which the positive feedback of actions and intent serves to reaffirm instantly that they are "doing all right." His description of this moment applies to my classroom: "We are in control of our psychic energy and everything we do adds order to our consciousness."

Indeed, I can now see the children acting as conceptual architects working at hyperspeed, almost beyond words, as ideas, solutions, and resolutions come coherently together. As Csikszentmihalyi describes it, "Thoughts, intentions, feelings, and all senses are focused on the same goal. Experience is in harmony . . . A bond like that with other people is in itself an ecstasy." Yes! The children now seem to realize that there has been a shift from their original roles as adversaries and opponents, a thrilling shift to the awareness that they are all on the same team. They are now playing together against, or perhaps even *with,* the Game. They have won the battle against the Game, but more wonderfully, perhaps more importantly, they have won the battle against themselves, against the negative, wrong-headed, selfish, or even brutish tactics that we often find ourselves succumbing to under the pressures of daily life. Their unique, differentiated selves — nations, ethnic groups, interest groups, religions — are all now moving toward integration, or, in Csikszentmihalyi's words, "a union with other people, ideas, and entities beyond the self." Certainly, they maintain their separate identities, but now they are in one team, one nation, one world, and they are bound to save it!

This is enjoyable learning at its best. There is no question of not meeting the goals of the "assignment." The one-size-fits-all model of education is out the window, for the ultimate solution that my students create each time has never been seen before in exactly this way. And when we are done, I am happy to inform each class, with heartfelt congratulations, "Girls and boys, you are true innovators, for the world has never been saved this way before. I hope you may use the thinking and feeling tools you have developed in the Game to help yourselves and to help the world someday. Thank you all."

## Sharing the Click; Releasing the Flow

In my classroom, I have often seen this remarkable experience of the group click catapulting everyone into the flow. I've seen it elsewhere, too. In church, sometimes, there is a moment when the congregation clicks, calling back to the minister as he preaches his sermon or singing with the choir. There is that same eerie suspended moment . . . and then the service *takes off*. At a jazz concert, too, you can feel that moment, like the apparent pause of an airplane on the runway as it seems to gather itself before lifting into flight—that moment when the music some-how *lifts off*, and the musicians and the music and the audience all become one. At a ball game or tennis match, you can feel it as well, the times when fans and players and the ball and the field are all somehow united, when the game is playing all of us, and the thrill is ours to share. These are spontaneous group experiences: first the click, then the flow.

Sometimes, in my classroom, a single student will inspire a click for the entire group. This was the case with Neela, daughter of the Tibetan lama who had come to study at our local university. Neela had been chosen to be secretary of state of the ecologically minded nation, the country mandated to promote peace and environmental protection for the entire planet. Despite this initial condition, however, the Game takes on a life of its own, and sometimes even that country does not remain as committed to peace or to ecology as it is initially charged to be. Depending on the dynamics of the Game as a whole, even the "pro-peace" country can get swept up into arms buildups or warlike responses to the mercenaries or any number of military maneuvers that seem warranted at the time.

Neela, however, had very high standards for herself and everyone else, standards that came not from a place of judgment or self-righteousness, but from her almost overwhelming passion for peace, justice, and harmony. At one point, exasperated with the amount of warfare going on in what she had expected to be a game about peace, Neela spontaneously stood up during her country's turn and began haranguing the entire class. Her stance was arrow straight, her feet were firmly planted, and she was charged with crackling energy.

"You people have got to be more compassionate!" she scolded. "You've got to show more compassion for everyone! There are people suffering on this planet, and you are not showing enough compassion! This is not right! This is not the way of peace! We need more compassion, every single one of us! We must start showing compassion!"

In the Game, students learn very quickly that when it is their country's turn, they must allow their prime minister to speak for them all. Neela's outburst was all the more striking because she was normally so committed to following the rules. Something in her frustrated words electrified the group, as if she were a lightning rod through which the crackling energy was channeled, and her impassioned words and her slapping palms were actually transmitting that energy to the rest of us. You could see the upsurge of intensity after she finished speaking, the sudden click as the Game kicked into high gear.

I don't think that Neela planned to have that effect—I don't think she even planned to stand up and speak. Sometimes in a group, one person is given the opportunity (or the burden) of calling the rest to a higher standard. Something in Neela's intensity communicated her energy to the entire class, and we rode that energy until the Game was won.

Another shared click was inspired by Ryan, who had twice been awarded the World Peace Game Peace Prize—once when he played in class and again in a summer program. Wherever he was, whatever he was doing, Ryan seemed to have the gift of keeping the entire planet and all its citizens in mind. I don't know how he did it, but when you looked at him, you could just see the largeness of spirit that kept him mindful of many dimensions at once and that enabled him to bring a broad, compassionate vision to bear on every layer of the Game. He had a clear goal—he was going to help the world overcome poverty and warfare and oppression—and that goal informed every word, every action, even every thought, it sometimes seemed.

One Game Day, Ryan had the opportunity to stand and speak as an officer of the United Nations, and he said simply, "We have to think about how to help *everybody,* not just some people!" He went on to list all the people who at that point in the Game were underrepresented, underserved, downtrodden, disempowered, disfranchised, or oppressed. He spoke about the Nin, whose sacred shrine was not being respected, and about the Kajazians, whose plea for an autonomous homeland was falling on deaf ears. He talked about the Krell, a newly recognized people who had no assets and virtually no political clout of any kind, and about our world's poorest country, which controlled so few resources and faced so many challenges. He named the outstanding crises to be solved, one after another, always speaking in terms of how these crises affected the people with the least political power, the least access to world attention, the least ability to make their needs known and respected. Ryan was determined that these people should not be left out of our global deliberations, and his plea that we remember them was essentially the click that put everybody on the same team, that kicked our intensity and focus and shared commitment into high gear.

But perhaps the most inspiring of all the shared clicks that I have ever witnessed—and certainly the most dramatic—involved a little boy named Gunther. Although Gunther's people in the Game were poor and homeless, and although Gunther himself faced many personal challenges, he was the key to the shared click that ultimately enabled the Game to be won.

## Gunther Solves Global Warming

Gunther was one of those children who looked like a little old man. He always wore baggy pants that hung down over his shoes and long baggy sleeves that kept sliding down over his hands, and his walk was like a shuffle. He was a bright, creative child, but you had to look closely to discern the intelligence and inno- vative thinking. Otherwise, you'd just see an odd little fellow who was easy to disregard.

The semester that Gunther was playing, I had recently added another element to the Game: a stateless refugee people called the Krell, who had just been recognized by the United Nations. These were truly the most down-and-out people on our planet, and they started the Game with basically no resources. I had made Gunther the leader of the Krell, so his challenge was to work out whatever deals he could with the UN, the World Bank, or perhaps a generous nation that was willing to donate, invest, or otherwise assist his struggling people.

As Gunther was trying to find funds for the Krell, the rest of our planet was trying to solve global warming. This is always the most challenging crisis in the Game—for the students as for the real world—and I had created a scenario in which the poorest country, called Cold Country in that session of the Game, had developed a special hydrogen fuel-cell technology that it was able to sell to the other three nations. In theory, this technology of- fered a solution to the problems of global warming and providing ecologically sound energy. The catch was that every nation had to build a certain number of these expensive factories and com- mit to using them. Oil consumption also had to be decreased across the board; otherwise, the solution wouldn't work. I am proud that my students have managed to solve the problem of global warming several times, but it does require an enormous financial commitment from each country, as well as a highly co- ordinated international effort. Invariably, of all the crises that must be solved before the Game can be won, global warming is the very last problem they solve, and often it has looked as though this will be the first time it won't get solved.

Poor as his people were, Gunther wanted to help solve global warming, too. But since the Krell were already not using any oil —they had no industry, and they couldn't afford oil anyway—it didn't seem likely that he could do much. Nevertheless, Gunther was deeply committed to making some kind of contribution, and putting an end to global warming was the contribution he wanted to make.

"I want to solve global warming," Gunther frequently insisted in his deep, gruff, old man's voice.

"You can't do it all by yourself!" one of the other children would reply. No one was rude enough to say what everyone was thinking, which was, "Gunther, you and your people have absolutely nothing! You not only can't solve global warming by yourself—you can't even help *us* solve it!"

But Gunther was adamant. "There must be something I can do," he said. He stubbornly insisted on having his say, even though he was having trouble getting the words out.

"*Well!*" he said. "We're gonna . . . we're gonna . . . we don't have *any* money. But if somebody *gave* us some money . . . if somebody *gave* it to us . . . We're gonna *solve global warming!*"

Nobody really understood what Gunther had in mind, and with all the other pressing global crises, it was easy to write him off. But when he got a little money—a grant from the UN, I think—he said, "Now we can help make it easy to solve global warming. We're going to give our money to Cold Country."

"Gunther," said one of the students patiently, "how will that help?"

"*Because,*" Gunther replied with exaggerated patience, "that means they can sell their technology for cheaper."

Nobody was catching on.

"And that means more people can buy it," Gunther continued. "And that means we can solve the problem!"

"Wait a minute," said the prime minister of the oil-rich desert nation. "Is that possible? Can he *do* that?"

"Oh, yes, he can," said the weather goddess, a tall, quiet girl named Keisha. "In fact, he has already checked with me, and I have ruled that if Gunther gives all of his people's money to Cold Country, they can lower their prices by ten percent."

It took a few minutes for the full scope of Gunther's idea to sink in. When it did, there was a lot of debate about how the process would work. How would the change in price affect the other nations' ability to buy the hydrogen fuel cells? What agreements needed to be in place to make the deal happen? How could they do it so that everyone agreed to participate and to start using the fuel cells at the same time?

Gradually, as the students began to understand Gunther's idea, their excitement and anticipation increased. And then . . . *click!* Suddenly, everybody got it, and the energy in the room just took off. Deals were struck, bargains were made, treaties were drawn up, agreements were signed—we were all in the flow, and all of a sudden, global warming had been solved—three-quarters of the way through the Game!

"Ladies and gentlemen," I said, "I must tell you. No one in the history of the Game has ever done this before."

The students burst into cheers. Everyone was hugging everyone else, and jumping up and down, and clapping, and stomping their feet, and yelling, "We did it!" And in the center of it all was Gunther, in his old-man pants and sweater, his arms thrown out to the sides, his head thrown back, as he spun around and around with an enormous grin on his face. I thought of a whirling dervish, or a dancing Hasid, or maybe even a Bacchic figure, overflowing with so much joy that he couldn't stand still. The poorest of the poor had, against all odds, enabled the world to save itself.

## What Enables the Click and the Flow

The click is impossible to predict or control, as is the flow that emerges from it. But it is possible to identify the conditions that inspire these precious states.

Scientific research reveals the circumstances that enable the click. Apparently, this type of creativity is generated by the brain's production of alpha waves, which are the type of brain activity that occurs in a person's most relaxed state. In one experiment, a master meditator was able to put his brain into an alpha state and go on to solve one creative problem after another. So according to the research, walking away from a problem rather than bearing down on it is often most productive for coming up with genuinely creative solutions.

I loved finding out about that, because it seemed to offer scientific support for the notion of the empty space. Making room around a problem and simply observing, or engaging in play rather than in focused, intense work, often allows a click to occur.

The other stimulus for a click, the research tells us, is reaching an impasse or breakdown. The frustrating impossibility of being able to find a solution pushes us to the point where we are ready to create a new approach.

I have observed this many times in my classroom, including with Pablo, Brennan, and the coup d'état collective. The shadow of confusion, overload, and failure somehow served to bring out new potential, new solutions, and new courage. Likewise, the prospect of nuclear devastation, which would leave them without customers, was what inspired Michael and Jamal to envision a whole other approach to arms dealing. And the frustration of apparent failure moved Neela and Ryan to speak passionately to the class, inspiring us in turn to experience the group click. Before the spontaneous group clicks that grow entirely from the "group mind," I often observe a kind of despair or low-grade misery, as though the class has to hit bottom before somehow freezing into that supercharged moment that then explodes into the flow. Experiences like these—on both the individual and group levels—are why I remain so committed to allowing my students to be confused, overwhelmed, and frustrated—and even, at times, to fail. As uncomfortable or painful as these experiences may be, they are often the necessary precursors of a breakthrough.

## What Clicks Can Teach Us

As we've seen throughout this book, each stage of the Game offers lessons that can be applied far beyond the classroom. We've seen the value of appreciating the empty space—the need to *wait and see* when feeling overwhelmed and the importance of not taking at face value even the most painful defeat or failure. We understand the need for individuals to wrestle with their own growth and the importance of learning how to collaborate. But what can we learn from the click and the flow, processes that seem completely beyond our control or even our cognition?

One lesson, I think, is to remember that such precious moments do indeed occur, and so whenever we are working with groups—whether an organization we meet with face-to-face or a larger community of which we are a part—we can know that both the click and the flow are possible. Often, as we have just seen, clicks are born of apparent failures, and frequently it is when things look the darkest that an individual is inspired to suggest a new possibility or that the group itself is somehow energized to move into a higher gear. Knowing that such transformations happen—seemingly in an instant—can give us the stamina we need to make it through the times when it seems that nothing at all is happening, even though a great deal may be happening beneath the surface.

It's also important to recognize that some problems are not so much solved as they are transcended. Before the click and the flow it sparks, we typically have a much narrower idea of what a solution might look like than we do afterward, when we are suddenly able to view the problem in a whole new way. Thanks to the click and the flow, some solutions that weren't even visible before come into view. Gunther's desire to give money to Cold Country so that it could develop cheap alternative energy, as well as Michael and Jamal's decision not to sell nuclear weapons, were effective because they revealed possibilities that had previously been unthinkable. Ryan's and Neela's speeches were powerful because they opened up new territory—in the mind or the heart or the imagination: a new vision of compassion on a global scale that somehow couldn't be seen until they saw it. Once that door to possibility has been opened—by any individual or by the dynamics of the Game itself—we feel the click and step through to a new perspective on how we analyze a problem and envision its solution.

Maybe what happens during the click is that we move from simply trying to apprehend reality to understanding, on an almost physical level, our own interrelationship with reality and our own potential effectiveness within any situation. *You matter,* says the click. *You can do something. Especially within the collective, you are powerful.* Everyone who has that experience feels his or her own possibility amplified as a result. It's why demonstrations are so powerful, or yoga classes, or group meditation. It's what draws people to church services, or ball games, or concerts. Shared experiences, especially when they involve effort or commitment or an opening up of our hearts and minds, take us to another level of possibility, where we are conscious in a whole new way of what we might be capable of, and where we feel, with our collaborators and companions, what we all might accomplish together.

Perhaps another way of looking at these states is that they are the process through which the progression from individual to collective finally becomes conscious. If we were to ask the heroic rescue workers I described in chapter 5 why they behaved as they did, many of them might say, "I just did what I felt I had to do" or "I just did what seemed right." But if you asked my students after the flow why they are acting as they are, they might say, "Because that's what the world needs" or "We all had to work together" or "It was how to make peace for all of us." Their consciousness of community — their sense of being responsible to it and guided by it — is also a consciousness of power.

Finally, I think the value of these states is to remind us that things are never going to remain exactly as they are now. Everything is always in the process of becoming something else, whether abruptly, via a click, or more gradually, by some other means. Therefore, selecting a perspective and then locking yourself into it is very hazardous. This may be true of all the states in the Game: none of them lasts; all of them change. But it is especially useful to look at the seemingly instantaneous "out of nowhere" changes produced by the click and the extraordinary quantum leap represented by the flow to really drive home the point to ourselves that we can and should expect remarkable success even when things look the bleakest.

# 7

# Gary and the Ecological Disaster

Generally in warfare, keeping a nation intact is best,
destroying a nation second best; keeping an army intact is
best, destroying an army second best; keeping a battalion
intact is best, destroying a battalion second best; keeping
a company intact is best, destroying a company second
best; keeping a squad intact is best, destroying a squad
second best. Therefore, to gain a hundred victories in a
hundred battles is not the highest excellence; to subjugate
the enemy's army without doing battle is the highest of
excellence.

— SUN TZU, *The Art of War*

THE WORLD PEACE GAME operates as a kind of crucible,
in which we have the chance to explore the relationships
between individuals and groups in new ways. As we have seen,
the Game allows individuals to discover new capabilities within
themselves, as their interactions with the group open up new
possibilities for strength, leadership, and courage. The Game also
allows individuals to be tempted by their dark side—their arrogance, self-absorption, and attraction to power. Perhaps most
important, the Game enables all of us to learn what a group is
capable of when it operates as a unit.

For many of us, the notions of group mind, group heart, and
group identity are often difficult to grasp. We are used to thinking

of life in very individualistic terms, and our main thinking about groups is often about the effect they have on us personally, as individuals.

But when you grow up in a close-knit community, as I did, or when you participate in a powerful group process, such as the World Peace Game, you learn to appreciate the power of groups that take on a life of their own. Just as much as an individual, a group can be wise or foolish, accurate or mistaken, compassionate or heartless. Sometimes a group is the only entity that can correct a misguided leader; sometimes a group requires a wise leader to set it straight.

In this chapter, I give one example of each: Gary, the misguided leader who needed the full wisdom of the group to set him straight; and Amy, the shy little girl who grew into her leadership and helped educate the group. Their stories will bring me to a discussion of the different types of victory I have known in the World Peace Game and the lessons each might hold for us.

## Fourth-Grade Hubris

Gary was a redhead with a crewcut that took an almost aggressive twist toward the front of his scalp. He was a sturdy boy, though not particularly large or tall or strong, and he had a very clear sense of his own abilities. He was smart and capable, and he knew it, and he had the kind of charisma that enabled him to dominate just about any social situation.

Gary loved being at the center of things, and because he had so much confidence in himself, he thought he could pretty much act independently, without regard for the cooperation — or the wishes — of others. He didn't behave badly — in fact, his behavior was very controlled. Although sometimes he could become mildly frenetic, maybe even a little wild, he always seemed to know exactly what he was doing, and he took a lot of pleasure in his ability to control his own environment and to manage the reactions of the people around him. I guess you could say that Gary was the master of his own universe.

Gary was minister of defense to his best friend, Todd, to whom I had offered the post of prime minister. Todd was probably surprised by the opportunity, because he was a somewhat passive kid who often deliberately withdrew from situations. He had sandy hair; a sallow, almost wan, complexion; and a very large, round forehead covered by bangs so long and thick that it sometimes looked as though he was trying to hide behind them. His posture added to the impression: he was always reclining in his seat or backing away from a group, and if you came right out and asked him to answer a question or offer an opinion, he seemed to shrink back into himself even more.

After the first few Game Days, I was forced to admit to myself that my hopes for Todd had not exactly come to fruition, as he had proved to be a very weak prime minister who took any opportunity he could to avoid making a decision. Looking back, I think his greatest fear was failing publicly, a fear so powerful that it prevented him from taking any risk or responsibility as long as there was an alternative.

And there was an alternative—Gary. When I invited Todd to become prime minister, he looked down sheepishly, and for a moment I thought he was going to say no. Then he looked over at Gary, who was smiling. I believe Gary wanted the role of prime minister for himself—particularly since the position in question was leader of the Game's richest, most powerful country—but knowing that Todd would have the post was good enough for Gary. So from the first, there was a kind of tacit collusion that led Todd to say, in a small, uncertain voice, "Mr. Hunter, I accept."

As soon as he could, Todd invited Gary to be his minister of defense. Gary immediately began counseling his friend, speaking in short, excited bursts. One of his first suggestions was, "Let's get Aton for secretary of state!" Aton was a very capable, balanced kid with large eyes and dark skin, and as soon as he was offered the post, you could see him assume the gravity and weight of the position. His shoulders actually twitched, as though he were taking on a literal burden. A sincere, devoted, and diligent student, Aton extended his hand to Todd, confirming his acceptance of this new responsibility. But no sooner had Todd responded with a shy, surprised handshake than Gary took over.

"Now, Aton, here is what we're going to do," he began, and then he launched into a series of extravagant plans for acquiring weapons, expanding their country's military presence around the globe, and forcing their most powerful neighbors into alliances.

Aton just stood there, looking stunned. It was almost as if this unofficial shift in power—the now obvious fact that Gary, not Todd, was running the show—had disoriented Aton, leaving him too discombobulated to protest. Aton took responsibility and hierarchy very seriously. He was the oldest boy in a large, somewhat traditional Nigerian family, and he had often spoken about the duties of the eldest brother. So when Gary usurped the prime minister's leadership role, Aton was uncertain how to respond. As the flood of words from Gary continued, Aton looked increasingly worried and confused.

While Gary was instructing Aton, Todd had gone ahead—perhaps at Gary's direction—and asked a boy named Nash to be chief financial officer. Nash was one of Gary and Todd's circle of friends. An earnest boy with a sweet, worried smile, Nash quickly settled into his role of number cruncher and record keeper. He was good with figures and calculations of all kinds, and he appeared happy to keep the books, leaving the political power brokering to the others.

When I saw the situation in this wealthy, powerful country —which the boys had named Greenstone, for its dark-green color on the game board—my heart sank. Gary had, in effect, established a puppet government, using Todd as his figurehead. Todd seemed comfortable enough with the arrangement, but he never expressed any happiness with his role. Every time one of the other prime ministers referred to Todd as a fellow leader, you could see his discomfort with the designation. When negotiations took place—those fast-moving periods between declarations when students dashed all over the room to create alliances, firm up treaties, and otherwise devise solutions to crises—Todd was often approached with questions, offers, or invitations. Whenever possible, he would literally back away, referring the question to Aton or Gary.

Gary simply took it for granted that he could step into any conversation that concerned his country, and he had several projects of his own as well. His primary delight was a series of negotiations with the arms dealers as he swiftly expanded his country's weapons program. So Greenstone was fast creating an enormous storehouse of armaments, a huge military budget, and a severely unbalanced power structure. Nash was content to do the books, Aton seemed to have been disarmed by Gary's boldness, and Todd had basically opted out. This left a power vacuum that Gary was delighted to fill, and I couldn't help dreading what might happen when he finally stopped accumulating power and began to actually wield it.

## Enter the Saboteur

I didn't have long to wait. As so often happens, the catalyst for action was the saboteur, who staged a deliberately provocative attack on Gary's territory with a small but effective band of mercenaries.

As I moved the little plastic soldiers across the board ("I have been instructed by an unknown third party . . ."), I made sure not to look at the saboteur, who in this session of the Game was Kai, a handsome little fellow with smooth, dark skin and bright, alert eyes. Kai was sharp intellectually, poised, and eloquent; he spoke his mind calmly and convincingly. He was the last person you'd suspect as the saboteur: he was always so clear and so definite, it was impossible to believe that he had anything to hide.

Kai had determined early on that Gary would be an easy target for his machinations. Arrogance is often a tempting target for those who work covertly, because the arrogant and the powerful find it so difficult to believe that anyone might ever use their self-confidence against them. In fact, when Kai first approached Gary, trying to convince him that Greenstone was vulnerable to attack (so that Gary would spend more of his nation's resources on their defense budget), Gary was skeptical.

"We're too big for that," Gary said scornfully. "Nobody would *dare* attack us! Especially not a little group of soldiers that don't even have their own country."

Kai kept after him, though, and eventually Gary realized that this piece of information, whether true or not, was to his advantage, as it provided a further rationale for his ever-increasing arms budget. Even while the mercenaries made their way from one nation to the next, Gary professed his fear that they would attack Greenstone, using that as his pretext to ask Nash for more and more money to buy weapons.

Finally, the mercenaries did attack Greenstone, setting up an outpost right on the border of the country's oil fields. By this point, nobody was even expecting Todd to act. We were all just waiting to see what Gary was going to do.

I couldn't interfere, but I could try to give some guidance. "The adults in the world also have the problem of small armies that move around like this one," I told the class as I moved the little plastic soldiers into place. "These small armies can attack here, can attack there, and we might not have any idea who they are—we might not even know why they're doing this. How can we deal with this problem? The adults have not figured it out. Can you do it today? Is combat the best way to stop the mercenaries? Is it the only way? Think about it. See what you can do."

Indeed, the mercenary attacks are always challenging for children in the World Peace Game, in ways that are intentionally similar to the actual difficulties that adults face in the real world. How do you negotiate with an anonymous group that isn't officially associated with any national government and that doesn't have a recognizable leader? How do you create peaceful solutions with people who apparently aren't interested in peace? How do you work things out with people of violence who don't even have any demands for you to meet?

In this case, the normal anguish of being attacked by an anonymous enemy was magnified for Todd by his deep unease at being the center of attention. True, Gary was willing to step into the spotlight, but Todd still had to endure the reflected glare.

Finally, it was Todd's turn to stand up and make his declarations. He was so reticent about speaking, he was stammering.

"I . . . I . . . I . . . I am going to ask . . . my minister of defense . . . to deal with this matter," he managed to say, and then, relieved, he sank back into his seat.

Gary leaped to his feet. He seized the silver telescopic wand that leaders use to move the game pieces across the board and waved it dramatically as he paced back and forth, like a general addressing his troops. When he spoke, his voice was firm and clear and proud.

"I am going to launch my ICBMs at those mercenaries who would intrude in my land, because I have to protect my territorial rights!" he declared. "I want to teach those guys a lesson, and I don't want them ever coming back into my country again!"

We all noticed his use of the first-person pronoun. It becomes natural, very early in the Game, for most of the children to speak in terms of *our* territory, *our* nation, *our* land. But for Gary, it was all *me, my,* and *I*.

His teammates sat behind him, shocked into silence. Nash looked down at his bright-yellow folder and the papers covered with penciled lists and calculations. With a furrowed brow, he carefully erased one set of numbers and began writing another. Aton looked both awestruck and despairing. I wondered whether he had gotten to the point of trying to put a halt to Gary's aggression, or whether he had even seen this coming. Todd was clearly not interested in challenging Gary's decision. Would anybody else challenge it?

I looked around at the class. Anytime there is any type of battle in the Game, everyone drops deeply into a disturbed and questioning mode. We all wonder whether the battle is really necessary, if for no other reason than that it puts us all in danger of losing the Game. This time, the risks inherent in Gary's plan were obvious to everyone except Gary.

The members of the United Nations have permission to speak at any time, and Secretary-General Kelsey rose to her full height, her long blond ponytail swinging slightly as she stood. A rangy lacrosse player with a wide-eyed stare and a seemingly inexhaustible fund of physical energy, Kelsey was very conscious of her role in the Game and always stood poised and powerful when she spoke.

"Defense Minister Martinson," she said, looking hard at Gary, "are you sure you want to do this?" Her speech was balanced, clear, and strong, and usually just a few words from her were enough to command respect. But Gary only shrugged.

Then, remembering who was nominally in charge, Kelsey turned her gaze on Todd. "Prime Minister Havilland, are you sure that you approve?" She darted a glance at me. "It's like Mr. Hunter said last week, you don't want to be shooting first and then asking questions later."

In many situations, that might be a difficult lesson for fourth graders to learn. And certainly, Gary's aggressive action might have seemed normal on the playground. But here, for any of us to win, we all had to win. It was increasingly clear that Gary had lost sight of that fact.

Todd could probably feel the growing hostility toward Gary, which was also, by extension, directed against him. He slumped so far down in his chair that he was practically off the seat. He kept his head down as Gary nodded vigorously in response.

"This is *exactly* what I want to do," Gary said. Then he glanced, almost dismissively, at Todd. "And the prime minister is okay with it, too. Right, Todd?"

Todd barely looked up, but his hands were flipping out of his lap, making a brushing-away gesture. "Okay, okay!" he said, his hands moving desperately. Then he pulled them back down into his lap and forced them to be quiet.

But Kelsey wouldn't give up. She had clashed with Gary once before, when she realized how quickly his store of arms was growing. Greenstone was already the most powerful country in the world, she told Gary then. Why did it need more arms? "Maybe you ought to spend your money on something else," she said.

Gary just shook his head and declared, "You can never have enough weapons!"

Now Kelsey was saying calmly, "Look, Defense Minister, you have lots of choices here besides attack. You could ask whoever's doing this to talk to you privately, before you start shooting off missiles all over the place. You could ask us here at the UN to send our troops to defend you—that wouldn't even cost you anything!"

Nash and Aton looked up hopefully. Todd slumped further into his seat.

"No!" Gary said firmly. "I've got to defend myself! I have the right! This is my declaration."

Again he glanced at Todd.

"I mean, *our* declaration," he amended. "Greenstone's declaration. And Prime Minister Havilland just said it was okay."

"You could ask us for help," Kai said, almost under his breath. He knew that only the country whose turn it was could speak, the only exceptions being the weather goddess or someone from the UN. As the saboteur, he had done a wonderful job setting up this volatile situation, but as the prime minister of the Game's poorest country, he was worried about the future of the Game. I admired again Kai's brilliant feel for strategy. As an ally of Greenstone whose troops were stationed right next to where the mercenaries had attacked, his nation could have entered into an exchange of favors, sending whatever troops it could spare to deal with the mercenaries. Even if Greenstone had paid for Kai's help, it would have cost Greenstone far less—and been far less dangerous—than a missile attack near the oil fields.

I don't know if Gary heard Kai, or if he was still answering Kelsey. "No!" he repeated, still shaking his head. "It's just got to be this way. Attack!"

I wondered whether Gary really couldn't grasp that other responses were available to him, or whether he was simply excited about getting to "blow up stuff with missiles," as I'd once overheard him say to Todd. There was something very American in Gary's reflexive reliance on brute action and naked power. It spoke to something that I find both admirable and disturbing in the American tradition: the individualistic attempt to use one's personal power to achieve one's goals, at all costs and regardless of the consequences. At this moment, standing poised and triumphant on the balls of his feet, Gary seemed to embody the American desire to overcome all obstacles despite the odds. Looking at this redheaded nine-year-old boy, I felt I was looking at the archetypal tough guy, the rugged individualist who served as his own model, his own mirror; the man with no need for others, who brooked no challenge to his own ideal of self-worth and competence.

Still, others in the group were ready to question his actions. Kelsey was sitting down, defeated, but Tessa, our weather goddess, got to her feet.

"I hope you know exactly what this means," she said grimly, but at the same time exhibiting supreme calm.

Tessa was one of the best weather goddesses the Game has ever had. She had a sense not exactly of right and wrong—nothing as moralistic as that—but of *correctness*. She didn't care about winning an argument or taking the moral high ground. She cared about actions having the consequences that they were supposed to have and people seeing clearly the meaning of their actions. You might say that she was *gleefully judicious*. For a nine-year-old girl in glasses and braces, she was awfully like a figure from Greek mythology, one of those impartial dispensers of justice who mete out consequences without fear or favor, but taking a certain divine pleasure all the while.

"Look, Gary," she said. "I mean, sorry, look, Defense Minister Martinson, you have to understand that if you send missiles that close to a huge field of oil, you are likely to cause a huge disaster. I mean, really, really big! Mr. Hunter, if Gary—if Defense Minister Martinson—sends those missiles, we'll need to have a coin toss to see if he hits the oil."

As I've said before, we always use a series of odds-weighted coin tosses to determine the outcome of a contested situation. I agreed that a coin toss was in order now.

Behind Gary, Aton winced, and even Nash involuntarily shook his head. Todd leaned even farther back in his chair, his body slumped so far down that his bangs almost hid his eyes.

Tessa bounced on her toes, as she always did when she got excited. "Think about it, Defense Minister Martinson," she said. "Just think about it. If your missiles hit the target, okay. All right. No problem. *But if they don't . . .*" She bounced again. "If they miss even a little bit so that they hit the oil fields . . ." She paused dramatically. "Well, then, you are going to have an ecological disaster that could spread across the entire planet. I'm just telling you."

A tall, awkward boy named Joel stood up. He was the leader of the Nin, whose land adjoined Greenstone.

"Um, our tribal burial lands are right next to those oil fields?" he said, turning every statement into a question as he usually did. "And so, um, we would rather that you not . . . uh, you know, that you not do it?"

Gary shook his head. Far from being cowed by the opposition, he relished it, savoring this chance to show the rest of the class how much more he knew than they did. "Nope," he said. "I know what I'm doing. I'm going to fire the missiles."

He gazed at me expectantly, and I did everything I could to keep my feelings from my face. They had to be allowed to play this out their own way.

"Get out the coins, Mr. Hunter," Tessa said with a mischievous smile.

I looked at Gary, giving him one last chance to change his mind. I don't think he even noticed.

"Fire!" he exclaimed.

## Disaster

"Come on, Tessa," Gary said impatiently. "Throw the coins!"

I watched intently, not even sure what outcome I wanted. If Gary's missiles hit their target, the world would be spared an enormous disaster—but Gary would have learned, once again, that might makes right and that he was indeed always right. But if Gary's missiles missed the mercenaries and hit the oil fields . . . I couldn't even imagine a disaster on that scale.

We all watched the coins in riveted silence. And the results showed . . . disaster. Gary's weapons had hit the oil fields.

A shocked silence settled over the room as Gary's face took on a frozen look of disbelief. Nothing in nearly thirty-five years of playing the Game had ever gone so dreadfully wrong. I admit that I had never even imagined this possibility: an ecological disaster that could destroy us all.

Shock and rage paralyzed everyone in the room. We were furious with Gary for causing the problem, with the United Nations for not preventing it, and with ourselves for not somehow pre-cluding it. A vision of certain defeat descended on us, weighing more and more heavily as each moment passed.

Only Tessa seemed unfazed. "Well, Defense Minister, this is going to create big problems, as I told you it would."

She looked around the room.

"Mr. Hunter, can I use that black paper?"

I didn't know what she had in mind, but I nodded my agree-ment. She went over and grabbed some scissors off my desk. We watched her, rapt and uncomprehending, as she slashed the black crepe paper into a large, jagged shape and brought it over to the game board. Quickly and firmly, without any hesitation, she positioned the paper over the oil fields and spread it into the surrounding airspace.

"Your missiles have caused a raging oil fire that has compro-mised the atmosphere of the entire planet," she said calmly. "For many, many Game Days, oil smoke and ashes are going to com-pletely block out the sun—which is going to cause economic damage and a whole bunch of other problems."

A growing mutter of dismay spread throughout the room as the children glared at Gary. As the teacher, I felt that I should do something, but I had no idea what to do.

Tessa took a step backward, and our attention returned to the ominous black crepe paper that covered most of the sky. We imagined the acrid clouds of oily smoke, the ravaging oil fire, the dead wildlife, the ensuing famine. We imagined the toxic oceans, poison swirling in their currents. All of us—including Gary—were in shock.

"Madame Weather Goddess," the Nin chieftain, Joel, finally managed to say, "how many Game Days will it take before the pollution evaporates?"

"Yes," added Prime Minister Kai, speaking on behalf of the Game's poorest nation, "and how much will it cost to fix this?"

"*Can* we fix it?" UN secretary-general Kelsey chimed in, looking pale and shaken. "Is it even possible?"

Somehow, finally, Gary managed to speak. "How much damage?" he croaked. "How many problems?"

Tessa looked at all of them and shook her head. "I'm not completely sure," she said. "I'll have to research that tonight and let you know."

Slowly, sheepishly, Gary sat down. He shrugged once, convulsively, as if his whole body was trying to disown what he had done. One by one, the children looked at him.

"Way to go, Gar," a boy named Marco said sarcastically. Normally, I would have said something about that kind of insult, even at a time like this. But before I got the chance, Gary launched into the kid with a punch, and a scuffle began.

"*Excuse me,*" I said loudly, and everything came to a screeching halt.

Gary looked up at me, his face blazing, and then, chagrined, he dropped his head and backed off. His lips were trembling, he was blinking hard, and his fists were clenched tight. Trying to slow his breathing, he sank back into his seat.

"Gary," I said, "you know what the rule is." He nodded.

School policy on any type of physical violence is very clear. The child involved has to be given a time-out so that he can work through what he has done. He may have to visit the principal's office so that he can talk about what he has done. And then, if he has been playing the World Peace Game, he has to be put completely out of the Game.

As I looked at Gary's bowed head and the shocked, frustrated faces of his classmates, I knew that this could not be the end. Somehow we had to find a way to restore Gary to the group. Somehow we had to find a way to solve the world's problems —together.

"The rule is that Gary needs a time-out," I said carefully, trying to buy time. Gary shrugged slowly into his backpack, utterly defeated.

"While he's gone, there is another process we have to complete," I heard myself say. I was making it up as I went, word by word. "We have to hold a *tribunal.*"

## The Tribunal

Gary and the other children looked up at me expectantly. I explained that a tribunal was a kind of court in which world leaders are tried for crimes against humanity. While Gary was out of the room, the rest of us would consider whether he could be forgiven for his actions and allowed to return to the Game, or whether he should be punished by being permanently kept out.

Slowly, his feet dragging, Gary left the room. I went with him, carrying a chair that I placed against the wall, positioning it so that the class wouldn't be able to see Gary, but I would. Gary dropped his backpack onto the floor and sank into the chair. I briefly rested my hand on his shoulder, then went back into the classroom and closed the door.

"Now, ladies and gentlemen," I said, still finding the words as I said them, "we have an opportunity here, to either restore Defense Minister Martinson to the group or leave him permanently out."

"It's *his* fault if he's out!" someone exclaimed.

"Yeah, first he fired the missile, then he hit Marco. He's *supposed* to be put out."

"Maybe," I said. "Those were his choices. But now we have our choice. In a tribunal, there is one person to bring the accusation and another person to defend the accused. We will also need a judge, in case there are any disagreements about procedure. And when the tribunal ends, all of you will vote on whether Gary is in or out."

One by one, the hands went up. Tessa, the weather goddess,

was to be our judge. Kelsey offered to play the people's representative and bring the charges. Kai volunteered to be the defense attorney. Each student made a clear, logical, and compassionate case. Then it was time for the class debate.

When the students were ready to vote, I brought Gary in. I told him he had the option of facing the tribunal and pleading his case.

Gary blinked. You could see how emotional he was, how different from his usual cocky self. He agreed to hear the evidence against him, which Kelsey ran through quickly, recounting the disaster he had caused and the destruction that had resulted, but also bringing up his previous reckless arms buildup and his usurping of Todd's proper role. As she spoke, Gary seemed to be listening, really listening, in an honest, open way. Some of what he heard pained him, some appeared to confuse him, but all the time, it seemed to me, he was listening.

Then Tessa took over. "The question is, should you be allowed back in the Game," she said. "So explain it to us, Gary. What did you think you were doing? And why do you think we should let you back in?"

Even more shaken than before, Gary began to speak. "I thought I could stop the missiles from going into the oil fields," he said. "I thought I could control where they went." He said he thought that his plan would work to stop the mercenaries, but now he saw that maybe that hadn't been the best way to handle the situation.

"If you let me back in the Game," he concluded, "I'll be a better minister of defense. I won't do things the same way anymore." His lip was quivering again, and he seemed to be near tears. It was a remarkable sight to see such a haughty kid brought so low, and I'm proud to say the students treated it with respect. They were solemn, almost somber—no jeering, no teasing, no contempt.

They took their vote. It was a close decision, but they let

Gary back in. The decision was accepted very quietly—no one cheered; no one even smiled—and then they went about trying to repair the disaster he had caused.

## Restoration

"Madame Weather Goddess," I said after the decision about Gary had been rendered, "can you let us know what will be required to repair the damage resulting from the fire?"

Tessa shook her head. "I need some time to think about it," she said. "I'll let you know tomorrow."

That night, Tessa did her research. The next day, she said, "Mr. Hunter, I'd like to speak first."

I agreed, and Tessa stood up. "I, the weather goddess, have made a decision about the damage that Defense Minister Martinson's missile attack has caused." For three or four Game Days, she told us, a huge cloud of oil and smoke would drift above the world. The weather goddess would move the cloud around according to the wind currents.

"Those currents, of course, are up to me," Tessa said. She continued to detail the ecological devastation: the destroyed farmland, the polluted atmosphere, the increased danger of climate change. When she had finished her catalog of horrors, we sat stunned once again. The focus on Gary had caused us to forget for a while the disaster itself. Now we were forced to return to a crisis that, by this point, had engulfed the entire planet. It was beyond any crisis I would have assigned to the children—a crisis so profound, and involving so much economic and ecological misery, that it was almost too painful to think about. But there it was—and we had created it. Somehow, then, we had to fix it. I couldn't imagine how.

Then something extraordinary happened. It was as though this whole series of events—the disaster, the tribunal, the forgiveness, the consequences—was the click that this group needed to push it into overdrive, into the flow of extraordinary super-collaboration, in which all of us were suddenly working as one. Somehow necessity had forced us into a much deeper level of connectedness than we had previously been able to achieve, and you could almost see the individual minds in the room meld into one single intention as we confronted our vast problem. The only possible response to this crisis was to come together. In that sense, Gary had actually been our best catalyst.

And so the hyper-negotiations began. Usually the different entities in the Game proceed with separate agendas and individual policies, but today we all leaped into action as one. The room became a blur of activity, and the noise level went through the roof. A huge cyclone of energy swirled around the game board, fueled by everyone's desire to solve this problem *now*.

When I finally rang the bell, the students returned noisily and reluctantly to their seats. As always, we began in the east, with the poorest country's declarations. Prime Minister Kai stood up to speak.

"I am Kai Tanaka, prime minister of Frozenland, and I speak for my country and for the entire planet," he said. "We have agreed to solve climate change by planting one trillion trees on each continent."

"No, Kai, that was *ten* trillion trees!" someone corrected him.

"Oh, right!" Kai said quickly.

"But those are just seedlings!" the weather goddess objected. "They can't soak up the carbon dioxide as quickly as full-grown trees."

"Don't worry, Tessa," Kai assured her. "We have a plan." Then he went on to lay it out: they would also plant shrubs; they would seed the clouds to create rain; and they would set up giant fans to blow the smoke away, creating a huge vacuum that would in turn produce a cycle of wind to break up the dense clouds of smoke. The weather goddess had to rule on the feasibility of a lot of these ideas, and some of them she sent back to the drawing board. But somehow a combination of solutions was cobbled together.

"Okay," Tessa finally ruled. "This'll work. But it will take two or three Game Days to get everything done, and the cost will be astronomical. So who is going to pay for all this?" And the negotiations began again.

Before the oil field disaster, financial negotiations among the various entities in the Game had been somewhat contentious, not least because Gary had been so focused on using his country's budget for armaments. Now, however, with the tacit agreement of everyone in the Game, Gary was centrally involved in the finance operations, where he devoted his arms budget to "planetary repair work." I think he felt lucky to be able to participate and grateful for the chance to make amends.

And so the Game continued. And so, eventually, we won. And so my students had the chance to see that individual hubris and will and narrowness of vision can create crises of epic proportions. And that the only solution to a power-drunk individual who acts recklessly and selfishly is a unified, wise, and compassionate group, which somehow finds solutions when there are no solutions and makes a way when there is no way. Gary's disaster taught us that the group has a collective wisdom that transcends each of us. If we are lucky and careful and compassionate, that collective wisdom can lead us all to peace.

## Using Aggression to Ensure Peace

Amy was a small, shy child who didn't say much, even to her closest friends. She was scrawny, with wisps of hair sticking out from her two stiff brown pigtails. Her glasses sat oddly on her small, angular face, and to add to her generally awkward air, she wore braces.

She was a quiet little girl. But hers was a sharp, intense sort of quiet. She was the kind of child who never seems to miss anything—although she spoke so little, you could never really be sure of what she had actually seen.

In the Game, Amy served as the minister of defense of the poorest nation. I don't quite know how that happened—how silent little Amy ended up in charge of the tank corps and air force and ground troops. I only know that Amy took her responsibility for her nation's defense very seriously.

Amy's poor country was next door to a very wealthy, oil-rich nation whose power had gradually been growing throughout the Game. Prime Minister Paul, the leader of that wealthy nation, enjoyed his power and sought to increase it, while Amy's impoverished nation had to figure out how to make its way in the world. Its strategy seemed to be to stay out of trouble and not provoke any problems with the larger powers. So it was all the more surprising when one day, without any apparent provocation, Amy suddenly attacked her next-door neighbor's oil fields.

This unassuming little girl launched a full-blown military operation against her prime minister's orders. She marched into the territory that contained the oil fields, surrounded it, and, without firing a single shot, secured and held it. Her tank corps held the ground while she threatened tactical airstrikes to attack the enemy troops from above. Her military resources were small, like Amy herself, but unlike her, they were aggressive. All by herself, Amy had started a war.

Her prime minister was horrified and commanded her to withdraw the troops. Amy refused. The neighboring country was furious and threatened to retaliate, but it was unable to conduct any military operations because its fuel supply was all locked up. Amy had devised a brilliant tactical maneuver. They dared not fire on her forces for fear of hitting their own oil reserves.

Of course, we were all very upset with her. Everybody was shouting, "Why are you doing this? This is the World Peace Game. We're trying to get peace here! What is wrong with you?"

Her girlfriends pleaded with her—Marcie, her prime minister, and Ruby, the secretary of state, and Shanna, the chief financial officer. Amy just shook her head. Prime Minister Paul, the boy in charge of the wealthy country, accused Amy of ruining the Game. Amy just shook her head. As usual, I didn't interfere, but I did question Amy, trying, as I thought, to make her think more deeply about the reasons for her action and, more important, to recognize its potential consequences. But no matter what I said to her—no matter what anybody said to her—she just shook her head. All she would say was, "I know what I'm doing."

I couldn't help taking it personally. As you've already seen, I often take it personally, thinking I've failed, when I believe my students aren't learning—and even more personally, I'm afraid, when they don't follow the path I feel they should. I struggle against this tendency continually, but I don't always succeed in keeping it in check. And this incident with Amy was one of the worst bouts with failure I've ever had, not least because the Game was already going badly, and I felt that Amy had put the last nail in its coffin.

As a final insult to my pride, Amy was someone from whom I would never have expected such a warlike action. How had I misjudged her so badly? Amy was quiet and well-behaved—had I found it easy to neglect her? Or to attribute to her the stereotypical qualities of a fourth-grade girl—quiet, nice, a follower of the rules—without really seeing her or understanding what she was capable of? What would Sun Tzu think of a leader who had such a poor grasp of reality, who saw people in such general terms rather than noticing them in all their specificity? But most important, why would Amy do this?

A few Game Days later, I had my answer. It came out that Prime Minister Paul was planning a military offensive to dominate the entire world! Had he had his fuel supplies, he would have followed through on his plan. Amy, quiet and unassuming though she was, had kept her eyes open. Although her prime minister, the United Nations, and I had all failed to grasp the dynamics of the situation, Amy had seen them all along, and she understood all too well what was about to happen.

Without the help of her fellow citizens, Amy had been thrown back on her own resources, and so she'd had to go deep into her own creativity to try to find a way. And she did. She created a unique solution: her very own version of what Sun Tzu would have called "the unorthodox surprise attack."

## Amy Channels Sun Tzu

How had Amy come to understand that the other country was planning an attack long before any of the rest of us did? Years later, I happened to run into Amy as I was browsing in a local bookstore. She had matured into an outgoing, poised young woman, who still seemed able to hold a certain concentrated stillness, allowing me to finish some long, convoluted story about the Game that I had decided to share with her right there in the aisle. Just before we parted, I thought to ask her, "Amy, how did you actually know that Paul was planning a military sweep of the entire world? And how did you decide on the strategy you came up with?"

Her answer was surprisingly simple. "Well, Mr. Hunter," she began, "I knew who I was playing against — Paul. That told me a lot right there, because I thought, given the kind of person he was, that he might think like that. You got me started with something you read to us from Sun Tzu, I think, something like by watching the little details closely, we would know what big things were coming. So I was watching him all along."

I could only vaguely remember those readings, but they had obviously made a big impression on Amy. She continued, "I noticed that Paul would keep moving his armies up to his western border, a little at a time, but he kept saying it was for showing that he was withdrawing them from his eastern border to show friendship to his eastern neighbor. And that certainly wasn't like the Paul I knew!

"Then I saw him buying more and more weapons from the arms dealers when he had plenty already. So I put all of that together, and I realized that he was going to try taking over the world. That's the kind of guy he was, you know."

I couldn't argue with her there. Paul *was* that kind of guy.

"So," Amy went on, "I tried to get Marcie, my prime minister, to see what he might do. But she had, like, a crush on Paul at the time, I think. And the other cabinet members, Ruby and Shanna, they would always just do whatever Marcie thought best, so nobody supported me. Paul even overheard me begging for help, and he just smiled. He knew. He knew that I knew, and he thought that because I was in such a poor country, there was nothing I could do about any plan he had. I could just tell.

"So I thought, *How do I stop this guy? Because if we don't do it now, it will be too late when he's more powerful later.* The UN couldn't be bothered when I asked them to think about my hunches, and finally Marcie ordered me to just sit down and forget it. She *was* the prime minister, and I was her minister of defense, after all. So I got kind of desperate, I guess."

"So you took matters into your own hands," I said slowly, and she nodded.

"Yep," she said. "Had to. I could see so clearly what was going to happen if I didn't."

"But did you realize the risk you were taking, that no one would support you and most everybody would be against you?" I persisted.

She nodded again. "Yes, I knew. I didn't think it would be as bad as it was, but I knew they all wouldn't like it. Paul was popular and good-looking and smart, so I wasn't in a good position to challenge him. But you know, my mom always had talked to me about standing up for what I believed in. I guess I really believed in what she said."

Still puzzled, I asked, "But how did you know what strategy to use? How did you know that cutting off his oil supply was the key to defeating him?"

"Well, I didn't," she admitted. "I sort of guessed. But I knew that that part of his country was nearest to mine and that he needed oil to move that big army around the board. You remember, Mr. Hunter, how you used to say that every time we moved something on the board, we had to calculate the cost of its fuel and deduct it from our budgets?"

I smiled. "You bet I remember. I must have said it thousands of times."

"So," Amy went on, "I figured he'd need that oil to run his military if he wanted to take over the world. So I thought, *If I can stop his oil flow, he can't do anything.* And I knew that if I could surround the oil fields near me, he also couldn't attack me, because he might hit his own supply! I don't know how I figured that out, but Sun Tzu said something about controlling the countryside or the enemy's supplies, so that was my guide, really."

Hearing Amy's words, I had the best feeling a teacher can possibly have. Even when I myself had failed to understand her actions, I had provided her with the resources she needed to make her own decisions, find her own courage, and step into her own leadership. My reward was that instead of destroying the Game, as I had feared at the time, she had actually saved it from Paul's hidden attempts to grab power. My greater reward was that Amy had gotten to experience the best that she was capable of and had taken it with her into the world.

## Spotlight and Shadow

Sometimes the greatest changes come from the least of us—the poorest, the smallest, the most obscure. Amy was one of these, and yet she was able to make a move that changed everything.

This reminds me of a story about my parents, who had an affiliation with a black Baptist church early in my life, but who left that denomination when I was a teenager. They went on to become Catholics and to attend a church a few miles away.

Although this new church was geographically not that far from our old one, culturally it was quite a distance away. At the time my parents joined it, in 1967 or so, it was an all-white congregation, and my distinct memory is that when we walked into the church on Sunday mornings, we were completely isolated. I mean literally, no one sat anywhere near us. They didn't just avoid our row—they avoided the rows behind us and ahead of us as well. It was as though we were on a raft adrift on a sea of empty pews.

As a young firebrand, I would have nothing to do with such treatment, and I left the church as soon as my parents let me. In my mind, no self-respecting person could have acted otherwise.

My parents felt differently. They stayed put—in fact, they toughed it out for twenty years. And when I finally went back to visit in the late 1980s, I witnessed a complete change in their relationship with that church. They each headed different lay committees, and they were treated with respect by everyone in the building. Indeed, they seemed to be loved and hugged and kissed good morning by every single parishioner who entered through the church doors, and when the service was over, they could barely make their way down the aisle, so many people came over to chat with them and ask their opinion about this or that. Through some kind of invisible action, my parents had simply upended the entire social structure of that church. Somehow they had turned the whole situation around—except that seemingly, they hadn't done anything. Their relationship with each other and their own spiritual life had had a powerful transformative effect on the previously hostile white congregation, and this loving acceptance of my parents was the astonishing result.

Were they afraid to attend that church, week after week, to

face that initial ostracism? I don't know, but if they did feel fear, it wasn't evident. Perhaps in another era, I might have asked them, but in the African American culture of the South in the late 1950s and 1960s, there were two worlds in every home: the world of adults and the lesser world of children, and rarely did the two meet. There were no philosophical discussions or candid dinner table exchanges between the generations. In fact, children might never know what their parents or older relatives thought, and in many households it would have been the height of rudeness to ask. All we children could do was try to decipher the coded conversations that took place when we were around and to imagine what they talked about when we were not. If any one of us had been bold enough to ask, he or she likely would have been told, "This is not for children" or "This is grown-folks' talk —you all go out and play!" This message was so powerful that even when I was a full-grown man, I would not ask my parents about their private matters, especially where race and segregation were concerned.

Still, I wondered then and I wonder now, *What made them able to persist throughout those years, until things finally changed?* Although I cannot be certain, I realize that I grew up seeing two systems of addressing the seemingly intractable problems of racism. One was the *spotlight school.* Members of this school— leaders such as Malcolm X and Martin Luther King Jr., other activists, and even ordinary black folks—took it upon themselves to personally register resistance to the systemic prejudice under which they lived. They took the heat for those of us who were not able to or who were afraid to take such a visible, costly, and dangerous stand.

Others, like my parents, belonged to the shadow school. While they sometimes went where they were not wanted and insisted on being accepted, they did so as subtly and quietly as possible. When I revisited that church and saw my parents involved in so many ministries and leading a number of lay groups, I marveled at how tenderly and lovingly they were received. Tearful hugs and warm handshakes had replaced those empty pews. No fear, no hate—only love, respect, and total belonging could be seen. My parents had wrought this difficult change with a gentle and quiet persistence over two decades. They had stood next to a mighty institution that had arrayed all its power against them, and when it tumbled down, they acted as if they'd had nothing at all to do with it. What it cost them—what fear, frustration, or sorrow—I will never know. But I know that they tried—and they succeeded.

Sometimes change is a matter of a leader getting far out in front of the rest of us and calling us to a standard we cannot yet imagine. Sometimes change happens more slowly, subtly, even silently, inspired by leaders who invite us to act differently simply by their own example. Sun Tzu, I believe, was a master of both the spotlight and the shadow, the light and the dark and the gray areas in between, because he seems to me to have first accepted reality and then made use of any tactic that fit the time. Amy—who acted in the spotlight but kept her reasons for doing so firmly in the shadows—seems to me to have been his true disciple.

## Finding a Way When There Is No Way

Think for a moment more about what Amy did. She undertook her action on Game Day 6, but her true intentions didn't come to light until Game Day 8. Since we played the Game only on Tuesdays and Thursdays, that meant that Amy had to live with being misunderstood, misjudged, and ostracized for several days. Most of the children thought that she was the warlike one, not Paul. Her girlfriends were mad at her in a very personal way—Marcie because she had a crush on Paul, the others because they were friends of Marcie's. Even I, her teacher, was disappointed in her, and although she was too polite to say anything about it when we met years later, I was sure that had been difficult for her as well.

She also had to live with her own doubts. If the evidence was as clear as she believed it was, why couldn't anyone else see it? She must have asked herself that at least once. To keep faith with her decision, Amy had to trust her own intuition, her ability to see clearly and to interpret what she saw. She had to trust, too, that she had taken the correct action; that her smaller war would not somehow provoke a larger one; that by seizing her neighbor's oil fields in a preemptive attack, she would not bring down the wrath of the United Nations or spark an unexpected alliance between her mighty neighbor and another world power.

When we finally understood why Amy had mounted her attack, we realized how brave she was to strike at a foe many times her size. We also realized her tactical brilliance: she had seized the oil fields without firing a single shot, thus using the least amount of force and causing the least amount of harm. In this, too, she had followed the teachings of Sun Tzu, who explains that the enemy you attack today may become your friend tomorrow. Because your opponent may have resources that you yourself will one day need, because its citizens may one day become *your* citizens, or at least your allies, you must not ravage its countryside or destroy its army. Rather, in any battle, you want only to occupy the land and dishearten the army, leaving resources and lives intact.

This Amy had done, with impressive results. Her courage had grown not out of a naive idea about peace or friendship, but rather out of a deeply strategic understanding of how the power was distributed in her world and how best to defend her people. In surrounding her neighbor's oil fields, she had essentially gone straight for the nation's heart. She had discerned its weakest link —the source of its power—and she had deprived the country of it. She understood that for both people and nations, our greatest strength is often our greatest weakness. Cut a giant off from the source of his strength, and he is helpless. Perhaps even at nine years of age, Amy had had more practice observing the workings of power than we had given her credit for. Perhaps she had understood that those who seem the strongest may in their very strength be the most vulnerable as well.

I wonder what would have happened if at the time she had been better able to articulate what she was doing and why. Or perhaps her silence was also strategic. After all, as she told me later, everyone else was invested in believing Paul. Criticizing a powerful leader who still possesses legitimacy often makes the critic look bad, especially if she is from a powerless or despised people. If that is what Amy was doing, her action was even braver than it first appeared, because she was able to hold the truth of her vision for such a long time even as she felt the social ostracism of her community.

To me, Amy exemplifies the kind of courage we sometimes need from our leaders, the kind of courage that can educate us into a deeper, wiser, and more compassionate vision. Some individuals are so masterful at seeing the way events are flowing that they get to the truest vision ahead of the rest of us. When that happens, they often need a great deal of patience and courage as they wait for us to catch up. I think that great leaders and visionaries—Martin Luther King Jr., Nelson Mandela, Black Elk, Aung San Suu Kyi, Buckminster Fuller—often have that quality. They see the way the world is turning—toward liberation or equality or social justice or care for the planet—and they commit fully to those possibilities. Then they do what they can to bring the rest of us along. Until we catch up, their vision can look like stubbornness or eccentricity or even selfishness. When we are finally able to enter their vision with them, suddenly it all makes sense.

Even such leaders, however, depend on their relationship with a powerful group to whom they feel allegiance. Whether they have an actual group to lead, like King, Mandela, Black Elk, and Aung San Suu Kyi, or whether they simply see themselves as part of a larger human community, like Fuller and many other artists and visionaries, they are never really acting alone. Somehow, even when they are ahead of us, they are still with us. Belief in us is what enables them to believe in themselves. Commitment to us gives them their courage. When we are finally able to see what they see, they have their reward.

## What Does Victory Look Like?

When I think of the victories we won with Gary and Amy, I am reminded of the many different appearances a World Peace Game victory might take. Sure, on the surface you will pretty much always see children jumping for joy and shouting out their triumph when the Game is finally won. And just before the final victory, you will almost always see that flow state I described in the previous chapter, where the roomful of children moves as one and creates the victorious solutions together. But many different types of roads lead up to those wonderful endings, and each, I think, offers us lessons for the kinds of victories we might expect to see in our own lives and in the historical events unfolding around us.

Amy, as we've seen, created for her class a heroic victory because she heeded the call to do something unpopular, something that required sacrifice or suffering. This to me is a lesson for all of us. Perhaps in your own life, you have had a moment of clarity, of being able to see what was needed in a certain circumstance while others did not. You could see a path of action forming that would lead you into uncertainty or even danger. Yet it was, according to your understanding, the appropriate thing to do. Did you do it? Did you step forth into the spotlight of public opinion and judgment to do what needed to be done? Did you wrestle with your fear and emerge the victor, as Amy did? Did you withstand the aftershocks of the displeasure, censure, and outright anger of strangers and friends alike?

Another type of triumph in the World Peace Game comes from a step-by-step unfolding of courage — the kind of courage it took the coup d'état collective in chapter 5 to overthrow the bullying tyrant. No one individual can take credit for this type of victory — yet it requires many individuals to act alone, as each new hero comes to take the place of the one who has been defeated. In the coup d'état, one rebel stood, made the Game's ultimate sacrifice, and then departed. Then another student came to stand bravely in her place . . . and then another . . . and another, in a dedicated strategy that would not allow tyranny. We can see a parallel between this brave gang of conspirators and the black civil rights activists Jo Ann Robinson, Vernon Johns, Claudette Colvin, and Rosa Parks, each of whom took a seat in the whites-only section of a segregated bus in Montgomery, Alabama, before the ultimate institution of the Montgomery bus boycott in 1955. One after the other, they endured being harassed, verbally abused, and sometimes assaulted or arrested. Yet each continued to challenge the systems of power when others could not, coming forth from the shadow school into the spotlight school. Like the brave students in my class, they simply refused to allow what was not right to stand.

A quieter but equally far-reaching victory was the sudden enlightenment of the arms dealers Jamal and Michael in chapter 6, as they stumbled upon the realization that the ultimate success of their arms sales would result in the world's destruction. This horrific prospect so sobered them that they decided to diversify their business into less lethal products. Have we ever seen adults in the real world create a victory by changing course midstream? Do we know people who were initially dedicated to a certain way of thinking, being, and doing, but then decided to remake themselves, risking the loss of their old way of life? Michael and Jamal make me think of the villain who becomes a doer of good works, or the workaholic who abruptly and completely changes her life to make more time for herself and her loved ones, or the person who leaves an abusive relationship. There is a heroism in seeing that the road to which we have been dedicated — perhaps even the road we have sworn to stay on — has now become a dead end. And rather than stay the course out of a sense of duty, honor, or loyalty, we make a bold decision, at some cost, to leave this path.

An even quieter victory — involving only a subtle change within the black box of his own mind — was Rodney's in chapter 2. With no fireworks, meltdowns, or soul-shattering awakenings, Rodney simply learned how to ask for help and to be more honest and straightforward in his relationships — and only because he had essentially hit bottom and had nothing left to lose. Yet this very helplessness paradoxically allowed him to see a way to gain power and standing. Being brought low was his way up, so to speak. He won by admitting his vulnerability and exposing himself to others — and in doing so, he helped create a victory for the rest of us. I think of his victory when I am brought low, when I need to admit my own vulnerability and to let go of my pride and ask for help.

David's victory in chapter 4 was quieter still. He had won many battles and achieved much military success. Yet even though he was meeting his goals, he realized that he was not creating peace through his victories, but merely engaging in an endless cycle of war. David's was a subtle victory of deeper personal understanding. Although he did not immediately change his actions — and perhaps did not even need to change them — his new awareness opened up new possibilities for the future and might safeguard him against taking wrong turns that beckon. Sometimes it is less important to change course than to simply increase our understanding of the possible dangers of that course.

As we just saw, Gary's environmental disaster and subsequent tribunal was a victory for him — but not for him alone. His humble restoration to the group and his newfound cooperative spirit empowered the entire group to recognize themselves as one and then to implement their power to change their world. From a dark place of despair and fear, the group put aside its differences, first to show compassion to one individual and then to devise a solution for everyone. I think of that group's victory when I need to believe that we as a people can correct our wayward leaders and set them on a better course.

Perhaps the greatest lesson from our victories, though, is simply that they always emerge. Each time I play the Game, I have a moment—perhaps several moments—of fearing that victory will not appear; that this will be the first session of the Game (perhaps the first of many?) in which my students don't solve the crises, don't improve the material assets of each country, and don't, finally, achieve world peace.

And then the class somehow pulls it together, somehow comes up with a new creative solution or a new mode of cooperation or simply a better way to communicate among themselves. Somehow they always come through. And so what I want to share with you is this: There is never *nothing* you can do. There is always *something*. And that something, if viewed critically and creatively and with compassion, can often lead to something else . . . and then something else . . . and then something else.

We can be in the depths of despair, crushed by our seeming defeats, bewildered by all we do not know. And yet the commitment to self-reflection and to developing our awareness and to supporting and engendering compassion always seems to provide if not a way out, then at least a way up!

Keep a space open. Continue to play the Game. Trust in the collective wisdom of the group. And you at least open the door to the possibility that somehow, some way, peace will come.

*Epilogue*

# The World Peace Game
# Goes to the Pentagon

The general who does not advance to seek glory, or does
not withdraw to avoid punishment, but cares for only the
people's security and promotes the people's interests, is the
nation's treasure.

— SUN TZU, *The Art of War*

THE CHILDREN BURST into the empty conference room,
their faces alight with excitement and perhaps a little trepidation. Playing the Game in our classroom is one thing. Despite
the careful use of titles and last names, despite the reality that
our little Plexiglas planet takes on for all of us as soon as the
Game begins, the children understand that at the end of day, we
are still just playing a game. Now, though, we are in an enormous
building filled with thousands of men and women, all with a single purpose: to make the thousands of decisions that determine
how our country deploys its troops, its weapons, and its military
budget. Questions of war and peace do not necessarily begin in
the Pentagon, and they certainly don't end here. But some of the
most important decisions on the planet are made along these
corridors, and today my class of fourth graders is here to find out
as much as they can about how that happens.

We have spent weeks preparing for this meeting. We know that
one of today's activities will be a press briefing, where we'll meet

the real-life spokesperson for the U.S. Department of Defense and pepper him with questions. The students have taken their assignments seriously, researching the world's trouble spots and coming up with the most important questions they can think of, which they are ready to share with the press secretary and policy experts. We know that at some point, we will be meeting Secretary of Defense Leon Panetta himself.

In our little classroom, we have long since won the Game — back in December, when the semester ended, a few months before this late-March 2012 trip. We solved the fifty-odd crises I presented to the students, and we raised the asset level of every one of our nations. We even solved climate change! So in our world, peace and prosperity reign supreme.

In the real world, of course, not only do we not have peace, but peace seems almost like a mirage, a goal so elusive that we can barely imagine it, let alone achieve it. And now, here we are, deep within a building that, whatever its commitment to peace, is wholly preoccupied with war.

## *Sun Tzu in the Corridors of Power*

I spend much of my time teaching nine-year-olds about the wisdom of an ancient Chinese general. And yet even if you could argue that Sun Tzu was also a man of peace, he was certainly a man of war. *He* might be at home among the military leaders of the Pentagon, but what am I doing here?

Pacifism was an adopted creed in my family, and one that I accepted without question as I grew up. It was not just a matter of foreign policy in our household but a template for how we were all expected to deal with the difficulties we faced at the time. My parents taught my brother and me a nonviolent response to segregation and to all other forms of racism, and it was the approach we absorbed not just in our opinions but in our very bones.

Certainly, I could talk with, sympathize with, and respect military personnel. But had the Vietnam War–era draft not ended just before my number was due to be called, I knew I would have had to find a way to resist. I marched in protest against the war, and I did not believe that I could have pulled a trigger. Yet this is far from the whole story. As a young boy, I had devotedly watched the black-and-white TV programs of the early 1960s — *Combat!*, a World War II drama, among others — and then gone out into the backyard with my brother and reenacted the scenes of mayhem we saw on TV. I will go further and admit that I harbored a secret attraction to the rigid order, the polished medals, and the deadly lure of weapons, and I cherished fantasies of being that tough and noble sergeant who commands the loyalty of his troops even in the face of death. However I now rate the two approaches — my family's pacifism and my secret love of the military — they were surely both a part of me.

And now here I am, leading a class of nine-year-olds into the doors of the most powerful military institution the world has ever known. Are we really here, and am I, an avowed peacenik, actually leading the way? Have all my efforts in peacemaking come to this moment, face-to-face with the power I had so feared?

## The Empty Space Meets the Pentagon

There will be many surprises and ironies for me today. Before this day is over, I will see that the warriors I meet seem to be as human and ordinary as I. I will see that two-, three-, and four-star generals, both male and female, are all attentive, kind, and even gentle with the children, whom they seem to genuinely appreciate. I will be surprised, touched, and perhaps a little flattered to see that these military leaders accord me a kind of respect that I did not at all expect, viewing me as a "peace warrior" who is not one of them and yet entitled to meet them on an (almost) equal footing.

Yet I will also be disturbed by my encounter with the height of

U.S. military power. I will have to think about why our nation is so enmeshed in conflict in every part of the globe. I will have to ask myself whether my use of *The Art of War*—on whose wisdom I have relied for the past forty years—gives me a closer connection than I would like with this American House of War, as the writer James Carroll dubbed it. Yes, conflict is a part of life, but does that mean war is unavoidable?

My students settle in around the conference table that has been prepared for them. Each seat is labeled with a paper sign giving the student's title in the Game: PRIME MINISTER OF SANDIA RODRIGUEZ, UN SECRETARY-GENERAL CHEN. The long, polished wooden table almost fills the room. There is just barely room for a second row of chairs, up against the wall, where the adults sit.

The children are solemn in their dress-up clothes—some of the boys are even wearing suits—but they can't keep their excitement from bubbling over. I watch them struggle with their two identities: serious diplomats who have recently concluded a demanding but successful set of negotiations, and wide-eyed, giggly nine-year-olds on a field trip. I realize for the thousandth time that I can never really know what they are taking from this experience, either what it means to them now or what it might mean to them later. I can only know what I always know: that this encounter with the workings of our world will change my students somehow, and that change will echo across the generations as they go out into the world.

We are welcomed by Beth Flores, the Pentagon staffer who first encountered the World Peace Game. Beth saw Chris Farina's film and my presentation at a conference she attended, and she was so excited by what we were doing that she invited Chris and me to present the film at the Pentagon itself. After that showing, we had one of the most moving discussions I have ever been a part of. The Pentagon staffers marveled at the children's thoughtfulness, creativity, and profound commitment to peace.

They marveled, too, at the sense of calm and openness that they detected, zeroing in — to my surprise, I will admit — on the concept of the empty space. "We need more of that here," one woman told us. "We are often so busy solving one problem after another that we don't have the kind of time you're talking about to pause and reflect. We're too busy reacting to events. But I would love to have that breathing room, that empty space, to think about what we might want to see happen in the world, rather than being forced to keep responding, responding, responding."

I heard her words with mixed feelings. I have seen my government and its military take actions to implement a geopolitical vision that I haven't always thought was conducive to peace. Would the empty space help Pentagon staffers come up with more profound visions of peace, or would it only give them a way to make more effective war? To Sun Tzu, perhaps that question would be meaningless, but to me it feels as though the survival of the planet may depend on it. Yet I appreciated this woman's commitment, her dedication to our country, her willingness to speak openly with Chris and me. And I was moved by how the film had affected her — how it had affected everyone who had come to see it. I was struck by the way that everyone I met at the screening spoke of the Pentagon's job as being to create peace — or, as they put it, to defend our nation against military threats so that peace would become possible. Was I being, as I had been with David, too narrow in my thinking, too unwilling to accept the necessity not just of war but of arming oneself, training oneself, to be the preeminent military power in the world, so that one could win as many battles as possible? Again, Sun Tzu and I might have different answers to that question. After all, he was a general — and some of these people were generals. I was a teacher. Even if they were acting out of necessity, I still might question whether there was another way to meet necessity's demands than the ones that they — and David — chose.

I was struck, too, by how much these staffers wanted to connect with the energy that they saw in my students. Maybe that's why Beth was able to arrange this visit. Certainly, everyone we meet today seems to love having us here. All day long, people light up when they see my students. They marvel at the children's questions and seem to drink in their freshness, their innocence, their eagerness. I wonder if we really do represent the empty space to them, and what it would mean if they had more of that openness in their workday or in their approach to solving the world's problems. I wonder how any of us—from the three-star general who joins us for lunch to my smallest, youngest student—can put together these disparate realities: the comfortable conference room and the distant battlefield; the policy made here and the lives affected over there; these children's seemingly unbounded promise and adulthood's painful constraints. Thinking of the real-life terrorists and mercenaries and tyrants with which these Pentagon people must contend, I wonder, not for the first time, what value the World Peace Game has in a world where so many people are so decidedly not devoted to peace.

## Coins and Corridors

After the children have met Beth and some of the other staffers who will accompany us today, we're divided into small groups and taken on a tour. The Pentagon is open to the public, and I saw several families and even a couple of school groups in the waiting area when we arrived. I assume that our tour is similar to theirs, with one important exception—ours may end in the office of Secretary Panetta himself. First, though, we walk through literally miles of corridors, each of which is a kind of mini-museum dedicated to some aspect of U.S. military history. In one, we see paintings that commemorate the signing of the Constitution. We are told that if General George Washington had not chosen to resign his commission before becoming president, we might be a military dictatorship today. I am struck by the emphasis, here in the Pentagon, on that aspect of our democracy. I am proud that even in the halls of the Defense Department, we can celebrate having a civilian commander in chief.

Our students are very much impressed with our soldier tour guides, who tell us that to win these jobs, they had to memorize some twenty-three pages of text and walk a mile and a half backward, which they must be able to do so that they can face their tour groups. The Pentagon is only five stories high plus two basement levels, but it is huge—the world's largest office building, if you go by floor area. More than twenty-five thousand people work in this building, and the corridors, if laid out end to end, would run for seventeen and a half miles—though it's also true that you can get from any point in the Pentagon to any other point in only seven minutes. It's easy to see—walking mile after mile past the exhibits dedicated to Generals Douglas MacArthur and Dwight D. Eisenhower, African Americans in defense, the American flag, and POWs/MIAs—how this building becomes a world of its own. Our guides tell us about the many stores, fast-food restaurants, and other amenities in this little city, and one student pipes up to ask if you can sleep here, too. No, says the guide, but that's about the only thing you can't do.

Our tour includes a stop at the place where the terrorist-controlled plane crashed into the Pentagon on September 11, 2001, penetrating deep inside the building and killing 125 Pentagon workers, as well 64 people on the airliner. Now there's an outdoor memorial to commemorate those who died, as well as an indoor memorial and chapel. At the end of the day, many students will name this chapel as the most important part of their tour.

We also visit the snack bar at the center of the five-sided outdoor courtyard around which the Pentagon is built. We learn that during the Cold War, Soviet spy satellites observed so many people going in and out of this structure—which was then a hot dog stand—that they believed it housed an underground bunker, or at least something more important than hot dogs. My students are delighted to learn about the famous hot dog stand, and later several will cite this story as their favorite piece of new information.

Finally, all our small groups converge on the office of Defense Secretary Leon Panetta. When we are ushered inside, I expect a stern personage, a severe man of war. Instead, I find myself shaking hands with a kindly, jovial, almost grandfatherly, gentle man.

Panetta welcomes us warmly as we file in and asks if we know what his job is. Despite his genuine friendliness, the students are shy at first. Finally, Lakshmi, a little girl dressed in a sari, answers. (The students had asked if they could, as an official delegation, wear their national dress to the Pentagon, so we have one sari and one red brocade Chinese dress.)

"If there's a war," Lakshmi offers, "your job is to protect the United States."

Panetta beams. "My job is to keep you safe!" he tells us. "To do everything to ensure that our enemies don't attack this country." He is an exuberant man—you might even say joyous—and despite what must be a monstrously busy schedule, he seems genuinely interested in talking to my students and learning more about what they've done. To put them at ease, he asks them to explain how the Game works, and he wants to know some of the crises they encountered while playing it. My students rattle off the issues they have dealt with: ethnic conflicts, mercenary attacks, cyberspace issues, territorial disputes.

"Were you able to deal with them," the secretary asks, "or did you have to go to war?"

"We achieved peace!" my class choruses, glowing with pride, and the secretary beams at them again. I wonder if he is thinking what I'm thinking: that it is always extraordinary when anybody, even a group of nine-year-olds, works through the overwhelming complexities of ethnic crises and national conflicts and somehow, despite all the obstacles, still achieves peace.

"What was the hardest crisis?" the secretary wants to know.

"Climate change," the children say without hesitation, and Panetta leads them in a discussion of this challenging issue. "What causes climate change?" he asks, and when the children describe their findings, he tells them that climate change was one of his own major issues when he was leading the CIA. "Can you imagine why?" he asks.

"Because the ocean rises, and it'll flood!" says Lakshmi.

Nancy, our arms dealer, suggests acid rain. One of the boys says, "Drought!" Another student says, "Because volcanoes can start emptying."

Panetta listens carefully, and then he explains that while all of these are important reasons to worry about climate change, there was another that his committee considered: the altered shipping lanes in the Arctic, created by the melting of ice in the Northwest Passage. "So you guys are lookin' at the right issues!" he concludes.

When he tells them that, the kids are wide-eyed, doing their best to rise to the occasion of meeting one of the world's most important men. (When they are asked at the end of the day what they liked about meeting Mr. Panetta, one of the girls says soberly, "It was a once-in-a-lifetime opportunity.") Yet here he is, bantering, with sincerity and obvious respect, with the children now curiously roaming about his office and touching mementos on his desk—the same desk used by World War I general John "Black Jack" Pershing. I watch their tiny hands brushing a brick taken by U.S. Navy SEALs from Osama bin Laden's compound in Pakistan; I see them eyeing the plethora of gigantic telephones via which Panetta has most certainly affected the lives of thousands of individuals, families, and children around the globe in profound and sometimes irrevocable ways. The children want to know why Mr. Panetta has so many phones, and they laugh at his quick response: "Because these phones are all screwed up, and they don't work!" They nod seriously when he explains that he needs to be able to reach the White House on a moment's notice and that the line has to be secure. One of the phones actually has a red plastic strip on its back. I picture him picking up the famous red phone during a moment of crisis and try to imagine the orders he might give. The terror of such a moment seems impossible to reconcile with the warmth and friendliness of the secretary, joking and laughing with my students as though he had all the time in the world.

I'm moved by Panetta's gentleness with the children, his distinct compassion for them, and his appreciation of their efforts to achieve the same goal he also strives for. But I also feel a dissonance that I don't know how to deal with. I keep trying to find the accord between this thrilling visit and the painful business conducted in this building—some connection between the lively cheer of the soldiers and officers we've met and the harsh necessities that are their reason for being. I'm trying, too, to link our small game and this enormous enterprise. But so far, I'm still seeing double: no way to merge the large view and the small one —all I can do is shuttle back and forth between them.

As our meeting concludes, Secretary Panetta shakes our hands and gives each of us a coin with his own name and seal on it. An officer tells us, when we file out, that these coins are special. If we meet the secretary and we don't have ours, we have to buy him a soda. If we meet him and he doesn't have his, *he* has to buy *us* a soda. (Actually, for adults, the tradition involves a beer, but they've translated it into child-appropriate terms.) The children are delighted with this tradition, but I learn later that these coins are a considerable honor—you can work with someone for quite a while and never get one. They are meant to acknowledge a person's membership in a unit, but they are also given to those who have provided outstanding support to a leader, a literal token of the leader's appreciation. So these coins are a sign that we met and that our meeting mattered.

## *Pizza with the Generals*

After meeting Panetta, we return to our conference room for lunch, during which we hear from representatives of the four branches of the armed forces: Army, Navy, Air Force, and Marines. With friendly rivalry but genuine devotion, each explains why his or her organization is the best. Our tour guides seemed to be enlisted men and women, but our lunchtime speakers are high-ranking officers, including several generals. We are taught how to leap to attention when they walk through the door, how to fold our hands at our sides ("Pretend you're holding a roll of quarters in each hand," our "boot camp" instructor suggests), how to say "Reporting for duty, *sir!*"

The students love it. All of them have watched countless TV shows or movies or have played video games featuring soldiers, not to mention our weeks of playing the World Peace Game, but now it's real. These men and women have seen combat, commanded troops, faced real-life versions of the problems we confront in the Game. Walking down the corridors lined with generals' photographs and flags scorched in the flames of battle, seeing the chunk of bin Laden's bunker, pausing at the memorial for staffers killed on 9/11 in this very building, we have been welcomed into this military world, at least for today, and being taught how to show respect for the men and women who command it seems like an integral part of being here.

When Major General Jay G. Santee of the U.S. Air Force strides into the room, he plays along. "This is the sorriest bunch of peaceniks I ever saw!" he roars at us. The children laugh, and he does, too. Then he tells us, with palpable pride and devotion, about the three core principles of his branch of the service.

The first, he says, is "service before self," which means that you think first of the people you want to help, while putting yourself and your own needs last. I think of the spontaneous rescuers who dove into the icy Potomac, trying to save the lives of people they had never met. Pentagon staffers made up part of that self-created rescue team. "Service before self" is a motto Sun Tzu would probably applaud. And yet I wonder, too, how this jibes with the basic job of a bomber pilot. This contradiction is inherent in Sun Tzu, but it is one thing to encounter it at a remove of several centuries and quite another to meet this smiling man, who has both overseen rescue operations after Hurricane Katrina and flown several dozen combat missions in Operation Desert Storm in Iraq. Saving lives and possibly ending them — all in the name of service. I don't know how you have a military that thinks any other way, but again I wonder about the uses to which that service is put.

That is not something Sun Tzu ever discusses. To him, it was axiomatic that a general's duty is to obey his ruler and preserve, or even expand, the military power of his country. But I have questions about the notion of surrendering oneself to a higher authority, allowing oneself to become a mere instrument of policy. I understand that if soldiers do not surrender themselves in this way — if they do not agree to unquestioning obedience to their superiors and, ultimately, to their civilian commander in chief — we simply cannot have a military. Soldiers sent into battle cannot stop and debate the wisdom of either the specific maneuver or the war itself. Nor would I be comfortable with a military that played an independent political role, questioning the wisdom of the civilian politicians who are supposed to have the ultimate say.

At the same time, how does anyone — from the lowliest foot soldier to the most decorated general — simply remove his or her capacity for humane moral questioning and cede that responsibility to another human being? How do you say, "I am simply an instrument of policy here; command me, and I shall obey"? What is the ultimate alchemy you have begun within your mind, your heart, and your spirit by relinquishing your moral authority and handing it over to another? What is the residual effect on your life, to have removed that ethical questioning mechanism as you go into battle or command others to do so?

Meanwhile, Major General Santee is still laying out the key principles of the Air Force, another of which, he tells us, is "excellence." He defines this as doing the best possible job in anything you take on—nothing halfhearted or mediocre. Also part of the Air Force motto is "integrity," a word the children do not know.

"It means you respect the truth and tell the truth," the general explains, and one of the boys says, "Oh, I thought that was honesty!"

Santee takes this distinction seriously—he isn't smiling now. "Integrity includes honesty, but it goes beyond honesty. It means that everything we do is in harmony with the truth."

I look at his whole bearing, and to me he radiates those principles: *service before self, excellence, integrity.* You might even say that he embodies them, that after a lifetime of devotion, he has literally become the principles he serves. Life-and-death decisions are part of his job, and I cannot believe, even in this brief meeting, that he makes those decisions with anything less than the service, excellence, and integrity of which he speaks. Must his decisions be the same as my decisions? Do I want my students—my victorious players of the World Peace Game—to follow in this man's footsteps, to join his Air Force, to aspire to his rank? I must confess that I would prefer them to follow another path. But as I have seen throughout three decades of playing the Game, I am so often wrong when I wish that—or perhaps not wrong, exactly, but limited. Don't I want our nation's generals to have played the World Peace Game in my classroom, to have read Sun Tzu, to have carried the collective wisdom of peace into the halls of the Pentagon and the ranks of the armed forces? Can you follow the ways of peace and still make room for war?

My students, at least, are as flexible as ever, taking in the events of the day but somehow keeping their own views, too. When the representative of the Marines says that "everyone gets that warm spot when they think about the Marines," Abigail pipes up, "Not *everyone!*" provoking a surprised pause and then a burst of general laughter. When a lieutenant colonel in the Army Special Forces asks the group who they think has more boats, the Army or the Navy, another girl says triumphantly, "The Army!" adding shrewdly, "'Cause you would only say that question if it was the Army."

The officers invite questions, and the students eagerly call them out. "My dad says they have a plane that can go at Mach 6. Is that true?" "Did a plane ever go so fast it blew up?" When asked by the officers how many children want to join the Army, the Navy, the Air Force, or the Marines, hands shoot up eagerly for every branch.

## Tough Questions

My students have spent weeks preparing the toughest questions they can think of for any policy experts they might meet and for the press secretary, with whom a meeting has been planned. I have armed each of them with a colored folder—red, purple, blue, green, yellow—bearing the words TOP SECRET DOSSIER in big black letters. They ask some of their questions at lunch, using the formal presentation style I have taught them.

"Ma'am, I am Ms. Giametti, chief of the South Korea Desk, and my question is, How is the president going to normalize relations with North and South Korea?"

"Sir, I am Ms. Lawrence, part of the China Desk staff. Why has this dispute between China and Tibet gone on so long?"

"I am Mr. Hoy, of the Israel Desk. How can the Pentagon help stop Israel from bombing Iran?"

Larissa, chief of the Mexico Desk, asks how the Mexican drug war affects the military planning going on in the Pentagon. She sits still and alert as two or three staffers chime in to give her an answer. When one of them says, "It's important for us not to use just the military tool," she responds with one sharp, decisive nod. I can imagine her years later, asking this question as a reporter or a policy analyst, but I also see the nine-year-old girl struggling to understand her world.

After lunch, we are taken to the press room, whose door bears the imposing sign ACCREDITED MEMBERS OF THE PRESS ONLY. Today, however, that is us. "Do you ever watch the news?" asks Terry Mitchell, the staffer who is preparing us for our briefing. "This is where it happens!" He stands at the podium at the front of the room, the Pentagon logo hanging behind him. The room is a comfortable auditorium with a few rows of theater-like seats, equipped, as we are told, with plugs that allow the major networks to feed footage directly back to their studios. Explaining how a briefing works—that there isn't time for everyone's questions but that the senior correspondent always gets called on first—Terry points to Mara, who happens to be sitting in the center of a row. "You, in the pink shoes, are the senior correspondent," he tells her. "You're sitting where the senior correspondent always sits." Mara preens and pulls her skirt down over her knees.

We are introduced to the press secretary, George Little. "The Pentagon has one of the most important missions in our country, and that's keeping our country safe," he tells us. Some three million people are associated with the U.S. military, which maintains five thousand bases around the globe. In fact, he explains, the U.S. military is the largest organization in the world.

Then he takes questions, and once again my students are on their feet, asking one tough question after another.

"What can the United States do about Yemen if al-Qaeda is up there?"

"What new tactics will the U.S. use in fighting the war against terrorism?"

"How do Nigeria's security issues relate to U.S. security issues?"

The questions are challenging enough to provoke some mock protest from the staff. "That is a very good question, and I would refer you to the State Department!" the press secretary says at one point, before laughing with the students and giving a thorough answer. When Mei asks, "Is America ready to protect Taiwan at all costs against China?" the secretary pauses long enough for Abigail to sing out, "She stumped you!"

The questions continue.

"What, if anything, is being done by the president about the European debt crisis?"

"What is Bashar Assad doing to make his people so angry?"

"What if the al-Qaeda attacks upon the United States relate to Pakistan—what would the United States do about it?"

"If Iran gets its own nuclear weapons, how will Saudi Arabia feel about needing its own nuclear weapons, and what will the president do about it?"

The staffers answer as best they can, and when we are joined by NBC News national security producer Courtney Kube, she tries to answer as well. But there are no easy answers to these questions, even when a fourth grader is asking them. My students have solved all the crises on our imaginary planet. I cannot imagine what they will make of the crises on our real one.

## Hot Wash

Now our day is ending, and we're returning to the conference room for a final discussion about what we've learned. In Pentagon lingo, this is called a "hot wash," which Beth Flores explains is an unblinking critique of oneself and the action just completed. The goal, she says, is "getting the most you can from every experience that comes in front of you," and to make it work, we have to "leave our egos at the door." I think again of Sun Tzu and his endless flexibility, which entails that type of clear, relentless, ego-free gaze at reality—and at oneself. I like thinking that is part of the warrior code, part of what makes it possible to fight when needed and to make peace when needed, with no judgments or biases, but simply an acceptance of what is. The catch, of course, is that we might well convince ourselves that the most desirable or convenient action is a necessity rather than seeing other possibilities. In the World Peace Game, peace is always possible. Is that equally true at the Pentagon?

Beth begins by asking the children what their favorite parts of the day were. They go around the table volunteering their replies: meeting Mr. Panetta, learning about the Pentagon, visiting the 9/11 memorial, finding out about the hot dog stand. Abigail says her favorite moment was stumping Mr. Little, and she flashes her mischievous smile.

Beth says that these kinds of days are "why we got into this business in the first place." She adds, "We need this kind of inspiration. We need those new ideas in order to do our jobs well."

After the students have finished discussing their visit, Beth asks them what they learned from the World Peace Game. The answers come slowly, thoughtfully, as the adults listen intently. We all feel we might learn something, too.

"I learned to plan things out just a *bit* more before I do something. People have to plan things out a *lot*."

"Instead of everyone on a team doing the same thing, have everyone do a different job. Let one person look at everything, and let other people just pick off certain things."

"I learned that violence isn't always the answer to every problem."

"Know who your allies are."

"Do your best with all you have."

"There's not as much fighting as you think there would be."

"Talk to your teammates before you do something," Abigail says. And when Beth asks her why, she grins. "'Cause you could mess something up!"

"I think I learned to take a more diplomatic position and have more foresight," says Rory. Beth asks him if that was difficult, and he says, "Yeah!" Beth asks him for an example, and he pauses. "I'll get back to you on that!" he says finally, and everybody laughs.

"That's a phrase that's commonly used in the Pentagon," one of the staffers says.

The students' answers continue.

"Look before you leap. You don't want to jump in an alligator's mouth!"

"You may have allies who are your friends. You may have others who disagree with you. Don't try to believe everything everyone says, or you could get yourself killed."

"It's good to have peace."

"War is usually not the way."

The kids are asked again which branch of the service they might like to join, and the answers, to me, sound just like those of any nine-year-old.

"The Air Force—because I want to jump out of an airplane!"

"I like the Marines because they're known as the tough guys."

"Why be on the ground if you can be in the air?"

"In the Navy, I could jump off a boat and maybe go scuba diving. And I wouldn't have to carry around my own beds and my own toilet, like they do in the Army."

Abigail points out that in the Army, "you get to shoot bombs out of the tank thingie."

Finally, Beth asks what advice the children have for her and her colleagues.

"Keep moving forward."

"Keep doing what you're doing."

"Before you do something that you'll regret later, think about it."

"Sometimes it's good to change your priorities if it's not working."

"Don't act like a hero."

"Don't give up."

## Looking Back

Our visit to the Pentagon put me into a whirlwind of mixed feelings. As a child of the U.S. peace movement of the 1960s, I had learned to see things in black and white. Like many of my youthful peers, I opposed the Vietnam War and then had to explore exactly how far my antiwar sentiments extended. Was I just against this war, or did I oppose all wars? Were wars in the name of a greater good valid? Did the ends justify the means?

When I think about how the World Peace Game has changed over the years, one of the things that strikes me is how children now are almost hesitant to go to war. During the early 2000s, when we were hearing a lot about the war in Iraq, students seemed more militaristic, or at least more willing to consider military solutions. In the last four or five years, however, the Game has seen fewer battles, more careful planning, more strategic thinking, more negotiations. I have seen far more of the "peace at all costs" kind of thinking, in which students—perhaps unrealistically—will do virtually anything to avoid war. I have to work harder, consequently, to redesign the Game, so as to undercut their initial responses and force them into the unknown. I have to find a way past their impulse to say, "Let's just not fight, and we'll win this World Peace Game in five minutes." Of course, I wish they could do that! But since the real world doesn't work by peace alone, I don't want the Game to avoid conflict either. Accordingly, I have refined the Game so that it's really not possible to win quickly. To win, students actually have to face whatever crises I have given them—not just "accommodate" their way out, but actually deal with the real conflicts and challenges.

Someone asked me recently what effect the world around us has had on my students' thinking about war and peace, and I honestly couldn't say. How do TV programs affect them—or the rest of the media, or the culture in general? How much influence do their parents have, and when does the culture at large trump what they hear at home? I don't know. I only know that they seem to be growing more thoughtful, more careful—and perhaps also more fearful, or maybe simply more aware that negative consequences exist. Certainly, they know more about the world's horrors than I did at age nine, and they live, as I did not, under the shadow of what might come to seem like daily disasters: political, military, ecological. The nine-year-olds who come into my class actually find ways to solve climate change—every year, somehow, they manage it! But it is sobering to realize that they are already familiar with climate change, already somewhat aware of its potentially dire effects.

I still cannot come to terms with the warmth and generosity of the Pentagon's treatment of us when I recall its mission of making war. It's one thing to appreciate the wisdom of an ancient Chinese general and quite another to think about the entity whose troops go marching in my name, whom my president commands and my tax dollars support.

Certainly, the Pentagon officials we met were eager to learn more about the Game. At every turn, it was clear that no effort had been spared, no detail left unattended, and there was a sincere interest in how the children learned to achieve peace, how they understood Sun Tzu and used his insights to discover their own. A Marine Corps general entered gravely into a discussion with a nine-year-old minister of defense, who was accorded the courtesies befitting her rank as they argued about how much force is necessary in the world. I have heard that generals hate war most of all, because they know firsthand its cost. They have met the men and women who go into battle and die, and they understand combat, not as an empty abstraction or as a chance to score points on the world stage, but as an actual experience that changes people forever, even when they survive. Certainly, Sun Tzu understands the realities of combat, which is why I have always trusted him to instruct me in apprehending other types of reality. So perhaps the welcome we received at the Pentagon represents a genuine openness to our mission of peace.

And yet the entire building is dedicated to war. Perhaps war is a mistake that we cannot stop making, but I continue to hope that someday we will learn not to make it. This might be a possibility Sun Tzu never considered, but in his time wars were not the all-pervasive force they are today, where every child with a game box can kill thousands of realistic-looking enemies, where video games are actually used to prepare real soldiers to kill. In his day, soldiers had to kill in hand-to-hand combat. Now we kill at a distance, invading lands far from our borders, leaving poisons and mines behind when we depart. Our wars are very different from the ones Sun Tzu wrote about. In our time, unlike his, global war is a genuine possibility. It is both sobering and hopeful to reflect that global peace is also a genuine possibility —indeed, perhaps a genuine necessity, if we are not all to destroy one another and the planet as well.

When I asked my students to do our own "hot wash" back in our classroom, their responses ran the typical fourth-grade gamut from goofy and trivial to thoughtful and profound. Lakshmi said that her high point was "talking to Mr. Panetta as if he were our equal." I am glad I could give them that lesson—that even powerful men can be addressed directly, that they might even have something to learn from us.

Rory said that his favorite moment was visiting the Pentagon memorial. "It was actually kind of cool to sit in the same spot where the plane had hit," he explained.

"It was really touching to me!" Lidia agreed. "I was tearing —to be in a room where some people might have died."

The attacks of 9/11 happened before these students were born, but they have grown up in the shadow of that day. I'm glad I could help make it accessible to them, give them something concrete to imagine beneath all the rhetoric. I'm glad, too, that they could imagine it at a protective remove, seeing the memorial rather than live TV footage of the disaster itself.

"I liked learning that everybody was really nice and made jokes a lot," Mei said. "I thought it was going to be really strict, but every single place they could squeeze in a joke, they did it, and some of the jokes were really funny!"

"I learned that violence isn't always the answer to everything. Sometimes it is good to be peaceful, too," Colin said.

"I saw these people, and I saw that they were just people trying to do a job, and I felt sad that they had to go to war," Abigail reflected.

And then, of course, there were the children who liked learning about the hot dog stand.

I loved hearing all their answers, not for the specific conclusions they had come to—it would be surprising if those did not change many, many times between now and their adulthoods —but for how thoughtful they already were, how alive to their experience. I loved how open they were to what they had done and how ready they were to let it change them.

The talk moved on to what the children had learned from the World Peace Game.

"I learned that sometimes people can't find peace, and some people think war, and the other person might think peace, and so that normally leads to war."

"I learned that war is not always the answer. You need to learn to figure out the problem first, before you do war."

"War is bad because you get hurt, and some people die, and it's sad when people die. So you should always figure out the problem first, try to make peace, and *then* if it's not working, then you can do war. But the better solution is if you don't have to do war."

## The World Peace Game Meets the World

When I began the World Peace Game, many years ago, I wondered how my students' parents would feel about it. But parental response has been uniformly positive, even over three generations and several different school districts. Many parents have come in at the end of the day to express a deep gratitude for the transformative effect the Game has had on their children.

"Mr. Hunter, it's like night and day, how Eva is now compared to before she started the Game," one mother told me. "She actually talks to me and her father about something other than sports and video games!"

"Mr. Hunter," a father began, "our dinner table conversations are all about global diplomacy now—what to do about climate change and what do we think about U.S. policy on this issue and that one. I mean, we are grilled at the table about our political sentiments . . . every night . . . for months on end, even after the Game is over."

Yet another parent told me that although it thrilled her to have her daughter and three of the girl's friends who were also playing the Game discuss diplomacy in the back of her SUV as she drove them to an out-of-town soccer match one weekend, it also drove her nuts. It seems they talked nonstop for three hours about global policy, refugee problems, nuclear proliferation, the potential effects of national inflation, and a dozen other such topics. "I mean, I'm grateful, Mr. Hunter," she told me, "but you can imagine, three hours locked in a car with four, loud, policy-debating nine-year-old girls!"

One of the things I've realized about the Game is that despite my supposed "peaceful" intentions, the Game is actually neither left, right, nor even center politically. This is because the children begin with my original premise but then make of the Game what they will. Sometimes they move more toward the right, sometimes they lean to the left, and most often they appear to be a kind of supergroup of compassionate centrists.

The children themselves report that after so many weeks of wrestling with such enormous global problems, they feel a greater kindness toward their younger siblings, or they want to take better care of their pets, or they are motivated to make some change in a larger way, so that they can make the world better. And they do! In the year following their Game experience, Prime Minister Amelia's team organized its own charity. The children decided to collect coins from their fellow students to send to Mozambique, to build a clean-water well. Amelia had read studies about clean drinking water being a problem there, and the Game she had just concluded featured a water-supply problem in a desert country. I was proud that she had taken the lessons to heart. I love what Brennan told me, too: "This game taught me about being compassionate and helping others, and that if you work together, you can achieve anything."

Sometimes the most rewarding comments come from the more reserved students who didn't say much during the Game. James, a slight, rather morose, timid fellow who acted as his nation's chief financial officer, stood up during our weeklong post-Game reflection period and spoke poignantly about how deeply the Game had affected him, how much he cared for his teammates, and how much respect he had for the opposing players who had made the Game better through their skillful opposition. His brief, wistful speech touched me and reminded me that still waters do run deep.

Certainly, the most touching feedback I have received over the years is from students, often years or even decades after they have played the Game. I might think that they will forget it, as they do many childhood activities. But many of them remember. Here's what Holly said in an e-mail years after her family moved away:

> Dear Mr. Hunter,
>
> It's been such a long time since I've seen you in person, but I watch you talking about the World Peace Game on the TEDTalk show every week. I feel very fortunate to have met you, and I have never been so proud as a student. It's because of you that being here in Hawaii is tolerable, knowing I have something to look back on. News of the World Peace Game has spread through our school, and I feel so blessed to be able to stand in front of my class and say: "I played the World Peace Game. I was the General of Defence [*sic*] in the first game I played, and was the first Facilitator General to run the World Peace Game under Mr. Hunter. And if I could, I would relive those moments every day." That is how proud I am to be one of your students, and when I come to visit, I'll be sure to stop in and see you.

An even farther-reaching effect can be seen in this e-mail from Irene, a student who played the Game twelve years before she wrote to me:

> Mr. Hunter,
>
> I just watched your TEDTalk on the World Peace Game and cried for the entire last ten minutes. Some of my clearest memories from elementary school are those I spent in your room, particularly gathered around the World Peace Game. I was privileged to play two years in a row, and I will never forget the day my parents came to observe and were a little concerned by the way I fearlessly purchased black-market arms and defied the U.N. The World Peace Game has never left my mind; I've continued to mull over the issues we discussed and to apply those concepts to today's conflicts.

For some of my classmates, the World Peace Game may have been just another awesome experience in the Quest classroom, alongside Jewels of Wisdom, video projects, and other endeavors. For me, the World Peace Game shaped the entire course of my life. I am currently a Peace, War, and Defense major at the University of North Carolina at Chapel Hill (along with another major in American Studies and a minor in Creative Writing). My concentration is in National and International Security and Diplomacy. Rarely does a day go by that I don't think about the World Peace Game. I can't describe the feeling of adrenaline and excitement that starts in my fingers as I take notes in my Public Policy classes and runs to my brain as I begin to meditate on current global issues. It is an indescribable feeling, but one well known by anyone who has played the World Peace Game. I am sometimes frustrated in class when our lectures focus on problems and I want to discuss solutions. My Peace, War, and Defense professors comment that I approach current issues and conflicts differently than many of my classmates. I believe that this difference exists because I've been thinking about global peace since my formative years. When I approach a conflict, I don't try to think like a seasoned politician or diplomat. I try to think like the nine-year-old girl who sat amongst her cabinet in a Venable classroom, who focused on her plastic tanks and troops and weighed options with the utmost gravity.

I don't know what the future holds for me, but I do know that I hope to take the skills I acquired in third and fourth grade and make a tangible difference in the world. I sit in my college classrooms and outline plans for conflict resolution and global education, and I hope that I can one day make those plans a reality. If I could solve the world's problems at age ten, there's no reason I shouldn't be able to at age thirty or forty.

Thank you so much for your dedication to my class, for your encouragement as we wrestled with the ethical dilem-

mas we encountered in pursuit of peace, and for your ability
to transform a task that gives our world leaders headaches
into an experience that I love more than any other game
in the world. I hope that hundreds of schoolchildren will
be able to learn from this game the way I did, and that one
day a generation will be able to implement those ideas and
achieve world peace.

> Thank you, thank you, thank you.
> Irene

## Reaching Forward

Thinking of my students' trip to the Pentagon, I can't help wondering how they'll see that trip by the time they reach adulthood.
How will they take what they have learned into jobs at the Pentagon, or posts with the armed forces, or positions as policymakers
and diplomats and citizens who try to tell the Pentagon what to
do? I think of our Pentagon visit and of the Game that preceded
it stretching forward into a future that I will only ever partly
see. And I think that all I can do—as a teacher, as an adult, as
a human being—is to transmit to my students this little experience of war and peace, so that whatever it was to them, they can
carry it forward. If I can succeed in doing that, it is as if I am
stretching out my hand over the decades. It's as though each of
my students is a window into time, and if I have the correct view,
I can look through that window and go forward through the centuries—each student I have reached, each person he or she has
reached, each future he or she has affected. And, of course, my
extended hand is ultimately just a continuation of my mother's
gesture, which itself continued something in *her* past, and so on,
and so on, each of us just another link in the lineage. I just happened to be in line to help shape the next link and to disperse
this wisdom in a new form, but it neither begins with me nor

ends with me, just as it didn't begin with my mother and won't end with my students.

A word or a gesture can be so powerful. For good or ill, it can penetrate walls—it can penetrate centuries. If your intent is pure enough, you can do so much good with that one gesture. At least that's my experience.

*Appendix*

# The World Peace Game and "Teaching to the Test"

AS THE WORLD PEACE GAME has grown in prominence, I am often asked to relate it to current trends in education, particularly the most prevalent trend of "teaching to the test" and the growing tendency to penalize educators and administrators financially or even by the loss of their jobs if they don't "produce" high or improved test scores. Of course, some forms of assessment are necessary. But I'm concerned about what seems to be an overvaluing of quantifiable test scores over the more intangible forms of learning. The World Peace Game offers precisely this type of learning, and while I believe it is supremely valuable, it is nearly impossible to quantify.

After three decades of teaching in a variety of settings, I believe there are other ways to ascertain student growth—a "photo album" rather than a "snapshot" of student development, to quote educational researcher and innovator Jay McTighe. The premise of the World Peace Game is that assessment can be self-evident to the students, so that they not only know "where they are" in their own understanding but also are invited to share in the creation of their own assessment tools. Student self-assessment then becomes a vehicle for self-awareness.

As opposed to traditional forms of grading, which create pressure, transparent assessment relieves pressure, because all the students know at all times where they are in the learning process and how they are progressing. This is better for both students' psyches and their actual achievement. I remember a high school math unit that I was sure I had figured out. When I failed that test, I was stunned for weeks. I had had no idea that I wasn't doing well, and after I took the test, it was too late to make a course correction.

Contrast this rude shock to the new approach to evaluation that my fourth graders and I created together a few years ago. Imagine four vertical thermometers side by side, marked off in equal increments of 1 to 10. (The students drew this out on a big sheet of paper as we drafted the concept.)

The first thermometer is a measure of *function:* how well an idea, solution, approach, or problem-solving technique has worked. Students use their pencils (no computers needed!) to shade in their self-assessment on a scale of 1 to 10, while I share my own assessment on a duplicate sheet. Sometimes smaller teams of students elect also to use this rubric together.

The second thermometer registers *elegance:* the beauty of the design, solution, or idea. Again the student self-assesses, while I and perhaps also a small group evaluate simultaneously. "How gorgeous was your thinking?" I ask. "How elegant was your idea?"

The third thermometer measures *effort.* This measure can be tricky, because sometimes we can achieve great results with little or no effort: a brilliant solution or a wonderful idea just "comes to us." Other times, we strive mightily but don't have much to show for it. Even so, our thermometers at least allow us to record our assessment of how hard we worked.

The fourth thermometer shows us the *number, name, and kinds of resources* we have sought out in our work. Students are asked to list their sources of information, providing a handy catalog of the range of their research.

Finally, there is a large empty box on the far right-hand side of the paper. Here I ask students to write or illustrate the evolution of their thinking about this particular project. Their response provides, quite literally, a map of their thought process. Sometimes I also ask them to add a box for mapping the emotions they experienced during the work.

It's all a bit of fun at first. But when I ask them to pull out their thermometers for a number of projects completed over time, they are astonished to discern patterns in their approaches to problem solving. We sometimes even add a column to indicate which type of intelligence we are using—mathematical, musical, visual-spatial, literary or language-based, or kinesthetic—according to education researcher Howard Gardner's theory that many different types of intelligence exist.

This kind of approach actually encourages the children to take things further. Once we have amassed a set of thinking maps and assessment thermometers, students often begin to share and compare. Instead of comparing his or her grade to a classmate's and feeling either elation or despair, a student can regard someone else's thinking history and become intrigued. I even see students spontaneously wanting to "try on" different thinking modalities in their next project. "Let me see your thinking map," a student might say. "Cool! I don't think like that, but I might try it next time."

## Acknowledgments

The writing of this book became possible only after I met my cowriter, Rachel Kranz. Her warm, radiantly effusive personality and striking ability to construct a vast conversational landscape at first overwhelmed my more limited concept for this book. Yet the more we talked in that first meeting, the more it became evident that she used language as an architectural construct to encompass every bit of what I offered in describing my ideas. She would listen deeply to me and then, with no delay, capture the essence of my thought and, as if spinning silk from straw, speak back to me a volume of astounding insight. It was like listening to an x-ray of my own understandings. The illumination of the book's subtle anatomy was a revelation to me, and I began to quite literally "see" the book forming right in front of me. The result is as close as I can imagine to conveying the actual story of the World Peace Game. I will be forever indebted to Rachel and her wonderful agent, Janis Vallely of Flaming Star Literary Enterprise, for the months of unwavering, loving, and heartfelt support in seeing this work through.

With folded hands, I thank Eamon Dolan, my editor at Houghton Mifflin Harcourt, whose openness, vision, and masterful guidance brought this book into being; my steady and diamond-eyed copyeditor, Barbara Jatkola; and Cynthia Cannell, my literary agent, whose gentle, farsighted shepherding, humor, and graciousness took me beyond my hopes and dreams.

Immense gratitude to the visionary creator of the film *World Peace and Other 4th-Grade Achievements* and the nicest guy ever, Chris Farina, who began our whole journey, and to his entire crew: adviser Jacqueline Dugery, audio and sound technician Ben Clore, associate producer Kyle Copas, tech adviser J. J. Cohoon, director of photography Gene Rhodes, photographer and conceptual adviser Will May, and editor supreme Bill Reifenberger. Special thanks to the Paramount Theater of Charlottesville, Virginia, for hosting the film on several occasions.

I am deeply indebted to Brad Martin and Jamie Feild Baker, executive director of the Martin Institute for Teaching Excellence for their mission-sustaining partnership and vision; Don Batchelor, board chair of the Presbyterian Day School (PDS) in Memphis; Lee Burns, headmaster of PDS; Steve Hearn, chief advancement officer of PDS; and Winston Baccus, director of communications of PDS.

I am who I am because I am standing on the shoulders of the many masters, master teachers, mentors, and educators who came before me or assisted me in this work. I want to acknowledge especially Anna Aaroe and the staff of the Special Program for Academic and Creative Excellence; the African-American Teaching Fellows; the staff of Agnor-Hurt Elementary School and Albemarle County Public Schools; Rosa Atkins, superintendent of Charlottesville City Schools; one of my greatest mentors, Ethel J. Banks; Adele Booker; Steve Bower; Ron Broadbent; Sally Brown; Michele Del Gallo Castner and Kevin Castner; Bev Catlin; master teacher David Ferreira; Paul Fleischer of the Richmond Peace Education Center; my teaching partner, Lisa Harris; Myrtle Houchens; J. Malcolm Jarrell; the educators of Kingsland Elementary School; Jay McTighe; Pam Moran, superintendent of Albemarle County Public Schools; Valeta Paige; Jan Polo; Larry Roussell; Tenzin Thosam, translator, interpreter, and University of Virginia researcher; Dr. Carol Tomlinson at the Curry School of Education, University of Virginia; the staff of

Venable Elementary School; and the Virginia Commonwealth University School of Education's Paideia Program, including Nancy Boraks, Sam Craver, Jim Hodges, Dean Howell, Peter Madden, Cass Overton, and Nick Sharp.

Three people at the University of Virginia's Darden School of Business deserve special recognition for seeing early on the value of the Game to the larger world: Peter Rodriguez, head of the Center for Global Initiatives; Elizabeth Powell, assistant professor of business administration; and Don Stevenson.

For their careful oversight of legal matters and smoothing of complications, I thank Patrick Asplin of Lenhart Obenshain and Tim Flynn of McGuireWoods.

For their wonderful help in sharing the work of the World Peace Game with the larger world, I am indebted to Coy Barefoot of WINA Radio; Ian Bryan and Sensible City; Paige Russell of the Leigh Bureau; dear Bill Womack of Helios Design; NBC's Bryan Williams and Peter Alexander; artist Martha Saunders; and Brad Savage, host at WCNR 106.1 The Corner. For helping me think about the World Peace Game in a much larger way, I thank Sandy Speicher and Andy Switky of IDEO Design and Chris Anderson and Kelly Stoetzel of TED.

For his gracious support, I thank Thomas Huynh, founder of Sonshi.com, the Web's leading and most respected resource on Sun Tzu's *The Art of War.*

My students and I were able to visit the Pentagon to talk with generals and policy experts in the U.S. Department of Defense thanks to the efforts of General Martin E. Dempsey, chairman of the Joint Chiefs of Staff; Beth Flores, director of leadership and organizational development in the Office of the Under Secretary of Defense for Policy; and the secretary of defense himself, Leon Panetta.

The film screening of *World Peace and Other 4th-Grade Achievements* in Norway began with an invitation from a now dear friend, Tor Fosse, director of the Bergen International Film Festival. I must also thank his amazing staff and, in particular, Erik Aarebrot, who organized the subsequent First International World Peace Game in Bergen in 2011.

To the following dear friends, supporters, and sources of inspiration, I offer my gratitude for their gracious gifts of light and strength: Charles Farina, Robert Noell, Jacqueline Robinson, Raphaela Carriere, Juliette Harris, Gil Schmidt, and Dr. Lacy Peale.

And finally, I send my most loving thanks to all the students who have ever played the World Peace Game with me.